Memoirs of a Romantic Space Cadet

How LSD (and Pepsi) Saved My Life

Brian Carlin

Contents

(Chapter 0) Before We Get Started

Do you ever feel like you know something that no one else knows? I mean KNOW, absolute certainty? But articulation is just not possible? Yeah, you. You hold onto that one for a time-travelling minute. Everyone else, continue.

The road ahead, unless they can reverse the aging process, is a lot shorter for me than it is behind. I can't believe this body got so old when I'm pretty sure I'm still 24. Coincidentally, and I will admit that perhaps one out of ten truly are random - the rest, cosmic conspiracies of sorts, coincidences that is, what once was intended to be a full autobiography now ends at that enduring age.

The day that I met Andrea, and if the calendar and notebook scratchings from the period tell the truth, that would be September 4th, 1974, the expeditions with the Leary, Huxley, and Castaneda search parties started to wind down. I had found what I was lookin' for - sorry you two. (Ok, let's pause a second while some of you Google Tim, Aldous, Carlos and rock lyrics. Get used to it.)

With Mr. Toad's Wild Ride over, the next phase took us, no longer just me, down a relatively peaceful saunter over the rivers and through the woods, when suddenly life thrust us out onto, literally, the big highways. In 2014 we turned in most of our earthly possessions for a rock-star sized motorhome and have been living the dream ever since!

Somewhere in this recent tour, the rocky roads of the early days came back into focus and I started recalling stories.

Maybe the road metaphor does not really apply. Perhaps there's some Einsteinianism to apply to the seemingly analog path through life that bends, or perhaps, suspends the relentless march of time giving us a portal to "then". For when I revisit those events of the past, that muffling cloud, constructed by over one and a half billion seconds, dissolves like a morning fog. I can close my eyes and be there now. A little Baba Ramdasian, but then again, maybe I'm just getting it. You know, getting IT! This life thing? Maybe I'm slow, as I was as a teen, to get it.

The deal is, I started writing about our travels upon retirement in 2014. It began as a daily email to random family and friends until I figured out how to use the group function. The email list eventually grew to about ninety.

In the meantime, Andrea had started a blog intended to educate aspiring full-time RVer's. I thought the blog would include up-to-date posts of our travels, which were extensive that first year. It seemed to me the blog was being neglected so I took a shot at it.

Andrea was aghast (I think pissed off would better describe her reaction) about what I had written, washed her hands of it and abandoned the blog. My language and topics were not what she had in mind. She had already started posting beautiful daily photos on Facebook with succinct, clever commentary, a far cry from the psycho-babble accompanying the pics I was releasing.

It was easy to post to the blog - just add the blog address to my email list. I wrote nearly daily then as we were on a torrid pace and seeing so many beautiful places: Wrigley Field, Saugatuck, MI, Indiana Dunes sunsets, Niagara Falls, following the fall colors from Maine through the Shenandoah's and Smokey's to Florida's coast at Pensacola, through New Orleans, the wide open roads in west Texas and on and on.

Soon, I was getting some positive feedback, but mostly when I went off topic on a rant or some chemically induced reflection. I'd stay up past two drinking while occasionally taking a hit or two of some tasty weed, and was often under the glaze of the hypnotic sleeping pill, Ambien. Sometimes I was pretty fucked up when I hit send.

Andrea cringed (that would be an understatement) the next day, and I was sorry I hadn't done a better job of grammar and error correction, but not sorry about the content. I still thought, while drinking my morning tea, that they were sometimes pretty damn funny.

One thing I tried to do, when I attempted humor, was push the limit, to try to get the audience to think, "Is he nuts, or not?" Apparently, I succeeded. Rumors circulated among the family. The psychedelic drug use in my early twenties was well known among my five siblings. They knew I was nuts. The in-laws? Did it take that long? Welcome to my world.

Seriously, and I rarely swing that way - you gotta keep your sense of humor. Upon releasing some of those long, off-the-wall blog entries, I got a few responses stating, "You should write a book". By that time the idea had been festering but I had needed some encouragement, and that was it.

My original concept for a book was to convert the travelogue blog and throw in some more anecdotes from the past. At some point I had to write about my wildest experiences and that meant how much a certain chemical altered my state of being forever. When I got into the why, you know, why I went down that road and the memories leading up to that Thursday afternoon at Fort Polk that changed everything, it was almost as though I had taken a time machine back, at moments as an observer, others, in my youthful body, feeling the joy, the heartache, and the thrill as it "is" happening.

Time stops with that relentless forward march - perhaps that's just personal chemistry and maybe certain synapses in the brain were connected by the introduction of lysergic acid diethylamide unleashing memories from their hiding places and letting them feel like "now". Some folks report those dreaded "flashbacks" - like all of a sudden you're tripping again years later? I don't buy it – never happened to me. But, if the drug does provide some path to clear memory recall then maybe those flashback incidents are related.

Most likely, we all have such ability to recall to the depth of 'Being There' (great movie, by the way), and we just need to be prodded, like a hypnotist seems to. I thought at first that extreme emotion could ingrain those events for constant and clear retrieval, but as I turned my writings into an autobiography, many less extreme episodes surfaced in similarly "deja vu-ish" fashion. Open one door and lo and behold, there's another door.

Thanks to my writing class leader, Coleen Ehresmann, for introducing me to the book, 'Writing Your Life Story' by Barb Hofmeister. It contains loads of suggestions and questions to help you dig up those long buried moments, some bad, some good, some that will put you right back there, crying or smiling with the same emotion as that young and dumb version of you.

As I was saying a minute ago, after that time-memory discussion, the plan here was to reproduce the blog, but insert chapters of the life story between entries. Except for the background story behind choosing our motorhome's name, Odyssey, which goes back to translating 'The Iliad' in high school Latin class, I couldn't come up with a way to shift from travelogue to sections of my life. It would have been a disjointed mess.

As the stories of the crazy part of my life were put to page - and it was all done on my LG phones, which probably explains the arthritis in my left thumb joint from holding it for two years - it became long enough on its own to fill a book. And as I first mentioned, it only goes as far as meeting Andrea, my wife of forty-two years, when I was twenty-four! Turns out that, excuse my Brooklynese, I got some stories.

What a trip it's been, indeed! Join me? As S. R. Hadden says to Ellie, in one of my favorite movies, 'Contact', in reference to the coveted seat on a craft designed by an alien intelligence, "Wanna take a ride?"

Phase 1: The All American Boy

Chapter 1 - You Are There: Early On

Walter Cronkite Reporting

After a second consecutive 15 hour night shift at the firehouse, Al Carlin returned home that Friday morning to a beautiful day in Brooklyn - must I add New York? Everybody knows the only real Brooklyn is in New York, but not just the state, in the city also. It is a borough, or county-like entity of the city, and last I looked, if it was a city on its own, would be the fourth largest in the US. And watch out, Chicago, it's growing. But I digress.

As mentioned above, the weather was perfect. New York was experiencing an Indian summer in late October of 1949. This Friday, the 21st, the temperature would rise to 75. Al's wife, Anne, was up early, as usual, with baby Susan, nearly ten months old now. Al was on his way home for a 72. That is, 72 hours off. The way they work it in the New York City fire department is that you work two consecutive 6PM to 9AM shifts, you get 72 hours off. You work two day shifts, 9 to 6, then 48 hours off. Anyway, Al comes home and sleeps for a few hours.

Later in the day they take Susan, in her stroller, back then a little bed on wheels, for a walk through Leif Erickson Park, right across the street from their apartment on 66th Street. They finalize their movie date for the evening. Anne's mother, Mary, who with husband Gene, own the three story building they all live in, will take care of Susan.

After dinner at home, they walk the three blocks to the Alpine Theater on 5th Avenue. The movie is the recently released, original version of 'Gigi'. It has a kind of sizzling love story, you know, gets you in the mood.

Being Irish-Catholics, they are expected to raise a big family. To be clear, they started a bit early as Susan arrived on time, about eight months after their wedding date. Now, the first child always opens new parents' eyes to a world of responsibilities they never knew existed. So, after a ten month adjustment period, they were ready to continue that proud, Irish-Catholic tradition - reproduction.

Thus, after returning home from a movie seething with sexual innuendo, the tradition continued. As a million little tadpoles were gathering to be sent off to war in search of their target - an egg cell, on the other side of the world, another fighter was about to enter into the fray of life.

In a bedroom on 66th Street in Bay Ridge, Brooklyn, a million man army of swimmers were released and in a split second, the first to reach its target screamed a resounding, "Yahoo", while in a hospital room in Israel, a true warrior was born, Benjamin Netanyahu!

Hey, once you DO the research, you FIND a way to make it work. Come on, I looked up who was born at about the same time I was conceived. OK, a stretch, give me a break. Besides, with no faith in coincidence, it is my explanation for a rebellious spirit and attraction to Jewish women. OK, so I fucking DIGRESS!

Fast forward 279 days to the evening of July 27th, 1950. Anne, Al, and 18 month old Susan, now walking, are at their summer abode in the beach community of Breezy Point in Queens. It's the middle of the summer and it's a scorcher. Al took a vacation week as Anne is expecting any day now. Being a very slim woman, she looks like she has a beach ball under her sun dress.

Aunt Holly and Uncle Harry, who also have a summer home in Breezy, over on Tioga Walk, are staying with Anne and Al this night. Harry is Al's mother's brother and Holly, that is, Aunt Edith, or should I clarify, Edith L. Hollenback Cassidy, thinks Anne is about to give birth. She's looking forward to babysitting.

Sleep doesn't come easily to Anne and this night is very uncomfortable. The humidity is fairly high and the temperature is still in the high seventies near midnight when - uh-oh. Time to go. Her water breaks. Everybody gets up.

Lights are on at 40 Pelham Walk. It's not that unusual in this little world of young, Irish and Italian families, many of whom are policemen and firemen. Births in this boomer time and this community are pretty common.

Harry runs down to the parking lot to bring his '46 Plymouth to the head of Pelham Walk. Oceanside Ave, the crosswalk, is wide enough for a car. With a duffel bag full of Anne's belongings hanging over his shoulder, Al helps her walk the 250 feet to Harry's waiting car. By one AM, they are out of the Tioga Walk parking area and headed to the Marine Parkway Bridge.

The drive to Victory Memorial Hospital takes about forty minutes. If you're going to a hospital to have a baby, arriving at about two in the morning is not a bad time. It's pretty quiet this Friday morning.

Home phone service has not come to Breezy Point yet so no one has called ahead. As Al is checking them in, Harry finds a pay phone and calls Anne's doctor. Those were the days when doctors actually gave out their home phone numbers. By three, the contractions are coming in quick waves.

A short time later, Doctor Sefter arrives and immediately orders Anne's gurney moved out of the ward and into a delivery room. Al is told to get a cup of coffee.

At about 4:30AM, the early edition of the New York Daily News is delivered to the waiting room. Its big headline announces that the draft call is up to 100,000. Al turns it over to the sports pages. His Dodgers got clobbered by the Cardinals yesterday. He knows his baseball and is sure that if the relief pitching doesn't get any better, their good season is in danger. Jackie Robinson is batting .367 and just stole another base yesterday. Al gets lost in the article about the Dodgers.

Welcome to Planet Earth

"Mr. Carlin, it's a boy!"

Harry puts down his book, the best seller and so topically titled, 'Sleep Till Noon', and shakes Al's hand. "Congratulations!"

Forty-eight minutes before the sun would break the horizon out over the Atlantic, Brian James Carlin comes screaming into this world and doesn't stop unless he's feeding.

Out in the land of the rich and famous, out on the end of Long Island, in Southampton to be exact, a bright, George Washington University co-ed who was home for the summer, Jacqueline Lee Bouvier, turned 21.

It was noon in Middlesex, England where the son of a biochemist was celebrating his 7th birthday. That boy, Richard Wright, would later provide that newborn with hundreds of hours of pleasure, some in person, as the keyboard player for the band, Pink Floyd.

That's it, 9lbs, 19 inches, Brian James Carlin. Good luck out there.

One last word about that date - as I hear him signing off the show tonight (editing this in May, 2019), I'll remember to wish Scott Pelley a happy birthday next July 28th, coincidentally, a 60 Minutes Sunday.

Yes, at 5AM on Friday, July 28th, 1950, my head popped through that little, well, weighing in at about nine pounds, two ounces, maybe not so little, people hole through which most of us enter this world. My world was now in the care of Anne Carlin in Victory Memorial Hospital. My father, Alvin, was thrilled that it was a boy.

Just eighteen months earlier, Dr. Sefter delivered my sister, Susan, in that same hospital in the Bay Ridge section of Brooklyn, right off the infamous Belt Parkway. Four more siblings, Denise, Michael, Debbie, and Marilou, followed over the next seven years.

My mother was pregnant for the better part of nine years. How does that work? Apparently ok. I have lots of cousins. Aunt Clare had seven, Adrian (Uncle Bob) had five, Uncle Gene's wife (Mary?) had four or five (? Black sheep)

A few days after first breathing the exhaust fumes from those old Plymouths, Pontiacs, and Packards on the Belt, my chubby little body was transported over the Marine Parkway Bridge to our summer abode, 40 Pelham Walk in Breezy Point. If you think we had money, think again. We were like all the blue collar families at Breezy.

There was, apparently, enough money to feed me as I was so round I didn't walk until nearly two. I'm told I sat on my butt, shaking my hands around my head while they wondered if I was going to be one of those funny kids.

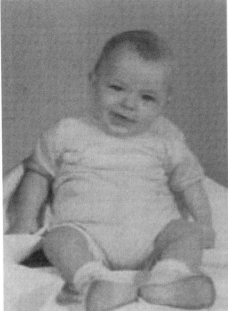

Yeah, there's a short yellow bus in your future, kid!

My father started his stint in the war as a Navy pilot. After cracking up a twin engine in training, his MOS (Military Occupational Status if you haven't been exposed to that lingo) was changed to air traffic controller. He spent the "rest" (operative word) of the war on one of the tiny Marshall Islands in the Pacific. One scout plane was stationed there. The front was much further west by then. I've seen pictures of him and his buddies in their swim suits and beers in hand, posing on a palm-tree covered beach. Tough gig.

The photo below is of the Carlin-Cassidy clan on the deck at Breezy Point, guessing about 1940, plus or minus a year. Let's start in the lower right – that would be Alvin, my father, at about 18. Over his left shoulder is his younger brother Bill who died at the end of World War II training to be a Navy pilot like his older brother..

To Bill's right is Helen, their mother, and then Fred, son number three, the afore-mentioned Aunt Holly, then Evelyn, the only daughter of Helen, and finally, lower left, Mabel, Helen's sister. Mabel was a nurse in WW I. In the front room in that bungalow hung a wide picture of over a hundred nurses from her days in the war.

Early Memories

After the war, the second one, Al's friend, Chris Hayden, talked him into becoming a New York City fireman. Great, steady job, decent benefits, but salary? Not so much. Chris had married Clare Lynch, a girl from the Bay Ridge neighborhood they all lived in. Chris introduced Al to Clare's younger sister, Anne. They fell in love, started making children, and got married. Yes, that sequence is right, by a month or so. My sister, Susie, was not early.

Anyway, our little, two-bedroom, seasonal bungalow in this beach community on the

Rockaway barrier island in Queens, New York, came from my father's side of the family. His father died at a young age but his salty, Irish mother, Helen, made a good living as a secretary. Breezy Point was a blue collar community, literally. It seemed that police and firemen lived in every other home, but they all had one common love, the beach.

For kids, this place was heaven for the summer months. After you parked your car in the lot and loaded up the Red Flyer wagon - it was magically there after dad had come back a week earlier and turned the water on - you walked along concrete footpaths to your bungalow and took off your shoes, for the summer. No streets. Walks!

Our unheated house stood on low stilts, twelve feet across a walking path from another identical home. That walking path was the street. Ours was Pelham Walk. Actually, each home had a wooden deck in front to provide a bit more separation.

Those decks were a place to converse with friends across the way, passersby, and a place to buy the morning newspaper from the man pushing the steel-wheeled cart which also carried magazines, comics, cigarettes, and cigars, and who knows what else back then. He announced his presence if the decks were empty but folks knew the daily routine and sat out on their porches waiting for him. You could hear those steel wheels rolling on the concrete a walk away.

Once a week another steel wheeled cart would come down the block and the man pushing it would repeatedly shout, stretching each word out, almost singing, "Tailor…..Shoemaaake..aah". This is New Yalk. Who pronounces that "r"? One more cart, the knife sharpener, would come through sporadically. I liked that one. Sparks would fly.

That's yours truly with cousin Pat on that old deck with sister Debbie. I guess. Could be Pat's sister Diana, born around the same time. The Lavin's deck is across the way. Pat spent half the summer with us. Good ballplayer.

The little summer homes were separated from the ones behind them by about fifty feet of fine sand that usually contained two troughs. The garbage trucks that picked up in the backs of the houses were fitted with tank treads to get through the deep sand and their tracks packed down a path that helped short legs walk between friends' houses. Between garbage pickups, those all-sand backyards hosted games of horseshoes, badminton, and whiffle ball.

Some early memories surround the birth of my sister Debbie. She was born a few weeks after my fifth birthday. We had to go back to Brooklyn then, playing it safe when Hurricane Diana (my cousin's name) stormed through the New York area. We came back to find the boardwalk strewn all over the place. Now, that's one of those memories I'm all over.

The home structures in our part of Breezy Point ended at least a quarter mile from the ocean. Each "walk" built their own narrow boardwalk that provided a means to more easily pull that Red Flyer holding lunch, drinks, chairs, and an umbrella down to the beach.

Every home on the walk was required to provide two eight foot long wooden boardwalks consisting of three ten by two's with three cross pieces, also of ten by two's. We painted our address, 40 Pelham, on our two. On the sides and ends of the cross pieces were large eyeholes used to run a heavy cable through dozens of individual boardwalks. Those cables were anchored up by the homes, the whole purpose of which was to keep the entire boardwalk together when a major hurricane brought the ocean up to the edge of the homes.

Usually, a formal block event was organized at the end of the summer to bring the boardwalk sections back to the homes for winter storage. The sections closest to the beach went first so that they could be transported by a Red Flyer Wagon - every home had one of them, also with a painted address on it. Then the home owner of the next section would tow theirs back up, etc. The same organized block party laid them down from 1 Pelham Walk to 109 Pelham. Pretty sure a lot of beer was involved. Lots of camaraderie among the cops, fireman, doctors, lawyers, accountants and others. A team effort made for a nice, friendly atmosphere.

More details keep bubbling up from those memory cells. Before that late-spring, board-laying block party, we repainted our boardwalk sections each year, white! Had to be white, otherwise they burned your feet. There was always some clown who thought redwood was nice - ouch, ouch, ouch, ouch. Pox on them.

Same as our front deck at the beginning of each summer, a fresh coat of paint. My sister, Susan, reminds me the deck was light grey. Why? I don't know. It got hot by the afternoon. We didn't have an awning on our deck. Our house faced east, so in the early afternoon we only had a sliver of shade at the front of the house to tip-toe on and then run down the ramp to the concrete walk. Even light grey got vey hot in the summer sun. Why didn't we have a white deck? I''ll never know.

Well, I suppose I have digressed, big time. That great idea of stringing the boards together with a heavy duty cable was no match for Hurricane Diana. The boards were scattered all over the little sand dunes around which our once flat path to the beach had been laid. My father found our boards and dragged them back to the head of the walk by himself. He was pretty strong. He had been a high school football player, a halfback, and during the summers at Breezy, he was a lifeguard. As a fireman, he kept in shape. He swam in the ocean almost daily. Tough guy.

You know, when he got into his eighties and reminisced, he brought up his father a lot – "greatest man he ever knew". His father, Wilfred, but known as Fred, was born without a right hand. He died when my father was about fifteen.

However, you never read a word about Wilfred's deficiency when his high school football exploits as a halfback at Brooklyn Poly Tech were reported by the Brooklyn Eagle, though even in their illustrations, as in every photo, his right arm was tucked behind his back.

My great grandmother kept a scrapbook of Wilfred's high school clippings.

Grandpa Wilfred Carlin, hand behind his back.

Every time I open that book, more pieces of hundred year old newspaper fall out. These are from 1908.

Back to the beach. Yeah, we actually did go to the beach. For all of us, swimming just came naturally. My parents brought us into the waves from, almost literally for us summer babies, day one. I was probably attempting to body surf by age five, maybe not out by the big breakers, but I tried to do what my father did, act like a fish. He didn't need a surfboard. You just learn to move with the ocean. Catch a wave and you're sitting on top of the world.

We sometimes brought our umbrella to the beach. That was our sunscreen back then. We lathered ourselves up with the bare-bottomed baby stuff but we were in and out of the water so often that the only protection was the umbrella. When she went to the beach at all, my fair skinned mother spent most of the day under the umbrella. Quite often it was just my father and other times we went with the neighbors. We ate peanut butter and jelly sandwiches out of the cooler, sometimes mixed with a little sand if it was windy. We had to wait a half hour after eating before going back in the water again, the one downside of eating lunch. In the meantime, sandcastles were built.

At first, it was just Susie and me, and then friends, Timmy and Donny Murphy, Kathy Lavin, the whole McElhinney family, Frankie Curly and many more. In the evening, after we rinsed all the sand off in our tiny shower, and after dinner, the big kids let us play hide and seek. That place was so heavenly. My siblings agree.

Some memories are aided by old photos. Here I am at three years old with my sister Susan, about four and a half, and our sunburned cheeks, and the next in line, Denise, seven months old, with the Mohawk doo. That photo was in Breezy Point.

547 66th Street

For the rest of the year, we lived at 547 66th St, Brooklyn, 9 NY. I've always remembered my street address, including the postal zone. It was drilled into my head, as was our phone number, Shore

Road 8-0197. We lived in the upper floor of a small brownstone in Bay Ridge.

My mother's parents, Gene and Mary Lynch, lived in the main floor and Aunt Eileen, another of their six children, and husband Uncle Deary - his real name was Chris but she only called him Deary, so he was always Uncle Deary - lived in the basement apartment with their ever present bowl of hard candies.

I do recall spending time with Aunt Eileen on many occasions, most likely when my mother was giving birth or just needed a break from two, maybe three or more, small children. Grandma Lynch was there too. I remember drinking tea with them, a real treat, having toast with jelly, and Velveeta cheese sandwiches.

I'm told that Aunt Eileen and Uncle Deary took Susan and me to the Statue of Liberty. Don't bother to spend that kind of money on preschoolers, nor try to impress them with natural or historical wonders. Instead, and now my memory is jogged yet again, try the circus.

I have vague recollections of going to Barnum and Bailey's Ringling Brothers Circus, and I'm 99% sure it was at the old Madison Square Garden. I remember walking through the area where they kept the elephants, with straw all around, and the side show with the freaky stuff I didn't understand, and the clowns, and, of course, the trapeze artists. One year I came home with a chameleon. It changed color a few times and died in a couple of days.

We also often visited with - perhaps I should say, were babysat by - my grandparents on the first floor. My grandfather had come to America from Ireland in hopes of a career as a singer. He became a plumber but his love of music infected all of us. We listened to his Victrola and sang along as early as I can remember. Most of what I recall from those days was Bing Crosby. Our Irish eyes are still smiling with the sound of music.

My father was always working - when he wasn't at the firehouse he moonlighted at a place called Retail Credit. I wondered years later if it was a loan sharking operation, just wondered because I think he was in collections.

My mother was always pregnant so I played in the street with Jimmie Lee and Wayne Campbell, not the one on SNL. Wayne was a year younger than me but he was my buddy. We strapped on roller skates to our shoes and skated for hours. Leif Erickson park was right across the street. We'd spend a lot of time over there playing knock-hockey and hangin' on the monkey bars.

Here I am with Wayne in front of our house.
Cool sweater, no?
Wayne's got the Frankie Avalon coif.

Wayne's father dressed up as Santa Claus for Christmas and walked up the stairs to our apartment with a sack of presents. I bought it at first. Then I recall wondering how the real Santa got into our house. We didn't have a chimney. That reminds me, Aunt Eileen always gave us underwear and socks for Christmas.

Then there was Easter. We'd wake up to a basket of chocolates of all kinds, jelly beans, egg-shaped and candy coated malted milk balls, and those yellow, sugar coated, marshmallow chicks. They were all carefully placed around a large, hollow, chocolate bunny wrapped in colorful foil. We couldn't wait for those holidays. Of course, we also supported many a dentist for decades to follow.

I was lucky being born in July. I got more presents in the middle of the summer for my birthday. My youngest sister, Marilou, got screwed. She was born on December 23rd, but she says my mother always got her presents and made her feel special. Good job, Mom.

When my parents had some time off, they strapped us into amusement park rides and stood back (read the sign over my

shoulder). I was two then, the one in the Evil Knievel outfit, and wondering if perhaps this is what loan sharks do with customers when they are stiffed. Susan is saying, "Bro, smile and maybe they'll let us out".

But come on. We lived in Brooklyn. How great was life in the early 50's?

Chapter 2 - Brooklyn and Breezy

From "Those Thrilling Days of Yesteryear"

I can hear those words, conjured up by Fred Foy, long time announcer and narrator of The Lone Ranger TV show, as the William Tell Overture plays in the background. The lead-in to the show ends with our hero hailing his steed with the lightning speed with his signature, "Hi-ho Silver!"

I could tell stories related to some of those old TV shows, including that sad Saturday morning - and this might have been pre-school - when I got all dressed up for my pending TV show appearance. I had my Captain Video ring on which was my ticket to the real show. My favorite space adventurer beamed a lucky boy or girl, through the magic of TV, from their home to the studio to become a Video Ranger, every Saturday morning. It was a bit stolen by 'Star Trek' and its "beam me up" Transporter. The show ended and I was still in our Brooklyn apartment. Captain Video disappointed me. I had wanted to be a Space Cadet. (Who knew? One of These Days!) Next week I watched Commander Cody, Sky Marshall of the Universe (no relation to Commander Cody and His Lost Planet Airmen).

However, I didn't come here to reminisce about 'Leave It To Beaver', 'My Three Sons', or Ed Sullivan's most famous introduction, "Ladies and gentlemen...The Beatles". Maybe those TV ticklers count as a themed story but I don't have one, except that I was often compared to The Beav. No, we're here for some memories of Brooklyn and Breezy Point, mostly before moving out to the country in 1960.

That's mom and dad and, I guess, Denise, with mom. Puts me at three, unless that's Michael and

then I'm four, but then, why would we be in Brooklyn since he was born in June? Sorry it's so blurry. Susie probably took it and she was only four.

My recollections of early childhood are few and disjointed. I can see 66th Street and the roller skates we attached to our shoes and the key that tightened them. I see the concrete park across the street that had swings, see-saws, and a jungle gym. I recall playing knock-hockey there and the day I broke Jimmy Lee's arm.

A few of us neighborhood kids were playing in the park that day, including Jimmy, Wayne Campbell, and his nattily attired brother Don.

That's Don Campbell and me, off to the side, considering whether I should let him keep the title of "Don", when obviously, I was the Boss of 66th St – come on, look at that face! (They really dressed us like that? Holy Shit!)

Breakin' Bad

Jimmy and Wayne were swinging together. Jimmy was sitting and Wayne was standing facing Jimmy. Wayne was smallest so he always stood. You could swing pretty high when you both worked at it. I was watching them and thought it was time to let me take Jimmy's place. I pulled the swing next to them sideways and warned that if they didn't stop by the time I counted to three, I would let the swing go.

The count went to three. I steadied my weapon and aimed. I estimated the time it would take for a swing cycle and the time it would take for my weapon to swing into its target. With a little push, the loose swing sailed through its sideways arc. Jimmy and Wayne's swing was descending. At the bottom of their arc the weaponized swing met them and struck Jimmy in the right arm. He immediately let go of the chains on both sides of the swing, his left hand grabbing the arm just above the elbow where a bone had cracked. Wayne stopped the swing as quickly as possible but they both crumpled to the concrete below.

Jimmy was crying wildly. Wayne couldn't believe what just happened and was mad at me for ruining their ride. This was not going as planned. My best friend, Jimmy, was hurt and it was my fault. This is bad. I'm going to get in trouble.

I don't recall getting in too much trouble with my parents but a few days later they made me go up the block and apologize to Jimmy, now wearing a cast from shoulder to hand. But I do recall the Campbell boys telling me to lie low. Tommy Lee, Jimmy's tough-guy older brother was looking to beat me up. I was afraid to go out for weeks. Every time I hit the streets I feared for my life. It all passed and Tommy never said anything about it.

What else about Brooklyn? I remember going to Owl's Head Park when it snowed and riding sleds on the hills. I remember getting my tonsils out. I had to sleep in the hospital and I was scared. But, they let me eat jello and ice cream.

Hospitals

What I remember most about that hospital adventure was the minute we pulled up in front of our house the morning they released me. There were a few trees on the block and in the one next to where we parked was a male Scarlet Tanager. It remained still on the tree long enough to get a positive identification. My parents agreed that it wasn't a Cardinal but how did I know it was a Scarlet Tanager? The World Book Encyclopedia! I leafed through those volumes constantly, paying close attention to the birds section and the pages on trains and planes. As soon as we got inside I looked it up. Definitely, a Scarlet Tanager.

The tonsillectomy was not my only hospital visit in Brooklyn. A bunch of us from the neighborhood were on our way to the soda shop on 5th Avenue, a few blocks west of 66th Street. The kids my age were too young to cross the streets alone but Gary Minor was old enough. He was probably about ten, twelve years old but there were no kids his age on the block so he hung out with us a lot. Our street didn't have much traffic so we often played right in the street.

Fifth Avenue was a different story. It was busy, lots of commerce, busses and taxis. Crossing at a designated crosswalk with traffic lights just wasn't an option we considered much back then. The traffic lights were there but it was understood, by kids, that they only applied to cars and it didn't matter where you crossed, as long as you made it to the other side.

This day I didn't make it. As we approached the candy store/soda shop from the north side of 5th Avenue, the break in traffic seemed to give us enough time to run across the street in the middle of the block. You had to start running as the last car was passing. I knew how to do this. But today as I started running, suddenly, Wham! I'm on my back and having a hard time breathing. My stomach hurts. The tail end of a car is in front of me and a lot of people gathered around. Apparently, the driver of the car stopped short when he spotted a parking space. I had timed my run with his car passing my position. I hadn't taken into account the car suddenly stopping.

Off I go into a police car to a hospital. My father appears a few minutes later. He and the very apologetic driver talk for a while. A doctor has me lie on my back on a gurney and examines my stomach, pelvis, and rib cage. The diagnosis - "He had the wind knocked out of him." The driver came to our house, not sure why – did he write a check? Or just concerned? Concerned that he might get sued? I don't know. I never got hit again in traffic, just got better at timing those wild dashes across busy streets and sometimes, the Belt Parkway.

Cop Stories

That reminds me of another story. One day a bunch of us are down at Owl's Head Park, which butts up to the Belt Parkway on its southern end. Someone wanted to see what happened when cars ran over rocks. Cool, little rockets. Suppose the rock is bigger, like fist size. We didn't have big fists then but when traffic was light we started putting a line of rocks across the road. Cars started avoiding them. Each of us would bring an increasingly larger rock out further onto the highway.

Suddenly, all the other kids disappeared and I turned around to see a patrol car and a big cop looking at me. "Put the rock down, kid!" The other cop pulled the car sideways in front of the rock line, blocking all westbound traffic on the Belt. "Pick 'em all up!". I think I would have remembered if the cops drove me home and told my parents. They found out from the other parents anyway. Not good for me.

One more Brooklyn memory, inspired by the episode with the cops. By the time I was nine, just before we moved to Long Island, I was well on my way to juvenile delinquency, lighting fires in bushes, and just being disruptive. One day I was over in the park across the street. I had chalk and I was writing the word "Fuck" all over the sidewalk. A man came up to me and said he was a cop. He asked if he thought my parents would approve of what I was doing. "Maybe we should ask them." I didn't think that was a good idea. "Then erase it. All of it!" I gave up my career in crime.

Lost in Brooklyn

I had just turned six and was entering the first grade. The setting is my first day of school. As a somewhat streetwise kid in Brooklyn, I already knew a few routes to specific places. Grandma Carlin lived diagonally across from Our Lady Of Angels Church and grammar school, which was on 73rd St and 4th Ave in Bay Ridge. I lived on 66th St, between 5th and 6th Ave. You can Google the address, 547 (I did). It's still there.

We had walked to Grandma's apartment many times - up 66th to 4th Ave, turn left, then six blocks to 72nd St. Easy. OLA, Our Lady of Angels, was literally right across the street. And I knew how to walk back from there, alone.

That first day of school in September of 1956, I was confident that I could take that walk home by myself for lunch. What I didn't know was that the nuns had a sinister plot for us six year olds. It was a decision we had to make as we were let out onto the streets of Brooklyn without adult supervision. We were told to get onto either the 3rd Ave, south, or 4th Ave, north line (of other kids). I was not prepared for that. I didn't know the difference in Avenues, so I went with door number one, 3rd Ave.

As the nuns released us out into the world I was thinking I was diagonally across from Grandma Carlin. So, I immediately went left. Oops, wrong way. Nothing looked familiar. About a dozen blocks later, I knew I was lost, and tired. I sat on a curb and cried.

A minute or so later, a nice lady from the hair salon behind me came out and asked me what was wrong. I told her I was lost, but I had remembered my address, and phone number. She brought me back inside the salon and called my mother. A short time later, Uncle Deary and Aunt Eileen showed up to bring me home.

My mom, who didn't drive, had made me a peanut butter and jelly sandwich that I devoured in minutes. And because I had no time left in my lunch period, Uncle Deary drove me back to school. No more walking until school let out. By then, my older sister, Susan, was tasked with making sure I made it home. I'm sure my mother laced into the nuns for letting this happen.

Breezy Point

We loved Breezy Point. I think I've made that clear. We discussed it earlier. Lots of great little memories from Breezy but only one coherent story. Mostly I remember playing stickball, whiffle ball, and hardball and we had catches all day, played running bases at the waterfront, and threw a football once in a while.

The beach, though, was all about going in the ocean. You had to, to cool off. When it was windy, you could get away from the stinging sand and sometimes it felt warmer staying in the water. But the real deal was that if there was any surf at all, the ocean was there to ride waves.

When we were little, we didn't have one of those floating mats. We called them rafts. You didn't need it. To ride a wave you timed its motion toward the beach, ran with it if you could and leaped toward the shore at the crest of the wave, just before it broke.

Depending on the direction of the wind, building (into the wave) or breaking waves off (blowing from behind), the force of the wave would push you forward and if you streamlined your body like a fish, putting your hands in front of you over your head, which was face down (you held your breath), in a praying position and keeping your toes pointed back, you could ride it all the way to within feet of the shoreline. Like that sentence.

The less-than-streamlined technique was with the head out of the water. You lifted your head up and put your arms down by your sides, tight up against your body. Your shoulders created the most impedance as the ride petered out and the wave couldn't propel you as far as the fish technique. But, you could see where you were going and people could see you.

When a storm was brewing far out in the Atlantic, we'd get the biggest waves, sometimes 10-20 footers. They were too big even for my father. The ten footers though were everyone's dream. If they built up like walls and then came crashing down, riding them was impossible. There had to be a significant amount of water under the crashing wave from previous waves rushing back out. Taking off on one of those from a height was thrilling, for a ten year old – and a forty year old, my father told me.

When I was eight or nine, my father's firehouse friend, Dave Laverty, came down to the beach for a day visit. Dave was a big, jovial guy who seemed to like kids. He picked us up and flipped up us around like we were footballs. He liked throwing a ball around, running bases with us, and swimming. But the first day he arrived – and he visited more than once – he brought a canvas raft.

This wasn't one of those cheap rubber pool floats. No, This was heavy duty. If not specifically designed to ride waves, it sure had no other purpose at Breezy. We all got a turn on Dave's raft but when he went home that day he said, "It's yours."

Holy Mackerel! It's the best surf riding raft on the beach. It was about my body length, some four foot nothing, so it was perfect for me.

I learned how to ride even those big, crashing waves and used different positions while riding waves, like kneeling and lying on my back. Riding waves, that's what the ocean is for.

These memories are all sort of fragments, a flash here a flash there – taking the free ferry to Rockaway Point where the movie theater was located, seeing my first movie, 'Old Yeller' and crying. The movie 'The Mysterians' – I loved it. The penny candy store and arcade next to the theater. Playing pin ball baseball with a three-tiered outfield deck.

There was one solid memory/story from Breezy that really stands out and it was one of those intense moments that gets me feeling like I AM in that moment, that three and two count, looking Big Frank in the eye. I thought the whole story deserved a name and it seemed obvious. Becoming a teen is a thing. It's got its good, got its bad. One thing is certain, you're not considered a kid anymore. Pink Floyd named a song for this Arthur C. Clark novel. I hear the lines,

"Childhood's End your fantasies,
Merge with harsh realities":

Childhood's End

Summer of 1963 in Breezy Point. I lived and breathed baseball. I knew the names of every position player of every major league team, but, there were only eight teams in each league then. Frankie Curley and I played catch every morning out on the "walk" before most adults were up.

We played stickball at the beach with other friends nearly every day. We played whiffle ball in the sand behind the houses and we were all, every kid I knew, including Kathy Lavin, in the Little

League. When it rained we played a dice baseball game with cards that assigned each player hits/outs per roll based on past performance. Baseball, in any form, was in our blood.

Well, here I am at bat in a big, Little League game in early August. In the eight to ten league I pitched our Darts to an oh-and-eight record, but as a second basemen in the ten-to-twelve league, I made the all-star team. Thus, I had the confidence to leap to the teenage league as the summer of '63 began. I was 12 when the season began but had just turned thirteen a week ago.

Now, I back away from the plate, gathering my thoughts while looking out at the pitcher on the mound. The intermittent rain has become steady. The umpire is urging me to step in.

On the mound, Frank Cheswick is a 16 year old in a man's body who throws fastballs that nobody can hit. He's already set the league record for strikeouts in a season. He's a legend. But he can be wild - very scary. He usually has to slow it down to throw strikes, but even then, very few can hit that restrained fastball either.

Our star pitcher, freckled-face Billy Baldwin, throws giant, slow curveballs, mostly for strikes. Neither pitcher has allowed a run today and Frank has not allowed a hit. The two best pitchers in the league are in an epic battle, a great game.

It's the bottom of the ninth, two outs, both strikeouts, and, with the steadily increasing rain, the game is going to be called off at the end of the inning, if, of course, we don't score. However, Big Frank has just walked three batters. In any case, I will be the last batter. The count is three balls and two strikes.,

Frank waits for me to step into the batter's box. I'm the worst hitter in the league, and the shortest. He must be thinking, "Just throw strikes". I'm thinking "Walk, walk, walk, and don't hit me!"

Rumor has it his fastball killed somebody. In fact, a few weeks ago, his wild fastball beaned one of the league sluggers. The husky kid's helmet kept him from going to the hospital, and, maybe, his grave. Chezzy's legendary status has been amplified by reports of beanings in other leagues. Some call him a head hunter.

Frank has thrown me an assortment of pitches. The first was an inside fastball, the real fast one, that nearly beheaded me and caused the catcher to say, "Ouch". Ball one. Next a slow-pitch, softball type lob that I swung at, but fouled off weakly. The next slow pitch I whacked solidly down the left field line, but foul.

That was the last of those teaser pitches. But, the count was in his favor at that point, one and two. He tried to lure me to swing at two mid-speed fastballs that were inside. The count is now three balls and two strikes. Could the pressure be any higher, on both of us?

My whole team and some of the parents are cheering wildly, "Let's Go Brian". Sounds like the cheer for my new favorite team, The Mets. I hear the other Frank, Frankie, my good friend, stuttering the same cheer.

Meanwhile, Old Chezzy is trying to decide whether to let a fastball rip and, perhaps, kill the kid and lose the game or, take his chances and lob one more meatball over the plate to the 75 pound shrimp. I have to read his mind. I think, "You give me that slowball again and I'll kill it!" His most accurate pitch is his slower fastball. That's what he'll throw, I decide.

Here comes the pitch. Frank hesitates on his windup, signaling to that me it's a lob. I'm not buying it. Here comes the big one, a "heater", as a baseball announcer might say, that blazing fastball. It's right down the middle.

Uh-oh, hurry up and swing. The bat hits the ball late, but solidly. It speeds by the first baseman into right field. Yay, I did it. But whoa - the right fielder is playing so shallow he might be able to throw me out at first base. I run as fast as I can. The throw comes in, but just after my foot hits the base. Safe. The runner at third has scored. We win!

The entire team comes out to carry me off the field. The spectators are cheering, staying in the rain. I am, as Jimmy Cagney said in the movie, 'White Heat', "Top of the world, ma!". This is the greatest moment of my thirteen year life.

Frankie Curley, my best friend and only fan I know in the stands, walks home with me in the drizzle. We get to my house and with his extreme stutter, tells my father about my heroic hit. My father was busy fixing something and barely acknowledged us.

Chapter 3 - Getting Through High School

The Country: Bellmore

In 1960, when I was nine, we moved from our tiny apartment in Brooklyn out to the country, out in the boonies, to the village of Bellmore on Long Island. Pull up the Maps app on your phone and plug in 400 Washington Avenue, Bellmore, NY 11710. OK, I remembered the zip code. Anyway, if you use the satellite view and zoom down, you won't find the old house. A McMansion replaced it. Fa-get-about-it.

Zoom out a lot and center the map until you have Manhattan on your far left and Montauk on your far right. See how Long Island looks like a fish with a twin tail? Brooklyn is the head with the North Fork and Greenport at the tip of the top tail. Montauk is at the end of the slightly wider, bottom tail.

For future reference, you might zoom in a little and find Southampton, Hampton Bays, and the iconic bar, The Boardy Barn on that south fork. Sorry, I'm a big fan of geography and visuals. I want to see the places I'm reading about on a map, if they're real, and all this shit is real. Whadya want, me to print the damn thing here? Come on, get into it. These are actual places. 'Be apart of it now' (Badfinger).

Geography lesson over. Back to moving out into the wilderness. In the 1960 census, the village of Bellmore had a population of just under 40,000. North Bellmore, that part above Camp Avenue, was bigger, just over 40,000. It wasn't exactly "the country". We moved into a gigantic house across the street from St. Barnabus church and grammar school. Gigantic! I think it was slightly larger than

1,600 square feet, but after that apartment in Bay Ridge, wow! And the yard! Besides having grass in front of the house, we had a driveway on the side that made a right behind the house and then turned left into a two-car garage! Who has two cars?

The side yard next to the driveway was our sports stadium. Besides the typical whiffle ball, stickball, softball, hardball, and football games, the yard hosted both Winter and Summer Olympics with standard events such as high jump, long jump and mini-pole vaulting. Some special events included "burn down the front tree with glue as we tortured ants", "blow up world war II model planes with ear piercing ash can firecrackers", and the premier event, "swatting fireflies in the early evening with whiffle ball bats".

The backyard would be home to flowers of all kinds, a variety of tomatoes, and, a decade later, some flourishing marijuana plants.

With six kids, five of them school age, a new mortgage, and a New York City fireman's salary, my parents decided that we all enter the public school system. It turns out Protestant and Jewish kids were not children of the devil.

I adapted pretty well to public school, making the honor roll regularly, playing sports, joining choir, and even appearing in the fifth grade play, 'Tom Sawyer', as Ben, the kid Tom suckered into painting a fence for him. "Gee oh willickers, I'm a lucky fellow, Gosh oh willickers, I'm lucky to be me", so went the beginning of my first solo singing appearance. Pretty sure I nailed it but I don't recall reading about it in the local paper. Oh yeah, we didn't have a local paper. That's why.

I have no idea how old I was here but I'm guessing it was for sixth grade graduation. Geez, it's a wonder I didn't get my ass kicked every day. What a twerp!

You know, I got compared to The Beav quite often. Remember 'Leave It To Beaver'? He was just two years older than me. That's something. I've learned over the years - that Jerry Mathers, The Beav, and I have something else in common – no, I don't have diabetes. The Beav and I both have Bullshit Artist degrees in Philosophy. That's something.

Can You Hear What I Hear?

Music was a big thing in our family and as each of the siblings approached eight or nine, we bought 45's with allowance money. It was Christmas 1962 when, I believe, I got my first album, you know, the vinyl LP (long playing) record that held about a half dozen three minute songs per side. It was 'Sherry & 11 Others' by The Four Seasons.

I also listened to the soundtracks of many plays and movies, my favorite being 'West Side Story' and just about anything else my father brought home. He loved music and was always buying new records. We followed the bouncing ball and sang along with Mitch Miller and watched the bubble maestro, Lawrence Welk.

My mother was a big fan of Johnny Mathis and her heartthrob of 1942, Frank Sinatra. She was one of those thousands of young people who got on the subway and attended Frank's appearances at the Paramount Theater. None of us could play an instrument but we HEARD the music, we felt the music, we loved the music.

Our genes, maybe those in Grandpa Gene's gene pool, seem to turn carefully constructed sounds into endorphins, pleasure drugs our brains release naturally. Why do you think music makes you feel so good?

Anyway, got the picture? We all loved music in our own ways. I was developing my own taste. Of course, The Beatles changed everything, but before them I was buying records by another English group, The Searchers. My older sister, Susie, brought home lots of 45's and saved me a few bucks by buying most of the early Beach Boys hits.

Cousin Brucie, host of a New York City AM radio station, brought that music into our homes, as did Scott Muni and a dozen other local disc jockeys. One year Santa gave me a white, AM/FM clock radio that, besides accompanying me through many a homework assignment, pulled in WBZ from Boston and WOWO from Fort Wayne, Indiana on cloudy and rainy nights. AM radio worked better with cloud cover. There's science involved – look it up.

That radio, with skillful play by play announcers, put me on the field, court and ice for countless games - The Mets, New York Football Giants, Rangers, Knicks, boxing championships (Floyd Paterson, Cassius Clay, etc.), and The Millrose Games (track and field) – yes, I listened to high jump competitions on the radio. Radio broadcasters knew how to present a game then. Most had started in radio before TV and could describe the visual before them.

Though he had been long gone to Los Angeles with the Dodgers, I was able to hear a few Dodger games announced by the greatest of them all, Vin Scully. He did the World Series so everybody in America got a chance to experience his game calling but you had to listen to him doing a game on radio to appreciate his ability to let you "see" the game with him.

But, I digress. As ninth grade approached, I had a decision to make. My older sister was allowed to go to a Catholic high school. Should I go there also? I had settled into Grand Avenue Junior High School and was quite comfortable with all the heathens. Apparently, my father's promotion to Lieutenant in the New York City Fire Department provided us the tuition to continue our private education. Seton Hall was way out in Patchogue, fifty miles east of our home in Bellmore. Two of my older cousins went there as well. Even though I was doing ok in public school, I opted to go to Seton Hall.

Seton Hall High School - Hello Gina

That was nuts. The bus picked us up at six in the morning. Ironically, it turned out that horribly long and boring bus ride was the best part of going to Seton Hall. Three towns later, we picked up the girlfriend-like sisters, sophomore Rene, and the first love of my life, fellow freshman Regina Leary. Gina sat in the third row of seats. Through the driver's rear view mirror from my first row seat, I had a perfect view of the prettiest girl I had ever seen.

I sneaked peeks at Gina every weekday morning and most afternoons until December. At that point, the madness of four hours of daily commute, and the concept of uniforms, and girls on one side of the room and boys on the other, and getting shoved into a locker because the seniors thought I was the shortest freshman, among other humiliations, gave me a handful of reasons to not return for a second semester. I'll miss you Gina. See you later. I don't think I ever said more than "Hello" to Gina in those three months. Years later - well, read on.

It seemed that our move from Brooklyn halted my growth hormones. I didn't make it to five foot until tenth grade and I became painfully shy with girls. In the summer before tenth grade, I shared a few puppy love kisses with Joanne, an eighth grade hottie who wanted to explore sexuality. Perhaps she could have cured my disease, my lack of confidence with girls, but, there was a complication. I played basketball with her older brother, John, whose reputation as one of the toughest kids in town persuaded me to break it off. I never saw Joanne again.

Cool Factor

During that summer of '65, I started hanging out in the record shop in Bellmore with a few other soon-to-be-sophomores. The owner, a young guy named Gary, didn't mind us hanging out there, as long as we looked like we were browsing when customers came in, so it looked like he had a bustling business. We were customers too. Gary would play the latest 45 releases, which, besides the British Invasion groups, included some local Long Island bands. It was a great way to know what was hot in music, and thus, to be cool.

There were maybe ten of us who became regulars at the store including a group of about a half dozen girls, most of whom I knew from school and who were in "the popular group". Among them, there was a new one, a bespectacled, pig-tailed blonde who, I could see behind those big glasses, resting partly on those chipmunk cheeks, was really cute.

I could talk to these girls about music, TV, and pizza, but only as part of the crowd. I was afraid to go one on one with any of them, much less the most beautiful of them all, Alice Dolby. But, how could I not at least try?

Well, I was most worried that if I asked her out on a date that she would say no. Isn't that our greatest teenage dating fear – rejection? So, I went with plan B, the end-around option. I asked Gary at the record shop to ask her how she felt about me. She had been telling him that she hadn't had a real date yet, just some couples dates with losers. He was hinting to me that I should ask her out.

Gary did his little investigation, seeming to like the Cupid role. His report back was devastating. She told him, "Brian? Yeah, he's nice, but too short." I was crushed. I was five foot tall, one hundred pounds that summer. Alice was about five-two. Teenagers think like that.

September came and, as luck would have it, Alice was in my Biology class in our high school, W.C. Mepham in North Bellmore. I usually sat close enough that I could stare at her pig-tails for forty-five minutes. There wasn't another girl in school as far as I was concerned.

In the fall, record store Gary became trusting enough in me to open the store for him a few Saturdays. He was a partying kind of guy and usually looked pretty bad Saturday mornings. So I helped him and the experience really helped my confidence as well - fifteen years old with keys to the store and cash register. He even paid me a few dollars.

The best part was that I got to play whatever records I wanted, most of which are on my phone to this day. It was the golden age of pop rock. Go ahead and Google "Top 100 pop hits September 1965". It's the pop-rock hall of fame. For Christmas, Gary gave each of us albums. Mine was 'Rubber Soul' by the Beatles. That album will always be ingrained in the grooves of my internal turntable for reasons I'll speak about later. But, I digress.

Put another notch in my 'cool' belt, but it didn't help me all that much come out of my self-created shy-shell. I wasn't shy. I knew that. Except with girls. I was clueless. With four sisters. Go figure!

Short Shit, aka Stud

Around that time I started to play a lot more basketball. Most sports came pretty naturally. I loved playing and watching. Basketball was a good fit because it mostly required athleticism. Bulk, not so much. Height helps, but little guys have made it before in pro basketball. I really worked hard at getting good, out till dark many an evening. I figured that if I could get to five-ten or so by senior year, the NBA would start to notice. At the end of that sophomore year I had grown an inch.

Depression was settling in. There would be no more chance of seeing Alice in school. The school district was exploding with baby boomers so they built a new high school, John F. Kennedy, in south Bellmore. The good news - no seniors, just juniors and sophomores. That helped - seniors have a habit of finding the shortest guy in school and picking on him. No seniors made all us juniors feel cool. We were the senior class for two years.

The bad part about no seniors was the sports teams. We sucked. I tried out for almost everything but I felt my size influenced coaches immediately. My best sports were basketball and football, though I loved baseball the most, but the coaches seemed to want the biggest. Had I made the teams, we couldn't have done worse. The first year without seniors, our football team was zero and eight.

The basketball team did not win a game with a horrifying record of 0-18. Half of those basketball players would practice down at Newbridge Road Park and they faced fierce competition from 'short shit'. That was one of my nicknames on the basketball courts.

In the fall we'd play tackle football games with no pads. I was known as "stud". Five-four, one hundred and twenty pounds. My game was to play fast and fearless, which was foolish. I only broke one knuckle though and was rewarded with the nickname that stuck for a few years. So what? Without a school sweater and a letter, the girl thing was tough.

Soon, I realized there were no new girls from the merged school district that did anything for me. I was so picky. The only ones that I thought were very pretty knew they were pretty and that made them ugly. Of course, that was my thinking. I never asked them if they thought they were pretty. I just put up a barrier because I was too timid to talk to them.

The one new girl who I really liked was about five foot ten. I don't think she ever knew who I was, and maybe that's because I never approached her. I didn't think any girl knew who I was, much less liked me. I didn't like this jerk who was me.

Senior year wasn't much better. I had lots of friends but no one I felt close to, maybe John Feeney, one of the Irish kids. He was smart and athletic. He became the basketball team manager as he too was short. I hung out with hoods to brainiacs, but I was getting worse with girls. No practice makes Johnny a bad date. Hah! I wasn't close to a date and making no attempt. No one was as pretty as Gina from that Seton Hall bus ride.

I Hate Life

I started to develop this self-loathing that brought on a self-imposed ultra-shyness with girls. At least, that's what I made myself believe. All I thought I had was my sports and music. There was a song back then called 'Patches'. It was a guy singing about his girlfriend who had just died. I still recall the lyrics, "Patches, oh what can I do? I swear, I'll always love you. Oh it may not be right, but I'll join you tonight. Patches, I'm coming to you". That sick idea didn't seem all that sick to me then.

Many a day, while playing basketball with myself in an imaginary high school game where I scored sixty points or so, I would die in a car accident later and Alice and Gina would come to my funeral and cry. And I guess that would make my soul happy? Who thinks like that? I hated me.

Senior year and I had no idea what I wanted to do with my life, except, maybe end it. I finally grew a little, topping off at five-six, so the pro basketball career was not on the horizon. I was a B+ student, not quite scholarship material, and my parents made it clear that if I wanted to go to college, go for it, but there would be little in the way of family financial aid.

Airplanes and flying had always been an interest. Why not? My father was a pilot in the war. There were two or three colleges in the country offering pilot training, but I could only afford one, the local State University of New York Agricultural and Technical College at Farmingdale, just fifteen miles away on Long Island. No brainer. Get me out of this prison. That is what high school felt like.

Near the end of my senior year, I started hanging out with a new group of guys. Bruce was a year or two older who lived up the block. I had known him for years but he was always a bit of a jerk, a loud-mouthed spoiled child. He seemed to have grown up a bit now that he was in college. I take that back – he wasn't invited back to C.W. Post after the first semester and spent most of his time up at the firehouse. He was a volunteer fireman.

Artie was a year younger and the son of my Sunday school teacher. I knew him through his mother. He was also on the track team and led the marching band.

Paul was also a senior at school. He was in my homeroom but in none of my classes, so I didn't know him very well. He was big guy, a lineman on the football team.

In the early spring, I was invited to play cards and stay overnight at Bruce's house. His parents were going away for the weekend. The real purpose of their card playing was to get drunk. I had never even had a sip of beer at seventeen and a half. I was, to most who knew me, the all-American boy, albeit a self-loathing, suicidal one.

With much trepidation, off I go to get drunk. Of course, I told them I had had a beer or two before. And I was going to show them that I could uphold my Irish heritage and keep up.

The first drink was rather large, a couple of ice cubes and the rest, cheap scotch. No big deal, I thought. About halfway through that drink I was showing them what a good hand I had drawn. It went downhill from there.

At the start of the next drink, the game had devolved and the world was not moving as I expected. Shortly thereafter I was praying to the porcelain God. When I repeatedly said I wanted to sleep they got worried, undressed me and threw me in the shower.

I recall little else from that evening except opening up all my feelings about being such a short loser. Only Artie was awake by that time. He shared some of his closer thoughts and a friendship was born, lasting to this day. You know, that last sentence might sound like it's off the cuff. But, I can't emphasize enough how important that friendship has been. I love that man.

I felt so much better about myself after that. We had a few more similar sessions that year and we all became pretty close, Artie and I especially. It was fun having real friends. All of them had girlfriends, or had some experience dating.

Bruce was dating a girl at least three years younger than him, Judi. We thought he was kind of robbing the cradle. Paul had a steady from our high school class, Maureen. Artie had dated a few girls, none you could call a girlfriend.

Me? No, but right at the end of senior year, a school friend, Tom, asked me to come over to his house one night. His girlfriend, Debbie, also a classmate, had a girlfriend, Connie, who wanted to meet me. She too was shy so Tom and Debbie wanted to set us up.

After some early objection, I agreed to go, just for the experience. There was no attraction. According to Tom, Connie liked me, but I had this pure vision of myself - if I wasn't in love immediately, I wasn't going to pretend. What a naïve nerd!

As the evening progressed past small talk and chips, Tom and Debbie started making out on the couch, and Connie and I just looked at each other with a little, "Ick" on our faces. Shortly thereafter, Tom and Debbie went to another room.

Connie gave me an inviting look, whatever that is, but I suppose it is an instinctual thing, that is, my believing she was inviting me....to do what? She inched over in her seat next to me on the couch. Oops, I was right. I hated this. I hated being me. Any normal seventeen year old would have made a move. Mine was to move away. What a friggin' idiot. That was the extent of my high school dating career.

Escape From Prison

A few weeks later, I graduated high school and with it, was unshackled from that horrible image of myself - not so much the image I had of myself but of the image I thought everyone else had of me.

This picture was the second take, after school was over. I didn't like my first shots so I let my Beatles cut grow out a little. Some vanity along with hatred. What's with that?

My new friends soon assured me that no one else thought I was anything but a fun loving, sports enthusiast, and not particularly shy. I already knew that, I just needed to shed the appearance that I thought I had projected to my peers. That sounds so fucked up. It's a good thing we didn't have a gun in the house.

The teenage years, for me, were, without a doubt, the worst.

Chapter 4 - Life After High School

The BDC

In the summer of '68, my newfound drinking buddies and I gave ourselves a name, the BDC, Bellmore Drinking Club. That name was a little premature. Only Bruce and Paul were legally old enough to drink. My eighteenth birthday was coming at the end of July and Artie would remain seventeen through February.

Our new bond evolved into recruiting a few others to join us as a softball team, though we were talked into changing the team's name to the Bums, due to our mix of underage players and, more importantly, the jerseys were cheaper with fewer letters. We barnstormed the surrounding towns, mostly playing against volunteer fire department teams. It was just an excuse for everyone to drink beer.

On my eighteenth birthday, after pineapple upside down cake at home – my mother always made our favorite dessert on our birthdays, Bruce took me to a local old man's bar where I showed off my recently issued driver's license and had a beer.

A few days later, the BDC originals packed into Bruce's Buick and headed up to Lake George for a few days of camping. We rented a tiny cabin and drank the entire time. What else? None of us were interested in pot. Actually, Artie and I had discussed it but decided "nah".

One night we went to a lakeside bar - Artie had a fake ID - in hopes of meeting girls but instead were entertained by Hurricane Hattie, a bawdy comedian/singer intended to please a much older audience. My experiences out in the "night life" were not inspiring and I still needed a date.

The boys were trying their best to hook me up. They set me up with one of Judi's good friends, Laura. Despite her six foot height, she went along, I suppose because she had a hard time getting dates herself. She was very pretty but intimidating up there and kissing her goodnight from a higher step was comical to both of us. I went out with another one of her friends who was cute and nice enough but I just didn't know how to get conversations going and was, frankly, too nervous. She was too and that didn't help. She turned me down for a second date.

With my Beatles haircut, Bruce kept touting me as George Harrison's brother whenever we were around a few girls. That never worked but when I tried out my best Liverpoolian accent, it was kind of fun. I enjoyed being someone else. It was liberating, not being that nerd from high school. That guy was gone anyway. This new guy seemed to be turning out a bit like the old guy though.

Summer flew by. I had gotten a seasonal job at Jones Beach State Park as a parking lot attendant. It was a highly desirable summer job on Long Island. My father had taken me to a used car dealer and bought me a 1960 Ford Fairlane for $200 to get me back and forth to work. It had a shift on the column. I learned how to drive that shift on the way back from the dealer's lot.

We learned shortly thereafter that it got forty miles to the quart of oil. It had a simple AM radio, poor heater, but a rather unique air circulation/supplemental braking system. The rusted out rear floor had large enough holes in it to provide room for feet to drop through to assist in braking. I had to put wooden panels down to preserve the heat in winter.

There was an incident where I needed that foot-assisted braking. We stuffed about eight members of the Bums into that old bomb after a softball game and all that weight was too much for the brakes. We were lucky not to get killed after going through a red light with almost no braking. I made two guys get out and walk.

The ignition system could not handle rain, even though it was high up in the engine compartment. One splash and the engine died and was out of commission for at least a half hour. Snow had the same effect but needed no splash. That piece of shit was not worth $200.

College began and I was excited to meet girls. However, my Aviation Technology major curriculum included about three girls and the required other classes were loaded with farmers. I joke but there were no Ellie Mae's to be found. I did make a good friend in Jorge (pronounce Hor-(roll the R)-hey) Gonzales, an Argentinean import. He already had his pilot's license.

That first semester I had expected to get flying lessons but I later learned that because I submitted my physical exam for the pilot's license a day late during the summer, I did not get into the pilot training program. Knowing it was my fault, I bit the bullet, bore down, and did very well in classes, including welding!?! I still have and use the red toolbox I built in that class. It looks like it will last another fifty years. I was having some fun but still no girls.

First Girlfriend

Artie and I went to a New Year's party bringing in 1969, got drunk, and met two girls. Sue Gold became my first girlfriend. Shortly after the new year I got an evening and weekend job at Kee-Zac Pharmacy in Bellmore to fund my dating habit and pay the $160 tuition for the spring semester. The romance lasted about three months. I think she got tired of me not even trying for second base - still the pure, all-American boy.

Sue was not everything I had been waiting for but the experience was needed, as was the breakup. I never thought I'd break up with a girl and, though I technically didn't, I was relieved when we split up. I could be mad, sad and glad about it, and was. I had loved and lost. Loved? No, not really, not even close, but I could now say I had had a girlfriend. And a Jewish one to boot.

Yeah, that went over like a lead balloon in the Carlin household – a Jewish girlfriend. Get used to it. They were still getting over my older sister, Susan, dating an Italian. Well, Sue cured me of any animosity I might have had toward people of other religions. I got the fucking nuns back. Nah nah ne nah nah. I'm not going to hell for dating a heathen!

The spring semester, 1969, also did not include flight training. I was getting a little frustrated. On the plus side, Jorge started bringing me along with him on some of his flights, one an April day trip to Virginia. Now that was fun. And the Mets were starting to look like a real baseball team.

As summer approached, I got an early call for the Jones Beach job and suddenly I was working sixty hours a week, averaging about $1.30 an hour, and rolling in dough.

Cool Factor by 10, Right, Peggy?

With the promise of payback, my father loaned me $1500 so I could get a real car, a red, 1966 Mercury Cyclone, a muscle car with a custom four speed stick, souped up for racing with a huge

Shelby clutch. The big, 390 engine produced 335 horse power (how do they know that, and, which horses?), a tad bit better than that Fairlane.

My father test drove it and said, "A lot better

compression than that piece of shit you have now." I think he secretly loved it, maybe not so much when I screeched those tires.

Wow. My cool factor was climbing. Well, maybe not so much me, but the car was great. The next few paychecks added some big-assed tires, a

Thrush muffler, rear suspension lifters and an eight-track tape player with speakers all over. Vanilla Fudge never sounded so good, "Set Me Free Why Don't Ya Babe". Now all I needed was a babe.

Sometime in early summer, Artie hooked me up with his new girlfriend's friend, Peggy. We hit it off right away. She was cute and fun, but smoked. That was a problem I overlooked for a while.

We went out to dinners, movies, a Mets game, and watched Neil Armstrong walk on the moon together. I wanted to love and be loved. I thought this might be the one, just my second girlfriend, but she was going to have to stop smoking. And, I'm pretty sure, she wanted me to do more than make out.

I was very slow on the uptake then, wondering where respect ends, just waiting for a distinct invitation to go for it. By September it was over. I was mad at her for not even trying to stop smoking. She probably had had enough of my goodie two shoes approach.

Near the end of the summer I started to go out to a bar in Wantagh with Bruce and Paul. Artie didn't join us, for good reason. He had stolen Judi from Bruce. It was a bit awkward for some time. At the end of August they all went away to college. I finally went to The Tabard Ale House alone. It became my new home away from home.

The Tabard Ale House

That was a big step in my confidence. I went to a bar on my own to try to meet a girl. It didn't take long to strike up a friendship with the bartender at the back end of the bar, Roger. He was also the best looking guy back there and attracted girls. I learned strategic positioning and hung out near the girl's bathroom - you will see every girl in the place.

With a couple of beers in me, I got some courage and started looking at girls in the eyes and kept looking, not turning away at a glance back. That was a fun, confidence builder. When they looked back, I smiled, then went over and talked. Me?

That alcohol did wonders. Of course, you have to find out if she was wacked out, had special needs, or was actually as nice as she looked.

I started dancing. Me? Even when not asking someone else to. I was having a great time and eventually met girls I wanted to date. Those couple of beers loosened me up and I could talk to girls, like I already knew them. Where was that me in high school?

One of my first attempts at going beyond just dancing and actually asking a girl out on a date was with the very hot blonde, Sue Schramton. I was not expecting to fall in love. I wasn't even expecting her to say yes. I was all about physical looks then, at least to start things off.

Once Sue accepted the date and we were out, I was expecting her to encourage me to be more aggressive. I needed to learn from an experienced girl. What I wasn't expecting on the date was her telling me she'd be right back from the bathroom and never returning.

That sucked. It was a rather large setback. Sue and I had several mutual friends who all hung out at the bar. It was embarrassing. I took a break from the Tabard Ale House.

In the meantime during the fall, I did not get in the pilot training program again. That was very bad and all my pleading did not get me into it. I began wondering where I would go next year. The good news, the Mets win the World Series.

High school was more than a year in my rear view mirror. I had a very cool car. I had lots of friends. I was popular. Guys liked me. Girls liked me. The Mets were champions of the world. I was doing so well in school that I didn't bother to buy the calculus book for class. My confidence was growing every day.

On the down side, I was 19 and living with my parents. I never considered it a negative though. I was still a bit too nàive and the confidence was not that high. And, let's get real - I hadn't even attempted to get to second base yet. There was still a lot of growing up to do.

In the late fall, Jorge and I flew up to an airport near Colgate, where Artie was attending college, picked him and another student up, dropped off the other kid in Albany, then flew back to Farmingdale on LI. A great adventure. Jorge had also brought me and friends to his home turf in Astoria, Queens, introducing us to the legendary "Connecting Highway".

If you love cars, you must check out this website: http://www.connectinghighway.com/

This was a highway connecting the Brooklyn-Queens Expressway (known as the BQE to NYers) to the Grand Central Parkway. In the 60's and 70's it was the east coast Mecca of street racing. The brainchild of Robert Moses, the godfather of NY state parks, roads, and master planning, the Connecting Highway, part of Interstate 278, was dug deep into the ground rather than as a raised road.

This design provided instant grandstands for all viewing the races that would occur between two overpassing streets, almost exactly one quarter mile apart.

Designated crazies would stop traffic approaching the "strip" while racing machines of all kinds, including full blown rail dragsters, replete with deployed parachute at the finish, would stop at the starting line while another nut would stand in the highway between the racers and count down, 3-

2-1, drop an arm and hope that the clutch popping would not produce a blown engine part or swerve so severe as to endanger life as the highly modified speed machines tore to the next overpass where sometimes a flagman would indicate the winner.

Pandemonium would erupt in the streets above, lined with race fans. Who needed to go out to the Jersey drag strip for "Sunday, Sunday, Sunday!" - remember those radio commercials you NYers?

Steve McQueen's Got Nothin' on Me

So let's back up a few weeks to Halloween night, 1969. Jorge, fellow BDC buddies Paul and newly inducted member, Nunzio, and I were returning from an evening at the Connecting Highway. We were near to dropping Jorge off at his Farmingdale apartment near the college, sitting at a traffic light facing east on Rt24.

We're at the intersection with Fulton St which comes in from the southeast at about a 40° angle. Suddenly a speeding car goes flying by, skidding in front of me, unable to complete the turn and bounces off the north curb, smacking into my beautiful Cyclone's left rear quarter panel on that rebound

I'm pissed and as I'm about to get out, the car backs up and then speeds away on 24 to the west. I look around to see if any other drivers are aware of what just happened and the guy next to me on the right, in a gorgeous, new, powder blue Ford Torino flashes his police badge at me, nods up and down, and then tears out in front of me, pulling a full u'ey while burning rubber, and takes off after the guy. I figure, why not, I spin my tires and the car, now following and suddenly it's a scene from Bullitt!

There's Officer Joe Bolton flying ahead of me in hot pursuit of the bad guys. Approaching slowing traffic ahead, they make a right, bouncing through a gas station to avoid the red light. The blue Torino goes right through after them and we follow, all of us leaving sparks in our wake. Down the back streets of Farmingdale through stop sign after stop sign at 60-80-100mph. No Shit. Officer Joe either decides this is not worth it or attempts to try to cut them off going down another block. We never see him again.

We start prowling the back streets and then suddenly we're right behind them and Paul writes down their license plate number. We think we have them, pulling alongside when they turn around on a sidewalk, drive opposite traffic, and then disappear down another side street. This time we lose them.

So we head to a police station and tell our story. We're told to get in line, it's Halloween and they have bigger fish to fry. But, they track the plate and give us an address.

By now it's 2AM. We find the house (how did we do that without GPS?), see the car with the red paint on the smashed bumper, and knock on the door. The lights are still on and a middle aged dirt bag comes to the door - "Whad'ya want?"

"Whoever drove that white car over there with the red paint on the smacked up bumper hit me tonight and then took off."

He comes out and looks at the car and my car. He goes back inside and yells, "Hey Asshole, get your ass down here." Here comes Asshole. "Did you hit this guy tonight?"

"I don't know if it was him.". Smack upside the head.

Nunzio pipes up, "We have your license plate and reported it to the police who gave us your address."

Paul recognizes Asshole, "Yeah, he's the punk who ran away." Paul is big enough to kick everyone's ass.

Senior Dirt Bag says, "Whad'ya want?"

I say, "I want you to pay for getting my car fixed. Let's share insurance information."

"I ain't got no insurance."

Ok, now I'm fucked. I tell him, "The cops said that if you can't get him to fix it you call us and we'll arrest him for leaving the scene of an accident."

"Get me an estimate and give me a few weeks. I'll pay for it."

And that's what happened. You don't ever want that to happen to you but I can tell you driving through a gas station at 50mph and flying through stop signs at 100mph, throwing sparks as your muffler bottoms out, was one of the most exhilarating experiences of my life. It happened just like that. How did I ever survive my youth?

The Roller Skater

In December, back at the Tabard Ale House, I met a real cutie - unfortunately, one of the few whose name has gotten lost in the cobwebs of my mind, the 1968 roller skating champion of the USA. At least, that's what she said she was. I asked her out on a date for the following weekend. She was so cute, I couldn't wait and did a drive-by of her house at night so I knew where I was going and wouldn't be late.

The first date went very well, as far as I was concerned. No red flags and a very enthusiastic kiss goodnight. All-American boy wouldn't dare go further than a little tongue kissing and even that was pretty daring for a first date. Could she be "the one"?

Artie came home for Christmas and spent most of his time with Judi. We double dated with them at least once.

The roller skater was my priority but I also felt that she was holding back some, like maybe she was dating someone else. I was pretty confident with myself but not with love and my true feelings. So, I was also holding back a little. I wanted a girl a little more aggressive or perhaps responding to me a bit more positively. You know what I mean? Actually, I was too timid to get sexual. I don't know why. Any shrinks out there want to comment? We didn't make any exclusive dating commitments so I still went to the bar and kept my eyes open.

At about the same time, the owners at Kee-Zac, the drug store, were always asking me about the girls. They saw me grow from this very shy and awkward kid to a confident girl-getter in a year and seemed to enjoy hearing of my exploits. And then they wanted me to go after a customer.

Summer Blonde Sue

Sue Brock was a freshman at Farmingdale, daughter of one of the better dressed couples who frequented the store. I had noticed Sue several months ago as a customer in the store and had conversed with her many times. I could tell she liked me. And what was not to like about her? Cheerleader good looks with the biggest and blondest hair in town. Biggest boobs too. Did I just say that? Mr. All-American boy? What, am I blind? And the drug store owners, Al and Pete, who kept urging me on, were not blind either. Wink-wink.

Sue wore just the right make-up and was very pretty, a head turner. Maybe too pretty for me. After the Sue Schramton fiasco, my confidence had slipped a notch with the blonde beauties and then I was dating the roller skater by December so I never really considered asking her out.

Come winter, it seemed like Sue was in the store more frequently and when she came in, Pete and Al would ask me to wait on her while they pretended they were busy and went into the back of the store to leave me alone with her. Finally, one day in January, I asked her out and, to my mild surprise, she said yes.

On that first date, We went to a Santana concert at Farmingdale. That first date was kind of a classic. I had this thing, a negative thing, about really pretty girls, especially blondes. I was more drawn to the cute type, or pretty but not so sure of themselves - you get that? I was turned off by the nose-in-the-air, "look at me but don't dare talk to me" types, whatever that is. I thought it was a "type" then. Another projection.

Well, Sue was almost that "bad". She certainly had that look-at-me-but-don't-touch look, but, she turned out to be very approachable. So, with my growing confidence, I'm game for taming the beast.

Knock, knock at the front door and good looking, dapper dad let's me in and I take a seat near the door by the stairs. Most of the homes in the area were Cape Cods with the front door opening to the living room and stairs right in front of you leading to the two second floor bedrooms.

The still very pretty, I suppose she was no more than 45-50, mom appears. With an instant flash to Mrs. Robinson, I stand up to greet her. Now here's the part I so clearly remember, putting this date In the "classics" category: In a bit of a show, she then walks over to a portrait of Sue at the bottom of the stairs and, drumroll, clicks on a switch to a light at the bottom of the frame.

Ah, there she is. How lovely! I want to gag and run away. Here's one of those moments – what am I doing here? We small talk a bit before the princess descends the staircase. Should I curtsy? Gotta go, concert starts soon. Get me outa here!

Now, I'm still Mr. All American boy and have got proper manners and am instilled with chivalry, but every other girl I've dated has at least reached for a door handle before I tried to open it. Tonight I have to remember all my goodie boy skills. This could be a long night.

Well, right off she seemed quite relieved to be away from her rather strict parents so I began to think that this wouldn't be so bad. It wasn't. The concert kept conversation to a minimum. A good night kiss on the lips was the best that I could expect.

Second base was as big as I'd ever dated but having never been in the area, I'd just as soon leave those puppies alone for now. I don't recall whether there was a kiss on that first date but it went well enough to warrant round two. I was happy to deliver her safe and sound and be able to say I dated a bombshell. The boys at Kee-Zac will want details. They were probably more excited about the date than I was. Funny, I can't remember a kiss, but as clear as this page is to you, I can see her mom turning on that light below the portrait.

The fact was, I was dating two girls. When my father found out he said I better get another job. The next weekend I went out with the roller skater, the next with Sue again. Now we're into February but I'm still going to the bar. Why stop at two? I meet yet another cutie at the Ale House who I ask out.

So, the second weekend of February in 1970, I have three dates. Friday the 13th with the skater, Saturday, Valentine's Day, with Blonde Sue, and Sunday with a snake. What you mean by that?

Janet The Snake

Ok, here we go. Like many young men before and after, we used the numbering system to rate girls. Yes, despicable, I know. Well, fucking deal with it. (I think we now have a short version of "deal with it" – A Mulvaney!) I can't change who I was and what shaped me at the time. This is a typical 19 year old. Hell, the numbering system was a movie title (but I didn't think Bo was a 10).

Sue? My thought then was about an 8.5, but those bodacious ta-ta's put her up in the low 9's. Yeah, they count. The skater, a 9+ for sure. The snake? Snake! Ok, here's where we go off road. Think black hair, lots of make-up, a bit slinky – tight clothes. Hot! Today you might think Goth, without the piercings, not that extreme. Patti Smith-like. Maybe a motorcycle chick, but gotta have black hair and makeup. Kind of tough looking.

Here's another way to think of snakes. Just about every girl who didn't have long black hair, and didn't paint on a ton of makeup, and didn't wear the tightest and tiniest mini-skirts, called them sluts. Every guy's one night dream date. Well, some of us. You know, just once.

Snakes defy the 1 to 10 system. They are either yes or no, answering the question 'would you do her?' (as if – we dreamed) and you can precede the yes or no with an adjective like, "A definite yes, a knee pads only yes, a take-her-home-to-mom yes, a sleazy no." I'm not proud of how we objectified women. Just wish that one of those snakes would have snatched me for a few hours. Or did one?

My third date of the weekend, Janet, is a snake, a definite yes. Cute as can be under the make-up. Met her at the Ale House and, after Summer Blonde Sue, I felt magnetized to the black hair and makeup. Janet was hot and nice, probably just a sweet kid in snake attire.

This weekend! This weekend the All-American Boy's life will take a turn. Three dates with three cuties on Valentine's weekend. What a perfect life! Could it get any better?

Phase 2: The Life Changers

Chapter 5 - Life Changer One: Pam

Part I - The Weekend

Friday the 13th, February, 1970. No, nothing sinister or unlucky happened. I was on my date with the roller skater. At some point, completely out of the blue, she asked me if I had ever done LSD. She was interested in trying it.

That blew me away. I mean, she skipped right over pot. So, out of the deeper blue, I lied and said I had tried it and that the experience was bad. I actually said I ended up in a tree and didn't know how I got there. What was I thinking? Pretty sure I was afraid of what I had read about it. Shit, I wasn't ready to try pot. Drugs? Hell, I was afraid to try to touch a breast!

That line of bullshit, I believe, sealed it for us. She probably realized I was lying. But, the fact was, I didn't want to hang with anybody interested in doing acid. What a difference a year makes, but, later for that.

I suppose the biggest problem was that I just lied to her and I didn't know why, or admit why – that I was afraid. I felt stupid and ashamed but I also didn't think that this would be our last date. I still liked her a lot. We'll get past this. The drug thing kind of hit me out of the blue. Didn't she want to explore sex?

Saturday, February 14th, Valentine's Day, I have a date with Sue tonight. I'm not particularly excited about it, but it's cool. Not excited? I had surely changed in the twenty months or so since I graduated. Never dated in high school and now I'm almost ambivalent about going out with, arguably, the hottest girl in town. Well, come on, I have two other hot ones this weekend.

Maybe the real me didn't change. I tend to think that I just became myself. Now I'm me, not the me I hated. And maybe I just knew none of those girls in high school were for me. The girls I wanted were out there. Maybe I wasn't lookin' into the eyes of the sun? You know? Oh, later for that.

Of course, I still had no clue how to get this sex thing off the ground.

First and foremost, I want to respect women as human beings, as objects of love in the purest level of that concept (even the 8.1's – oh, come on, lighten up). Secondly, I want to get laid. How do those two goals coalesce? Hang in there, buddy.

Do-Wah-Diddy-Diddy Here She Comes

It was just another Saturday, albeit a Valentine's Day, working at the drug store from ten to six. I was in that slow period of the day, late afternoon, pondering last evening with the roller skater – Jesus, did I fuck that up or what? - and tonight's date with Sue. Sue was like a short Jayne Mansfield. What? You don't know Jayne-severed-head-Mansfield? OK, maybe not cut off but such a mess, who knows! Look her up. But yeah, that kind of figure. Second base was certainly on my mind.

At about four o'clock, my friend Bruce strolls in. Bruce is always loud enough to be the center of attention and I always cringe when he comes in the store, hoping he won't offend anyone or make too much of an ass out of himself and me by association. My father calls him the village idiot. He's a walking caricature of all the embarrassingly loud, sometimes rude, sometimes clownish men you have ever known. You never know what he is going to say. But today, Bruce is not alone.

At his side is the hottest woman I had ever seen. Pam was born three days after me but she was no kid. This was a woman. Long, wavy red hair, wide-spread glistening green eyes, beautifully symmetrical face with sculpted high cheek bones, those mildly puffy cheeks freckled for cuteness, small, slightly turned up nose, thin lips curved up in a perpetual Mona Lisa smile with one crooked, imperfect incisor bringing Venus down to earth, and, with her winter coat flapping open, her tight blouse accented jaw dropping curves.

My jaw dropped. I also quickly processed the heavy make-up, mini-skirt, fish nets and spike heels. Nah, she was too gorgeous to be a hooker and Bruce couldn't afford one. A red-headed snake! A gorgeous python! For the first time in my life I believe in love at first sight.

Pam and Bruce had just come in from Southampton College where Bruce was attempting to get a degree between drinks. Pam worked in the registrar's office. I don't know how they met but Bruce's outgoing manner and Pam's attractiveness might have had something to do with it.

At any rate, here they come blasting through the door at Kee-Zac Pharmacy and I am blown away that Bruce is with someone this stunning. He's very good at meeting women but then he'll be himself and they'll be gone, or, one of his friends, like Artie, like me, will pursue. Perhaps this one's drunk. Why else would she be with Bruce? Oh, I don't care, she's gorgeous. Pursue!

Introductions are made and the purpose of their visit disclosed - I lead Pam to the panty hose rack. They are going to the Bellmore Firemen's Valentine's Day Dance tonight. He's a volunteer.

Bruce's parents are away for the weekend. Well, have fun tonight guys. As they leave he tells me to come over after work for a beer. I can't, got a date, but he says "After work tomorrow. We're not going back until Monday." You bet I will. My Sunday date is at 9PM. I can't get Pam out of my head.

While Bruce is having fun I can't even imagine, Sue and I go to the movies, The Itch, the locals' affectionate nickname for the old theater in town. I tried putting my arm around her during the show but she squirmed. Oh well, my arm isn't very long anyway. Second base was safe. As the movie let out, we ran into a couple I knew.

It had started snowing and gentlemen were getting their cars and picking up their dates in front. We agreed to meet our friends at The Branding Iron, a bar in Wantagh, the next town to the east. We drank small pitchers of vodka gimlets. I loosened up considerably, as did Sue, and I started telling her what I really thought about snobby girls and that ridiculous show her parents put on.

Anticipating the worst response and at first encountering a look of incredulation, she totally surprised me by thanking me. She hated playing the pretty girl game. Her parents were always pushing her to be perfect. And suddenly she wasn't just a date, she was my friend. OK, it was still a date but it was so much more comfortable.

If it hadn't been snowing so hard we might have lingered when I pulled up in front of her house - second base seemed within reach. Unfortunately, dad was literally standing at the front door waiting for us, professing to be worried because of the snow. It was pretty late too, and we were drunk. I was sure that one more drinking date would advance my sexual horizons.

Minutes earlier, while driving back to Sue's house I had heard sirens and thought, "There goes the firehouse dance", but also realized that it was nearly two in the morning. On the way home, after depositing Sue with her father, I started to think about Pam and, yes, I was fairly intoxicated. Bruce's home was just up the block from me so I thought stopping by to see them would be a good idea. You know how thinking and drinking go.

Approaching his house I could see tire tracks in the snow in his driveway but no Buick. He had gone to the fire. Imagine all those loaded fireman helping somebody else? I couldn't. I only wanted to see Pam again. I pulled in the driveway and knocked on the door for five minutes. I found out later she was passed out drunk. What would I have said? God, that was dumb!

Sunday, February 15th, 1970 was my first date with Janet, the Snake. Hung over today, I was hoping for a quiet day at the store. My thoughts drifted between possibilities with Sue, feeling queasy, possibilities with Janet, feeling queasy, and possibilities with Pam. Pam? Come on, man. You're in Class A, she's Major league. But let's focus on tonight. I have a date with a cute snake. If I'm ever going to get laid it's with her. But suppose I really like her? I don't want her to think that's all I want.

As I have that conversation with myself for the millionth time another piece of my mind drifts to visions of Pam. Now I really can't wait for six o'clock so I can go over for that beer. I just want to see that face again.

Sunday, 6:05PM at Bruce's house. From Kee-Zac to his house it's three short blocks on Bedford Avenue in the village of Bellmore, across the Long Island Railroad tracks, across Sunrise highway, second right, Clarendon, a short block to Washington. Buddy, Bruce's twelve-year-old protégé from across the street was there with a beer in his hand. Little Buddy? Little Billy's younger brother? What is wrong with Bruce? Why is this kid here? Fuck it, I got a beer too.

Pam was doing some hand sewing, something like that keeping her busy, but also sipping a beer. I sat across from her and could barely keep my eyes from staring.

God, she was pretty. I have no idea where the conversation went. I recall she was fairly quiet. I kept looking at her and thought that I'd be caught playing the eye game but it was more like I had to look at her. Occasionally she would look up at me and our eyes would briefly lock on, outside of conversation.

At one point Bruce was talking and, there, that's the signal - we connected! Those beautiful green eyes lit up and a subtle smile washed over her face. It happened a few times. I wasn't sure but I really wanted to feel that something was going on between us - for a few split seconds. Oh, I was sure! Then I had to go on my date.

Really? We just fell in love? No? What was that? That was something. Why didn't I just tell her right there? Get down on my knees and ask her to marry me? Something just fucking happened!

That was myself screaming at me on the short ride down the block to my house. Preparing for a date with someone other than who you are thinking about is difficult.

I recall very little about that date. After my imagined eye-contact affair with Pam, I was just going through the motions. Janet was cute, sexy, and by the aggressiveness of her goodnight kiss, willing. What the fuck was I thinking? This was the hottest first date I ever had but in the middle of that deep kiss, I thought of Pam. You dumb shit! I forget how stupidly I must have acted but our date ended shortly thereafter. My ride with me on the way home was loud.

"Didn't Pam look me in the eye and send some kind of message? I felt it. She did too. Or was it imagined? She stared at me and we were eye to eye for a second. Nah, think about this, dumb ass - you've just been out with three cuties this weekend. You're on fire. These were all nice girls, my speed. Well, Janet could bring me up to her speed, but Pam is out of my league. Forget it. Stop thinking about her!"

Part II - What?

By Monday morning on the drive to school, I had talked myself down from the world of Pam. Back to the future. The aviation technology curriculum was going well enough but I wasn't in the flight training program and this was the last semester. The next step, a four year school with flight courses, was starting to look like a problem. I couldn't afford it. The only colleges with flight training were in California, Northrup, if I recall, and some place in Michigan. In truth, I really wasn't paying too much attention to school.

I had girlfriends, plural! That's where my attention was. One of these days I was going to meet "the one", and maybe I'll even have sex, but first and foremost, I want someone to tell me they love me. That was the real goal.

Tuesday, February 17th, 1970. After taking Monday night off from the bar, I was back at my usual seat after my evening shift at the drug store.

Around eleven, Roger, the bartender, calls me over, says I have a call.

Bruce is on the phone and asks me if I'm going to be at the bar Thursday night. "Yeah, from about ten-thirty on." Where else would I be on a Thursday night?

He says, "Last night I was out with a bunch of people and Pam was there and she couldn't stop talking about you. She was drunk but she kept saying she loved you."

"WHAT?"

"Yeah, I know, but today when she was sober she remembered it all and wants you to come out to a party at her house this Saturday night. She's going to call you Thursday night on the bar phone. OK?"

"OK, I'll be here." I give the phone back to Roger, wondering what the fuck just happened, and ask for another drink, telling him to pour himself one too. I tell Roger the whole story, he buys me another and wishes me luck.

I keep thinking, "What? What just happened?" That eye contact Sunday! It was real. Did I just get called up to the majors?

To say that Wednesday and Thursday couldn't go fast enough would be an understatement of epic proportions. As the memories keep filling my head, I'm back there that evening. I race home from work, change into my bar clothes, swallow some mouthwash and I'm at the bar by ten-fifteen.

Thursday is the best bar night for meeting someone. Weekend dates are made. It is the busiest night of the week for single girls, and this Thursday night is no different. With my mind on just one thing, the impending phone conversation, I see none of those single girls. Not tonight. I work my way towards the bar near the phone, order my beer and wait.

Pretty much on time, the phone rings. Roger waves me over and smiles, "There's a girl on the line asking for a Brian." Wise ass. Guess I need a little loosening up

Even knowing she was calling, I'm nervous as hell. I knew why she was calling. She knew I knew why she was calling. But, in the back of my mind, I wonder, "Is this some scheme Bruce cooked up - to what end? Oh, fuck that thought. We connected. She likes me. Here we go…"

Pam's nervous too as she invites me to a party at the house she rents with her friend, Alana, in Hampton Bays. I eagerly accept and she gives me directions. I'm in uncharted territory. What is happening?

Isn't it strange how you remember some experiences in detail and have no recollection of others? I suppose when the experience is so traumatic you tend to keep those memories nearer the surface.

Up to that point in my life, these were, by far, the peaks, maybe not traumatic but intensely dramatic, to me. A few years down the road I came up with another theory about memories. We'll discuss later.

As I retrieve the basics from those days, I see them more clearly, some hour by hour. It still blows me away – it's like a movie running on my head. I thought this would be a quick retelling of the general story line but as I go on, I'm back there. Some of the details are fuzzy and I'm filling in a few holes but this is pretty damn close to exactly how it all went down.

Part III - How High is High?

Saturday, February 21st, 1970. If Wednesday and Thursday seemed to drag, Friday and Saturday were the days the earth stood still. After working Saturday, I showered, shaved, and put on my coolest clothes, then picked up a six-pack which I locked in the trunk, with, I would find out later, the trunk key. And then I was off on the hour drive from Bellmore to Hampton Bays. Come on, Klaatu, move your fucking ass!

Anxious? Ya think? I did all I could to keep that Cyclone from speeding too much. Vanilla Fudge was blaring on the 8-track, "Take Me For a Little While". I'd be good with that, I think. Be careful what you wish for.

Finally, I pull up in front of the house and try to get the six-pack from the trunk, but no trunk key. So, just go up and ring the bell, dumb-ass. I talk to myself that way a lot, especially when I'm being a dumb-ass, or a shit-for-brains, or just a fucking idiot. Just before I ring the bell, I pause on the front step and get serious for a moment. I think, "How did everything I've done in my life get me to this point?"

You ever get to one of those moments where maybe something big is going to happen, or it is happening? You step outside yourself for a moment and look at the play that is your life. I thought about the last week, how if I wasn't Bruce's friend this wouldn't be happening, if any number of things were different I wouldn't be here. It was one of those moments that made me feel like this is something.

Remember Letterman's bit, "Is it Anything?"? This may be just a joke on me, and I was considering that, you know, that the clown-prince, Bruce, had Pam play some game with me, but, if he wasn't yanking my chain, it also might be really something. It might be everything.

I just stood there for at least a minute. It was timeless. I am standing there now, looking up at the stars, wondering what's next?

I heard music and talking inside. Here goes nothing. Ring-a-ding. Pam, with rollers in her hair and minimal make-up answered. My introduction was "Guess who's here?", or something idiotic like that. Dumb-ass was joining the party. I was almost expecting her to grab me around the head, pull me to her and suck my tongue out. After what Bruce had said about her loving me, I was ready for almost anything.

Pam calmly invited me in and introduced me to Alana and three other girlfriends. Alana, who went by Al, grabbed me a beer while Pam ran back into her bedroom to finish prettying up.

Great, me and four girls. I'm pretty confident speaking one on one when meeting a new girl now, but how do I pull this off? This is the party? Maybe the prank is that I'm gonna get raped. I work on that fantasy as I find a seat. Getting real, I'm wondering how I'm going to comfortably talk to four girls I just met. Well, this ain't high school anymore. I can do this and proceed to babble as I'm still wondering what the hell is going on.

Not sure how I survived those minutes. I recall that I felt a bit like I was under interrogation but when each girl asked a question, I turned to my recent friend, the look-em-in-the-eye-completely-absorbing-their-words-like-I-should-have-been-doing-all-along approach, and felt at ease talking to them.

Being the new kid who Pam invited, her friends wanted to know all about me. I locked onto some pretty eyes - whoop, here comes a name I haven't recalled in nearly fifty years, Rene. In a few split seconds I was hoping for some indication that clothes would soon be shed for the coming orgy.

With my shyness around girls a thing of the past, I rambled on about my not so exciting college life, leaving out the part of dating three different women last weekend. It kept my mind off wondering what I was going to say to Pam.

Some more people arrived including Alana's boyfriend, Bob, and it became a more normal party. End of the rape/orgy fantasy. Pam, looking ravishing, by far the most attractive girl there, and, in my eyes, on the planet, reappeared and sat next to me as the conversations spread out.

Now, as those memories of the night start bubbling up, I see myself sitting in that living room. I see Al. I see Rene. I'm back there. Time has lost its grip. I'm looking at Pam who says she's getting a beer. She calls to me from the kitchen and I'm there in a second. It's a small room.

We are alone and she faces me, "Did Bruce tell you what I said the other night?"

"Yes."

"What did he say?"

Oh boy, here we go. This had to happen sooner or later. I guess sooner is better. This is weird but, "He said that you said you loved me."

Here it comes, she's gonna say she was drunk. We are very close together in the little kitchen at this point. She gets closer. "I do. I love you."

What is a 19 year old to do, besides melt? What does anyone do in that situation? Who has had that situation? I mean, did anything like that ever happen to you?

My head is spinning so high. And again, time gives up the ghost and I see that face right now, writing this. Those are the words I've been waiting for. I echo back, "I love you." I kiss her on the lips, she kisses back, and we lock on for who knows how long. It gets deep.

Someone says "Excuse me", the refrigerator door opens and closes, but the voice is gone when we come up for air. Secret, if there ever was one, is out of the bag. We look around and laugh and go back at it. A minute or two later with shit eating grins, a beer in one hand, and the other hand holding the other's tight, we go back to the party. I am so high I can't see anyone down there. I only see the most gorgeous woman on the planet, and she loves me. I keep getting higher.

Try as I might, I don't recall any other moments after the kitchen scene from that night. Maybe I was drifting in disbelief. I do know we drank a bunch of beers and fell asleep together on the living room couch. No sex, though there's a chance I made it to second base.

On Sunday morning I realized I just slept with "the one". She looked absolutely slutty in a movie star kind of way with mascara running and that red hair all messed up. I loved her more. After cleaning up, we went to church. I still believed that if I missed a Sunday mass I would go to hell.

Yep, 19 year old, god fearing Catholic, All American boy, who is dating - is that what you call it? - whose girlfriend is, the best looking, hottest woman on earth. God's checking you out, dude. You better do this right.

At church I met some of her family and they invited us back to Sunday dinner. I met brothers and sisters and the parents. They were all very welcoming. I wondered if they cared that I stayed overnight with their daughter. I wondered if I was just another one. Pam made it clear that I was her new boyfriend. Late in the afternoon we said our goodbyes, planned for me to come out again next weekend and I went back to my sheltered life.

Part IV - Living in a Dream

It was a dreamlike existence. This was the dream I had been craving for, love. I needed someone to shake the shit out of me and make me say, "I love you". I was one of the pickiest assholes on the planet when it came to pretty girls and now the prettiest of all was in love with me.

Those thoughts consumed me all week long. I went to school and work in a fog. The drug store owners wanted to know how my thing with Sue was going and I told them it was over, I had a new girlfriend, a real keeper. I think I told everyone, my friends and family. I never called my three other dates again.

There were a few awkward moments at the drugstore with Sue that spring. Then I didn't see her again until Halloween, 1987, in Glen Cove, NY. She brought her daughter, similar in age to our three year-old, to a public Halloween party for little kids. I recognized her immediately – she looked exactly the same after 27 years, statuesquely beautiful. With my thick dark beard I went over and re-introduced myself. It took a minute for her to recall who I was. We had a short and awkward conversation. It was odd. I digress.

Back to late February, 1970. I was so happy, but Pam was sixty miles away. I called her every night, or she called me. I went to the bar after work because I didn't want to face the reality that I lived with my parents. I do remember sitting at the bar and fending off pickup lines. Oh, that did happen. Why does it happen when you're not interested? Somebody is always on the hunt on both sides. Maybe it was that shit eating grin I had on twenty-four-seven. Happy people are easy to approach.

The next weekend we did more of the same - heavy petting Saturday night, church in the morning, walking on the beach, more getting to know you. The Saturday scene was just Alana and Bob, who went out, and Pam and I who stayed in.

Again, we slept on the couch and I believe there was a long play at third base, once I found my way. I had no idea what I was doing. Just running on instinct and getting little guidance. I had assumed she had some sexual experience. There was no reciprocal handy-work so I took that as a sign to stop at third. For as forward as Pam was in verbally expressing her love, she offered little in the way of responsive sexual signals - at least to this pathetic sap. In hindsight, I was just slow. The entire package said "come get me".

I was afraid. Suppose I fucked it up? Suppose she didn't want my advances at all? Suppose she's like me and wants to save it for marriage? Well, that wasn't true. I wanted to go there now. I just didn't know how to get there. I still wonder why she didn't take the lead when it was obvious how inexperienced I was.

The next weekend she and Alana invited a few other people out, reducing chances for intimacy. It was also not the time of the month conducive to sexual activity. A few of my friends came out Saturday and we all got drunk.

Now it's March 8th. Again, church, say hi to the family, go home. I'm still deeply in love but feeling like more should be happening. Bruce kind of nudged me this week about being more forward. He said Pam wanted me to be more forward. She wanted to do it.

The weekend of March 14th involved a more concerted effort and with Bob and Alana retreating to a bedroom, Pam and I loosened up on the couch as side one of 'Rubber Soul' repeated for hours. With extreme awkwardness, and not even sure if my placement was correct, the deed was done.

Home run! Well, not quite. I was so drunk and the effort and angle of attack was so not favorable for proper stimulation that I could not finish the job. I don't think she was anywhere near climax either, though, with my total inexperience, she could have gotten off many times as I tried and tried and tried. My thought afterward was disaster as we both passed out.

In church I prayed that we wouldn't go to hell. I went home with both pride and shame. Shame that I was so awkward. Would she forgive me? Would she help out next time? But, I wasn't a virgin anymore.

Two days later, St Patrick's Day, 1970, at about 9:30PM I hear banging on the drug store window. It's Bruce and Pam. Bruce says Pam made him drive her all the way in so she could see her boyfriend on St. Patty's Day. I was surprised as hell and elated. Pete let me leave a few minutes early and we went to Gruber's, the local old man's bar.

Pure happiness. I even brought her home to meet my mother, the night owl - didn't go to bed until everyone was home (until I started making 4am normal). My mother's minimal comments, like, "She has pretty hair but wears a lot of makeup", made me think she didn't like Pam. Anyway, back they went to the Hamptons.

Saturday, a few days later, the 21st, I went out there again. But she didn't want to have sex. Uh-oh. Everything else was fine but that was a step back. Oh well. She still loves me. That's all I want.

Part V - How Low is Low?

On Tuesday night I'm at the bar with Nunzio and we get pretty drunk. At 11PM I tell him that I only want to be one place right now and that is with my girlfriend, Pam. I wish him goodnight and get in my 335hp Cyclone, hell bent on getting out to Hampton Bays quickly. On the Southern State Parkway, I keep the speed down to a few miles over the limit.

When the parkway ends at Sunrise Highway, I start inching the speed up until Patchogue where the traffic lights end and I can fly. Nobody's on the road so I put the highway dividing line under my steering wheel - I'm very drunk and there aren't many lights out there making visibility poor - and gun it to just over 100. I'm gonna set the record tonight. That is one of those things I remember clearly - driving down the center of the road so I wouldn't go off the side. Odd.

Incident free so far, I reach the Riverhead traffic circle. It has about five or six spokes. Every other night I go down the correct road toward Flanders and Hampton Bays but tonight in my stupor, I take the road to Westhampton.

A few miles down the road I'm not recognizing landmarks. I'm also doing 100 on the small, deserted road. Suddenly I hear a loud pop, feel a bump and slowly the car starts to turn left.

Tires start screeching and I know I'm going into a spin.

Oh shit! I had a blowout, left rear. Brakes on while completing a 360, the car starts drifting to the right and towards telephone poles. Uh-oh! Scrunch, bump, bump and I'm off the road in shrubs and come to a halt - between two telephone poles, sort of at a 90 degree angle facing the road.

"Fuck! My spare is flat." That was my first thought. Then, holy shit, I'm ok and the car is fine, though stalled out in second gear. Somehow, watching the trees go by while rotating to the left, my instincts took over and I started down shifting through the spin.

The car starts right up and I try driving but that shredded tire and nearly bare rim are going nowhere. I get out and look around and wonder why the hell I'm not dead. Well, I'm not but I'm without a spare, so I'm walking. But where the fuck am I?

"Where the fuck am I?" After shouting those exact words a few times - I remember that very clearly - I start walking and within a quarter mile come to, of all things, a bar. My little 100mph spin did wonders to sober me up. So, I had a beer, described my predicament to the bartender and he told me where I was - just another quarter mile to Westhampton and Rt 27A, also known as Merrick Road to the west, Montauk Highway out east. Before leaving I called Pam on the pay phone and let her know I was coming. She had been sleeping and gave me a groggy ok.

I was about 10 miles out of my way due to the wrong turn. I walked and ran to Montauk Highway and then stuck out my thumb. Two guys in a brand new, bright yellow 1970 Dodge Charger gave me a ride. That was the classiest hitch hike ride ever. They dropped me off about two blocks from Pam's house. I got to her door at about 1:30am. So much for record time. She let me sleep in her bed but her jammies stayed on.

Alana, Pam and Bob, all calling in late the next day, took me first, to find my car - I had a vague idea where it was, and then to get my spare fixed. Promising to come out on the weekend, I head home.

Unfortunately, the front end didn't fare too well in the crash. The right front ball joint broke so I had to nurse the car home at about 30mph. It went into the shop the next day but wouldn't be fixed until next week.

I wasn't missing a weekend with Pam but my father wasn't trusting me with his big Bonneville either. The argument about that was epic. With little money and no ride, I hitch hiked out to Hampton Bays that Saturday night. It took over three hours. My anger continued. I had called Pam earlier and she told me everyone was going to be at the roller skating rink.

The ride that finally got me to Hampton Bays dropped me off at Pam's house. Bob came back and picked me up. I knew most of the people Pam was with but there was also a newcomer, to me, one of Pam's old boyfriends who just got back from Viet Nam. She paid a lot of attention to him. We all went back to her house.

After a while and a bunch of beers, people went home. Pam went out to say goodbye to her ex - and then didn't come back. I looked at Al and Bob and they had the same bewildered look that I had. But they didn't feel my pain. They went to bed and I sat up and waited in the kitchen, nursing a couple of beers.

At about 3am I went to the spare bedroom and looked out the window, and cried - until about 8 in the morning. She had become, in six weeks, my world. I felt humiliated, betrayed, devastated and it hurt so bad. I had tried to sleep to make it go away but I couldn't. I felt dead, or, I wanted to be dead. I had had a great, promising life and I threw it away to be a notch on a bedpost. That's what I felt like. I hated myself. Not Pam, she was a sick little girl. I let a psychopath hypnotize me and suck the life out of me. I was falling down a deep, dark hole.

Al and Bob tried to comfort me over coffee in the morning. I wasn't the first one but they were hoping I would be the one she clung to. I didn't go to church that Sunday. I surmised that God really didn't give a shit about me or any of us.

When Pam still wasn't back by noon, Al and Bob drove me all the way to Bellmore. I went to my room and cried most of the day, and tried to come up with a plan to resurrect my life. I couldn't. I just wanted to die.

Then I figured a way out. I needed to get away. I didn't have the balls to kill myself but if someone else did it, that would be ok. I was plummeting ever faster into that deep, dark hole of despair. Just a lot of blackness.

Part VI - You Gotta Get In to Get Out

That Monday I skipped school and went right to the military recruiting offices on Hempstead Turnpike. My father was working so I used his fucking Bonneville. First stop, Air Force. I want to be a pilot. "You need a four year degree and about four more inches in height, but we need mechanics." No thanks. "Try the Army. They need helicopter pilots."

There's an idea. This was Spring 1970. Viet Nam was a roaring hell. Helicopter pilots were going down at a 50% rate. Perfect. If I don't get killed, I can fly for a TV station afterward, or get some decent job. But, I might get killed and that's just fine too. Into the Army recruiting station I went. And out I came with an appointment to take some written tests to see if I'm qualified and a date for a pre-induction physical.

I didn't want to tell anyone at first. I drove to Farmingdale College and officially withdrew from school. Then I drove out to Southampton to tell Bruce. He immediately brought me to the basement office where Pam worked. She listened to what Bruce said – about me signing up - but wouldn't look at or talk to me. She looked busy and did not say a word.

I left and went back up to the main floor. At the top of the stairs she called to me from below, "I love you."

Totally stunned, I responded, "I love you. I gotta go" and left.

"Call me," she shouted.

What just happened? That was a scene from a movie that just never happens in real life. Oh, the drama. But that really happened. I'm looking down those stairs right now.

That moment gave me hope, but it also made me cry again. She had broken my heart and there would have to be a lot of mending before I believed her again. I drove home alternating between smiling and crying. There's some light at the top of that hole.

My parents were not happy with my sudden, rash decision. Well, my father might have just been going along with my mother. They were teens at the beginning of WWII and my father eventually joined the Navy and flew. This military thing was not new, just new as parents and Viet Nam was not WWII.

I was, well, not exactly happy, but I had a direction. I was getting out of my current life that I now hated. I assumed I would be killed in Nam. That's really what I wanted. I wasn't giving the "if I make it" scenario much thought.

And that is the real story behind why I joined the Army. And the real story was that I was trying to get killed. I didn't tell a lot of people the truth, that bottom line truth. It's embarrassing. You let a girl do that to you?

I used the excuse that I wasn't getting the flight training I had expected and that this path will give me structure and lead to the career I wanted, and blah, blah, blah. Made me sound like I had my head on my shoulders, except the part about the 50% death rate which I didn't mention.

When I started writing the story of this part of my life, the memories of the great parts - those happy days, came rushing back in detail. It was fun. The more I put down, the more that came to the surface.

As I moved deeper into the Pam experience, the details became fuzzier after that kitchen conversation which absolutely happened as described. That was the pinnacle of joy. There were weeks of unbridled happiness that followed but I suppose the pain and sadness associated with it all just won't let me go there in detail, all rather vague. It hurts again. I've avoided going down in that hole before. Too dark.

Back to the life that was. It's done. Over. Well, not quite. We got back together again a few times, me to hopefully resurrect true love, she to explain herself. And she did.

She really did love me. But she loved a lot of people. There was no more sex, at least not with me. Bruce would tell me a year later about he and Bob getting blow jobs from her. Was that to make me feel better? Thanks, asshole.

I wondered if she and Bruce had concocted this whole thing just to get me laid. I finally stopped going to see her, directly, but I couldn't let it go completely.

I came out to the Boardy Barn, a popular watering hole then and now, to see if she was there. I had one sighting. It was early summer and I brought some friends from the Jones Beach job. She was sitting at the bar with Alana. Rich Zagardi, one of my co-workers, took one look at her and said, "Slutty whore". And with that we have come full circle. It was my first fleeting impression. It didn't make that deep hole feel any more comfortable but it was starting to feel like home.

Chapter 6 - Life Changer Two: Jessica

Rube Goldberg Runs the Show

You know what a Rube Goldberg machine is, right? OK, for you who don't, a Rube Goldberg machine is a complicated series of mechanical devices that are linked together in sort of a domino effect, and often dominoes are incorporated, to accomplish a simple task. Rube was a real person, a cartoonist who drew such machines. An example would be the breakfast machine at the beginning of 'Pee-wee's Big Adventure'. Another example would be life, except that it is built on the fly and the simple task is – well, it has to be death if you complete the analogy.

April 1970. No going back now. I'm down in that black hole. The only light I see is that escape to the Army. First up, a date at Ft. Hamilton in Brooklyn where I take a battery of written tests specific to warrant officer flight candidates - helicopter pilots, and a full blown pre-induction physical.

The night before the physical, I don't go to the bar but instead stay home with mom and watch TV. Mom drinks Pepsi, no Coke. No beer for me. I want to make sure my blood alcohol level is reasonable. Since I don't smoke but still need something in my hands, instead of beer, I drink at least a half dozen Pepsi's. Funny how one little change in your routine can alter that Rube Goldberg apparatus. Actually, those Pepsi's might have saved my life.

The written tests had many questions that were of the general aviation variety for which I was prepared - thank you, Farmingdale. The rest were, at best, GED caliber. The physical was just your garden variety draft physical.

The draft! I left this out - this was the first year of the draft lottery, a random system based on your birthday. Nunzio, Bruce, and I were winners. That is, we pulled double digit numbers, guaranteed to be drafted. I used that as an excuse for signing up, in addition to all the other bullshit. Nunzio also managed to get drafted into the Italian army. He never went into either. Bruce eventually got drafted after his college deferment ended a year later.

Anyway, two weeks later I get a call from my recruiter - my blood sugar level was high. I needed to go to St. Alban's Vet facility in Queens to get a glucose tolerance test. Now it's May. This test is a test of veins. You drink a cup of glucose. A half hour later, they stick a needle in your arm and draw blood. That is, nurses in training draw blood. Seems like a game, find the vein. This goes on for six hours. You look like a junkie when done. Back then you did. Today they would probably put in one of those intravenous valves. One stop shopping.

Then I wait for results. Since the day I signed my enlistment papers, all my friends and relatives have been trying to talk me out of my bad idea. I'm down in my black hole and hear nothing. Then Nixon invades Cambodia. A few days later the four kids at Kent State are killed. Four dead in Ohio.

I'm not deaf and I hate Nixon. Colleges all over the country are closing. Bruce calls me to come out to Southampton to join in the fun. Hmm, always a chance I'll see Pam.

So here I am, waiting to get in a helicopter and kill people but I also join in taking over the windmill at Southampton College, a symbolic victory in the local protest of the war. I don't really care. No Pam.

Artie comes home from Colgate - all colleges shut down - and becomes my number one voice of reason, trying to talk me down from the ledge, or should I say, talk me out of the hole. It kind of worked, but I knew I was going to hear from the recruiter any day now. I never considered moving to Canada. I still wanted to end all this.

At the end of May, no word, so I started working at Jones Beach again. Experienced people like me got a chance to start on Memorial Day. That was when it actually was on the 31st. Artie's getting through to me but I still don't have much interest in anything, maybe playing out the incompetence of the Army. Let's run with this as far as I can.

I also needed more money to fund my bar bill and feed thirty-three cent Sunoco 260 into the Cyclone. I got drunk every night and burned two gallons of gas each way to the beach. I also delivered drugs every night – for the drug store. Hah! Gotcha.

Somewhere about the end of May, I do something stupid, again. There's a girl at the bar I've seen – and she's looked back - for months, I think even pre-Pam, but just couldn't bring myself to talk to her, or any girl. I just want to get drunk and feel sorry for myself.

One day, and maybe she approached me, we start talking and I ask her out. I was sorry the next day. My mood wouldn't change and it would be a long time before I would trust a girl with my feelings again. The date was a disaster. When it was my turn for the tell-me-about-yourself question, I told her about the Army and Pam. End of date.

Getting' High, Ya Can't Beat It

Then there's my first experience smoking pot. My sister, Denise, started taking some of my hours at the drug store so I had more time to waste, or to get wasted. One Friday I drove out to the Boardy Barn and got there early afternoon, waiting for Bruce. I was sitting at the bar when the guy next to me says something like, "Wow, man, the colors are better."

"What did you say?" I ask.

"I ate some hash a while ago and it's just hitting me," says the wow-colorman, "colors are more intense."

"Yeah? I never smoked pot," thinking he's whacked, but I'm interested. Anything to make life go away.

"Really, man? Wanna try some? You're not a narc or anything?"

So off we go in his car to the little hippy house he shares with friends. After colors-man is questioned by his buddies about my trustworthiness, I get lightly welcomed in and he leads me to his room. He loads up a pipe, we smoke it and he puts on Sgt Peppers. He tells me to lay back and listen and he leaves me alone.

I can't believe how good it sounds. There are notes there I never heard before. I feel strange but it's a good feeling – and the music! Big wow! He comes back and I thank him profusely, noticing I feel a little different on a social level – many thoughts pop to the surface, but it feels good. I like pot!

We go back to the bar and my troubles have gone up in smoke for another hour or so. Great experience but I don't have the urge to go out and buy any. But that was goooood!

The Rube Is At It Again

End of June and the recruiter calls. "Hey Brian, what happened?"

I say, "You tell me. I've been waiting for the glucose test."

He says, "Well, your draft number, eighty-eight, is about to be pulled. Let's just do a new physical. Don't drink any Pepsi this time. Your written test was fine. You won't have to take that again."

I'm not so convinced that I want to do this anymore but being drafted is not an option I want to chance, even if it is for just two years. A few days later I'm in Ft. Hamilton again but this time I do not lie about the asthma and hay fever which I omitted on the first physical – a critical alteration of the Rube Goldberg machine.

At about the same time, a new batch of employees, the recent high school graduates (on the East Coast, school drags on into mid-June), are deployed at Jones Beach. A few days after they filter into our ranks I notice a really cute one. Ordinarily, I would have labeled her a snake. She had the prerequisite black hair if not a little light on the make-up. However, I was done with numbers and labels - objectifying.

This girl was short and cute with shiny, long, black hair – and she had the greatest cheeks. For a week or two I just looked and tried to catch her eye. One day we had lunch break at the same time and I came over to sit with her, introducing myself to Jessica (of Connecticut Ave in Freeport). She's even cuter up close. Look at those cheeks!

In just a few minutes talking, I'm thinking, "Oh my god, I really, really like this girl. She's so nice – and can talk! She can articulate. So fucking cute-pretty. Oh, damn, I'm getting sucked out of my hole fast. This isn't supposed to happen".

It didn't, for the moment. I couldn't ask her out – the timing was just wrong - though I sensed she would have been receptive. I went home thinking about it. The top of that hole doesn't seem so far away.

That night I got the call. The physical was good. One more step - an interview with a bunch of colonels to find out if I can do everything asked of me.

A couple of days later I'm at Ft Toten in the Palisades, up on the cliffs overlooking the Hudson River on the Jersey side.

"Yes, sir, I am aware I may be asked to fly into areas under heavy fire. Yes, sir, I am aware I may be asked to fire at an unseen enemy that may include women and children." Something like that.

It went on for about a half hour. I am sure I pulled it off - that I could kill and be killed. The panel included those colonels and a one star general. Except for the moustache, which made me look older, the sideburns, and Beatles cut, I looked the part. It was, after all, 1970 and everybody had long hair, though mine was barely on my ears.

On the way home I felt like this was really going to happen - I was going to be a helicopter pilot, and probably get killed. Shit!

In the meantime, that insane roller coaster of life is suddenly soaring upward. Jessica contacts were more frequent due to my suddenly showing up where she was assigned to work.

The job was parking field attendant. We wore sailor type uniforms, gray scrubs with the cool white sailor hats - girls wore one piece, above the knee, blue dress/skirts. The girls' uniforms were not appropriate for a lot of bending over so most of the time trash pickup went to the guys and standing guard at the entrance to the parking field to answer questions and direct traffic on busy days went to the girls.

Anyway, a couple of my first year buddies got promoted. They wore white uniforms and had an officer-type white hat. Fancy. I heard from one of the higher up managers, Tom Semanski, coincidentally a classmate of my older sister Susan from her Seton Hall days, that I was considered for a promotion but a couple of the managers said, "Carlin? He's just out to have fun."

And so my legacy was born at Jones Beach and my approach to life had been certified. Fuck that Catechism bullshit. This is where it's happening, not some bullshit they call heaven with a god that doesn't give a shit. I'll be finding out about that heaven crap soon enough, or not.

Whatever! Having a close relationship to my bosses helped. They asked me where I wanted to be assigned - there were a half dozen parking fields at Jones Beach - and I got to ask them where Jessica was assigned. At first I just stopped by to visit on my breaks and then I had them assign us to the same field.

Jessica – Love Again

It is now mid-July and the clock is ticking on my Army induction. Word about is that someone is planning a joint, mid-summer, employee/Brian Carlin birthday/going away party.

I finally decide I need to be with Jessica. Damn, I'm falling in love again. Oh, it feels so good, yet I know it's bound to hurt so bad. I ask her if she'd like to go with me to the party.

Sure, but she's already arranged to drive with a friend.

At the party, on July 20th, we became a thing, holding hands before too long. It was a first date that went better than any first date. I can't count the Pam encounter because that was out of my control and possibly bullshit. Jessica and I were like two peas in a pod (I like your thinking, Forrest).

Here come those memories again - the details, after so many years, of the happy days. And those precious few weeks at the end of July were among the happiest of my short life.

Closing my eyes, I see the picnic table in the trees near the entrance to field 4 where we shared lunch.

We're on the sand dunes at the party, kissing for the first time.

I'm a passenger in her little Chevy Nova. She's driving along the Jones Beach highway between parking fields and in her sing-song voice she says, "There's Brian Carlin, my puppy dog, and he's sittin' right next to me."

I can see the joy in her face – she really, really likes me - and I'm on top of the world again. I'm sure she loves me and I am totally gone.

Those first days were ecstatic. It was so good. So healing.

My going into the Army was to her, like everyone else, a mystery. Why would a fun loving, peace-nik join the Army? I told her the whole, fucking, ridiculous story. She understood and promised to try to make these days as fun as possible.

We thought alike. We kissed, a lot. We knew this was going to be short lived so we saw each other every day, at work and after. There were no other boys in her life and if there were she dropped them.

I met her parents, she met mine - Jewish, really? Like I cared about that. Top of the roller coaster! And then the call came on my birthday, July 28th. Induction day would be August 5th. Party's over.

We squeezed in as many minutes of the last week together as possible. She had a curfew of sorts so after going back to her home I stayed until one or two in the morning. Never did we go near sex. We discussed it briefly but agreed that it might ruin the best friendship/love affair ever.

We never said "love" either. I knew I was deeply in love. That broken heart was nearly put back together - I say nearly because the uncertain future and it's cause still ripped at it. I had to believe she was in love too. I was afraid to say the word. I think she took love very seriously and knew she was just about there, but the timing was awful. I didn't care. I needed to let it consume me.

The night of August 4th was beautiful and horrible. We spent the last few hours at her home. The last goodbye, some tears, the last kiss at the door - and my car won't start.

Been having weird car troubles lately. It is a stick shift so push starting works, but very strangely, only in reverse. I've been strategically parking it lately so I can give it a push backwards from the driver's door, then hop in and pop the clutch. But tonight I screwed up and parked it on a slight downhill. Pushing backward and up the hill was not working. I had to knock on her door for help.

Jessica answered and was laughing and crying at my plight. She got in her car and with front bumper on front bumper, pushed me fast enough for the technique to work.

She quickly pulled up alongside me and shouted in my window - my Thrush mufflers did not do much sound muffling - and all I heard was "Bye" as she sped off. I was stunned. No last kiss? I figured she didn't want to go through the pain again and I understood. I drove off crying one more time.

Next day at 7am I'm at Ft Hamilton for processing. They send me off to JFK with a plane ticket that routes me through Houston to Ft. Polk, Louisiana. I get to the airport at about 11 and have 4 hours to wait for my flight. I call the booth at field 4 at Jones Beach and ask Tom to put Jessica on the phone.

Tom and everybody at the beach knows of our thing. I ask her if she would come to the airport. She asks why I drove away last night. After telling her all I heard was "bye", she says her words were "Meet you in front of the house". Damn mufflers.

I ask her to come to the airport. Of course, she's working. Like that matters to me. I ask her to put Tom back on the phone and then ask him to let her go for the day. In forty minutes we're hugging in the terminal. No security checkpoint back then.

It is one last moment of happiness and sadness combined. Again, I'm getting choked up thinking about it. Another fucking scene from a movie. How much drama can we squeeze into one year? And then it's really goodbye.

Twice. Yeah, I was 19 and in love for the second time as I turned 20. Really, love? Did I really know what love was? Have you seen 'Titanic', 'Forrest Gump'? Nearly fifty years later, yeah. I knew then and I know now. It was and is what most of us crave. The pain? No, I could have done without that but it must come with the territory.

I just know that I experienced it, as immature as I was, or perhaps as innocent as I was, a deer in headlights. The fact is, I loved and felt loved.

Looking out that airplane window to Jessica, still standing by a window, I wondered what the fuck I was doing on that plane.

Chapter 7 - In the Army Now; Jessica Part 2

Life Changed

Here we go, new life. I'm out of the hole. I just left the greatest love of all and may be on my way to die. What a strange, strange world I live in, Master Jack!

This is my first time in a jet. I change planes in Houston to a Sky King Airlines kind of deal. For you young-un's, Sky King was a TV show about a guy out west with a twin engine Cessna (does it matter?) who went around saving people. Anyway, after my first big jet flight we're led out to the tarmac in Houston and I get my first exposure to the heat of the south on an August night, and then stuffed in that tiny, hot plane.

At about midnight, we land in Ft Polk, me and about three or four other fools. When the door opens, that blast furnace of humid, pine smelling air overwhelms me. Where's my fucking atomizer?

I mentioned asthma before on my second physical. Documented! I really had it bad as a kid. I needed to carry an over the counter puffer all the time. I was mostly allergic to animals and grass, thus also listing hay fever on that second physical where I had pretty much changed my mind about going in - that physical that somebody said was good enough to qualify me, health wise, as a helicopter pilot.

They checked us in quickly and sent us off to bunks. This isn't so bad. We spent a couple of days in the temporary quarters before assigning us to the basic training company, A-1-2. Two hundred guys – at 20 years old, I'm one of the oldest - living in four buildings. That's when the Army became everything I thought it would be and more.

There were the drill sergeants yelling at you all the time, 5AM wake up, 9PM lights out, guys lighting farts (yep, blue flame asshole blow torch burned the hair off Jim's butt), and then there was the "more", the bathroom, singular. One for fifty of us. You might ask how that works.

Here's how - one wall, about a half dozen of those splashy, waist to floor urinals, one wall with sinks for shaving, one wall showers, and one wall, drumroll, about six toilets, no nothing in between each.

Forget the structure, chain of command, loyalty. Taking a shit and wiping your ass next to three other guys will make a man out of you. Me? Not so much. I didn't shit for a week.

I finally figured out that everybody else actually fell asleep right after lights out so I regulated at about 10PM. That is, when the five inch red cockroach wasn't using the facilities. I never shit next to anybody else, that cockroach included. And that's all I have to say about that. Already too much.

So we begin the eight week process of turning boys into men, otherwise known as basic training. This group of two hundred consists of guys from all over the US with a fairly large contingent of national guardsmen from New York City. About a hundred guys are idiots like me, volunteers for the warrant officer candidate (WOC) program to become helicopter pilots.

For the first week or so, we mainly do physical training. My junior high school gym classes were rougher, though they weren't in ninety degrees and ninety percent humidity.

We were not allowed to leave our immediate area the first couple of weeks so phone calls were not permitted. I wrote to Jessica daily and waited for a response.

On August 25th, they sent all the WOC's for full physicals, purportedly to see if we picked anything up since our induction physicals. First, we filled out medical history forms exactly like the physical that we took to get in the program. I tried to remember everything I put down so they could see I wasn't lying or screwing around. I checked off asthma and hay fever.

"Son, you really have hay fever?" asks a lieutenant with a medical corp patch – it has a symbol of a staff with wings and two snakes curling around it. The guy who designed that must have been on drugs.

Uh-oh, "Yes sir!"

"Well, that disqualifies you from the program. Get yourself down to the adjutant's office and review your options."

Wham!

And that was the end of my dream of flying helicopters as a career and any chance of getting blown out of the sky and/or captured, tortured and, my once objective, killed. Hay fever, which I had pretty much outgrown by then, saved my life. But recall that night before the first physical when I drank all those Pepsi's? That started it. The first saved-my-life event. Now this.

And now I'm realizing that the United States government had lied to me. They promised me, in a contract, a new life. They knew that life was not going to happen. They knew this new physical would void the dream. They knew the contract was bullshit. I was conned and I was pissed and so began a deep distrust of this great, fucking country.

(A little postscript: years later at baseball games, I sat, with my old Army shirt on, at the playing of the Star Spangled Banner. Sacred, my ass. Like that fucking god on the coins we're supposed to trust. Liars!)

And Nixon was the fucking president! Who were the assholes who voted for him?

I was pissed at everything. They wouldn't just let me go get killed?

Here we go again. Dashed hopes. I knew what I signed up for but I wanted somebody legal to verify the terms of my contract. A young officer did.

I signed a contract that offered me training that would lead to me obtaining certification as a helicopter pilot which was estimated to take about eight months, something like that. At that point I would be obligated to sign a new contract with the title of Warrant Officer for three years. Lifer sergeants would have to salute me as they put me on a flight for Viet Nam and a fifty-fifty chance of coming back in a box. Of course, that wasn't going to happen now.

The contract had an out - if, for any reason, you don't make it to the completion of the training, the original contract is null and void and you are now committed to just two years of service, just as if you were drafted, but - you get to choose your job.

Wait - there's one more big out. If you were accepted into the program with a physical disqualification and are subsequently physically disqualified and can produce the original physical that indicates such disqualifier, you may apply for and, should the entrance physical records concur, you will be granted an "unfulfilled enlistment discharge", the technical term.

In that case, if you are classified for the draft as 1-A and your lottery number in the draft has been pulled already, or will be pulled by year end, you will be drafted for two years and the Army will choose a job for you. Or, and this is the big mother fucker, if you have completed six months of full time service, you are considered "regular Army" and not eligible to be drafted upon release, like guys who sign up for the reserves. Well, that wasn't me.

So, I had a choice. Stay in for two years with the job of my choice, or, get out and start the process all over - my number was 88. They gave me a week or two to make my decision. I immediately wrote to my draft board, explained my circumstances, and asked what my status would be if I opted out. They wrote back right away and said my number 88 had already been called, meaning I would be drafted immediately upon release.

Before I get ahead of myself, I'm just getting out of the AG's (Adjutant General's) office with my options when I find a pay phone. I call Jessica at home but no answer, she's probably at work. I don't have enough dimes and quarters to try the beach, and most of those kids are heading to college this week, so I call home.

My father answers and I explain the whole thing to him. He's relieved and tells me, "Well, maybe this is a sign that you shouldn't fly. Twenty-five years ago this day, my brother Bill was killed in a training flight in the Navy."

Now how about that for a coincidence? I was looking for some excuse to lessen the disappointment. I'm good with the omen thing or whatever. Flying is out! I feel better and tell him I'll be looking for an Army job as close to New York as possible. And could he call Jessica tonight and tell her? My mother does, and in that world of snail mail, which actually was better back than today's USPS, I would not get a reaction for days.

The next day I go back to the AG and go through a book that lists all the possible jobs in the army for enlistees. It describes the duties of the MOS, military occupational status - their convoluted way of saying JOB, and the location of the training facility. After basic training you go to advanced training, usually to a school specific to your MOS. For draftees, that usually means infantry or armor training - killing.

On my first pass at selecting jobs, all I could think of was getting close to Jessica. She was going to college on Long Island so I had my focus. You get five choices. My top pick was chaplain's assistant, training in Ft Hamilton, Brooklyn. The others were in Jersey and Massachusetts. They mailed away my request and sent me back to company A-1-2.

I continued to train and wait for mail. Most of my spare time, the first few weeks, was spent writing letters. I wrote a lot of letters. It felt normal conversing with people I knew.

Except for the New York national guardsmen, who mostly kept together, I couldn't understand half of what the southerners were saying. I got some education through Stan. He was from Tennessee and he too had been ousted from the program with a punctured eardrum, a medical history item that he had listed on his entry physical. We were in the same boat. Screwed by the Army and disappointed that our future was now in disarray, but kind of relieved that if we played our cards right, we could avoid bullets. We had women waiting for us.

Now What?

Just about the beginning of September, they let us leave our immediate area, the four cell blocks - that's how I thought of them - so we could go to the PX to buy Cheetos and beer, or go to the row of pay phones a few blocks away. My first phone call was to Jessica, of course.

Her mother picked up and sounded genuinely happy to hear from me. Then she put the sweetest sounding voice in the world on. Jessica sounded so excited that I wouldn't be flying the death machines and that my time was now so short - only twenty-three months to go. There had been no promises of waiting for me before and none made now. I knew that one glimmer of hope was a long shot but it was the one thing that kept me upbeat. I didn't want the call to end but it put me in a really good mood for days. The letters started arriving and the hell hole became bearable.

Basic training wasn't so hard. Well, I was very fit to begin with so the physical training was more toning. I felt bad for the overweight guys who struggled with all the seven mile hike-jog's in full gear. I sweat my ass off but actually gained fifteen pounds.

They fed us so much food. Having been a night owl for a couple of years, I never ate breakfast at home. Now at 6AM I'm feasting on bacon and eggs, French toast, pancakes, shit on a shingle (chopped beef on a muffin), fruit, juice and coffee in one sitting. Lunch was usually a full hot meal as was dinner. Even when we camped out they brought out the mess truck with the same meals.

Basic training certainly improved my physical well-being, though my friends thought I looked fat in this photo. Well, my draft card, which I still have but has some privacy numbers on it so I won't show you, says I was 5'6, 130lbs.

This was taken behind our barracks in the middle of basic training.

At the end of basic they ran you through some timed obstacle courses and made you run a mile in full gear. A couple of the heavy guys failed and had to do basic over. That's one way to keep out of harm's way. I was ok with my mile, 5:45 with an extra fifteen pounds of meat on my body and another ten or so on my back besides those big Army boots. My high school time was 5:15, so not bad. But, I'm getting ahead of myself.

One day in early September, while marching out to the range, I notice one of the guys who had been hanging with the drill sergeants, had new sergeant stripes. He had the single private stripe a few days ago. I congratulated him in a questioning way.

He said "Shut up". Later, when not in view of the other drill sergeants he said they made him an "acting jack" because they didn't have a job for him yet. He didn't want to talk about it further. Hmm.

Besides Stan and I, two other guys in our company had stuff on their original physicals that should have been red flags that indicated that they never should have been accepted in the program. "Something happening here. What it is ain't exactly clear." - Stephen Stills/Buffalo Springfield.

But it was late September now and I didn't know where I was going next. It took almost four weeks after I applied for the jobs with training close to New York to get a response from whoever the hell the applications were sent to.

The response was - all those schools have been filled, please select five other schools. What? Come on, man! So, back to the AG's office or the Jobs office or wherever and select five more.

It's now the fall equinox in bumfuck, Louisiana and I still sweat as I lie in bed waiting for sleep to put me out of my misery. Every day the heat and humidity in those heavy Army fatigues drains you.

Fort Polk is actually in the center of the state, maybe, geographically, a little west, and the closest town is Leesville. It's a shit little town. By the fourth or fifth week of basic they let us go out on the weekend. That meant getting on a bus and going to a cheap hotel in Shreveport, Alexandria, or Lake Charles, going to a bar and getting drunk, and sometimes getting into trouble. We had uniforms on and didn't exactly fit in.

First time out, a group of us, including a big African-American guy named Lenny from Detroit, went to Lake Charles. We went to a jazz club. We go up to the bar and order drinks when I get my first taste of southern ugliness.

That hospitality is a load of bullshit. The racist motherfucker at the bar says he can serve us white boys but your friend has to go out and come through the other door and get served over there.

Lenny is dumbfounded, Stan is used to this, and I am boiling.

"Take your fucking drinks and shove them up your ass," was my less-than-considered response. I was so pissed that my thoughts just came out. You never know what buttons will trigger that hot headed Irish temper.

Stan grabs me, pushes me, and carries me out the door. A couple of patrons stand up looking for trouble but Lenny is about six-three, two-thirty and no one wants to mess with him, though I suspect the shotguns are being readied in the kitchen.

When we're all out of that shithole, Lenny starts sobbing. "I never had to deal with that before. I want to go home." He was an eighteen year old kid.

Thanks for that great first impression, Lake Charles. We find an integrated bar and enjoy ourselves though Lenny struggles to have a good time. Fucking 1970 and we're still dealing with this shit. We're in the asshole of the world.

My view hasn't changed much in almost fifty years. Sorry, all you "normal" people down south, fix it. If you just stand by and let it happen then you're part of the problem. Same with all you frightened white assholes all over the states. Get with the program. We're the minority now. And that's all I have to say about that, for now.

I don't tell that story much because I bury a lot of those early Ft Polk memories. A lot of ugly, racist stuff.

We went to Shreveport and Alexandria other weekends and made sure we saw black people in a bar before we went in, even if Lenny wasn't with us. The music was always good.

Anyway, when applying for five new jobs in the Army, all I could now think about, besides keeping in mind proximity to New York, was a job in an air conditioned building.

Hospitals! They're air conditioned. I'll clean bed pans. Make me a nurse, a brain surgeon. Get me out of this heat! Off went my new list. In a few more weeks basic training will be over and I don't have a job yet. Neither does Stan.

Late October - Graduation Day! I had kept my mouth shut, never volunteered for anything, never got singled out for screwing up and got my promotion to private class two, or whatever the next step up from rookie is. Actually, you start at E-1, Enlisted, Grade 1. So the graduates become E-2's. You get a stripe like a wing, something like that, to sew onto your uniform. A few guys had to do basic over.

Stan decided to hang around and do OJT, on the job training, as the company clerk - mail, laundry and a couple of other clerky things. The other two guys like us had picked schools that they got in - tanks or something really stupid like that. I guess they had real death wishes.

So I still had no job but the basic training company had something in mind. First, we got a week off but I couldn't go anywhere because my orders might come through. I could be going to a hospital any day now. But, alas, right about then that same letter comes - your five selected schools are filled, please select five more. Back to the AG, pick five more indoor jobs but re-thinking the geography, anything northeast or just north, near a big airport. Keep me out of the freakin' south.

In the meantime, Jessica and I wrote and I called as often as possible. At one point, in a letter, I dared to mention love, not specifically proclaiming my love for her, but sort of throwing it out there for discussion. She had sent me a photo I requested and wrote on the back, "I look like a statue. Love, Jessica". She wrote the word "love", so there it is.

The response was puzzling and disappointing. It immediately, though gently, quashed any notion of the kind of love I was talking about while explaining her view of, oh, let's call it, "the big love". So, is she a hippy? Hope it's not another "I love everybody" thing. I'm more interested in "I love you", you know, the kind where you want to spend the rest of your life with someone. Well, maybe she's just not ready and that's ok given the circumstances.

Or, this is the first step to let me down slowly. So, I have hope, and I have the first reason for doubt. I'm going with hope. She's all I have in that regard. My heart is in this. I'm all in.

A basic training company in the Army, at least back then, runs trainees through in eight week cycles. Then there's at least a week off where the drill sergeants, cooks, clerks and whoever else supports the day to day operation of the four barracks and office building, just sort of fade away.

When they prepare for the next group to come in the next weekend, they put Stan and I in a private room in my old barracks. I was now one of the guys in the company, lowest rank but I wasn't treated like a trainee anymore, just another young man in an Army of young men. A week later I was presented with three sergeant stripes. Acting Sergeant Carlin. The new trainees didn't know any better.

Soon I was leading physical training and taking the place of drill sergeants while marching. The real drill sergeants rode on the follow up medical truck. That's what they had in mind for me.

The Michael T. Gross Era Begins

As part of the cadre, I didn't have the strict hours of the trainees. When they went to classrooms or hand to hand combat training, I hung around the office, where Stan worked, and in the kitchen drinking coffee. By the end of October it started to cool down to bearable temperatures.

As a trainee, you pull KP, Kitchen Police duty, at least twice. The cooks sometimes talked to you, some were more personable than others. Michael T. Gross, from Philadelphia, was kind of a pain in the ass when I was on KP but once I was part of the company, he was a good guy. Kind of rough around the edges, he turned out to be kind of a rebel, even had a moustache, and he was younger than me. He got drafted and was luckily assigned to cook school. He's also from a northern city and speaks the kind of English I can understand.

Michael and I drank beer together a few times and then one day he asked me if I got high. I said I did, which was true, if only once. We went to his private room in the barracks next door and he rolled up a joint.

Those building were old, wooden, and took a lot of wear and tear from the heat and humidity. Lots of space over and under the door for smoke to seep out. It was during training hours so the young soldiers were out.

Michael stuffed the door with towels and we smoked that joint. He had a radio, found a rock station and we sat back and enjoyed the head. Hell, this ain't gonna be so bad after all.

My life could be worse. I'm in great shape, marching and running with the troops who all respect my sergeant stripes, I eat well, I can get beer at the PX and Michael keeps it cool in the kitchen fridge, and I'm getting high regularly. But something is going on in Jessicaland.

She writes about going to hockey games with a "friend". No more does she write about us. She's sounding more like a sister. I can see the writing on the wall. Getting high helps me postpone those thoughts but when I lie down in bed again waiting for nothingness, I wage war with hope and despair.

Well, I'm meandering now. Love is hanging on by a desperate thread. The future is a complete mystery but at least I'm not getting shot at, yet. It's now mid-November when the next letter comes regarding those great schools I applied to get into.

The letter is a duplicate of the first two, "sorry, try again." For the last couple of weeks, Michael has been trying to talk me into just staying here and becoming a cook. The company was short one cook.

The cook's hours in a basic training company were a mix of good and bad - twenty-four hours on, twenty-four off. You always have a minimum of six KP's who help and clean up. If any of them gives you lip, they get disgusting grease trap duty, or if they are real assholes they get the wrath of a nasty drill sergeant. Two cooks are on a shift, one usually a bit more senior than the other.

A shift typically starts at about 1PM, as lunch is finishing. They immediately start preparing dinner which is served at 6PM. The food line is open for one hour. Get it or forget it. Cooks supervise and help clean up to get out ASAP, usually by eight. Next morning you open the doors at four.

Now, I can't speak for other kitchens but in BCT A-1-2, when you flip on the light switch a strange thing happens. The first time you see it you don't quite understand what you're looking at and then as the black refrigerator doors transform to white you see them - hundreds of cockroaches swarming for the cracks in the walls. And then they're gone. Absolute truth. Every morning at four.

Back to the shift - you prepare breakfast at six, then lunch at noon, staying until the last guy is served or one hour later. You hand off duties to the next shift and then you're off for twenty-four hours.

Every other weekend you're off. When on for the weekend, the hours are a little easier. You start at six for brunch and open the good line at eight. That lasts until eleven when you close the kitchen, clean up, make a lunch/dinner buffet and open again at one. That lasts until four and you're out by five.

The really good perk for cooks in a basic training company is the week, sometimes two, between training cycles. They tell you to get lost but leave a phone number, basically free leave. That sold me.

I had already applied for leave around Christmas but now the prospect of going back to see Jessica every eight weeks was just too good to pass up. It took about a week to get all the paperwork processed and then they threw me in the kitchen, on-the-job training.

Bye, bye sergeant stripes, hello cook whites, goofy hat and all. The timing was a bit weird - my first day In the kitchen was November 26, 1970, Thanksgiving Day. I think I was trusted with salad for that meal after a few simple instructions. It wasn't your typical day in the kitchen.

Once that day was over I got into it. My first partner was the head of our department, Master Sergeant Ronald Dealy. He was a lifer from Maine who, as a regular Army guy, followed the rules to a T and strictly enforced those rules.

Dealy had a sense of humor and was personable enough but he was a prejudiced red neck. I kept my distance while I learned. I could follow rules, as stupid as they might be - that was the way to promotion and a raise. Follow orders.

I was astounded at the chain of command in the enlisted ranks - that is, from private, E-1, all the way up to Sergeant Major, E-8. Astounded at the stupidity. It seemed like an inverted cone of idiocy. Let's equate an E-1 with a 90 (out of 100), like a grade on an intelligence test, E-2 an 80, E-3 70, etc.

By the time these shit-for-brains life timers got to E-8, they had stopped thinking for themselves so long ago that their reasoning process had all but ceased to exist. At least, that's the way I saw it. The higher the rank, the dumber they were.

Officers were a different breed. They had some smarts right out of the gate but even with educated people, if you're constantly trained to follow orders – and may not question them, you're going to lose some creative, progressive, and out-of-the-box thinking. I understood the environment and adapted to it, trying not to dumb down, just play the game.

Anyway, dumb ass Dealy taught me how to be a cook. I never did get a satisfactory answer to my question, how long does it take for the roast beefs to cook? "Till they're done." Never got an approximate time so we were constantly opening the oven and cutting one open. Just fucking stupid. I knew that when I got my own kitchen there would be new rules. Fuck the Army.

Jessica Part 2 – A Life Changer? How so?

So here comes the two week Christmas leave. I'm excited but trepidatious. The last few letters and phone calls with Jessica have not been inspiring, but, she is going to meet me at the airport.

Flying in 1970 was an adventure. They had something called Military Standby - not sure if that exists today. I think we got a low fare but nothing was published publicly so who the hell knew? We had travel agents on post and they arranged everything. That Christmas trip home was kind of fun.

The first flight was on that small airline that stops in Ft Polk, but the plane was a bit bigger than the little thing I came in on. First stop, Jackson, Mississippi. During the stop, a flight attendant, they called them stewardesses in 1970, came on the PA, "Military Passenger Carlin, please come to the front of the plane." Damn, I'm getting kicked off. I grab my stuff.

"Private Carlin, would you like to sit in first class?"

"Yes, ma'am." And with that I get two vodka bottles with my OJ for the twenty minutes or so to Montgomery and two more to Atlanta, where I change planes. I'm pretty happy. I refrain from getting further blitzed on the flight to New York. Jessica is waiting.

Actually, she's not. She's late. Finding someone in an airport before the advent of cell phones and security lines is a challenge. At last, she's there. The kiss is halfhearted. She tries to put on a happy face but I know something is not right. The conversation home is not easy. She drops me off but can't stay. We make a date for Sunday night.

Reconnecting with family and friends was nice but I just wanted to see Jessica. Finally, the date, but a last minute twist - she's driving too, and will meet me at my old stomping ground, The Tabard Ale House.

I remember this scene clearly, driving behind her little, black Chevy Nova as we approached Wantagh Avenue eastbound on Sunrise Highway and turning left. I remember sitting at a bench in the rear of the bar. I remember oh too clearly her blurting out, "I can't see you anymore."

She saw the look in my eyes and, over the loud music, these were her words, "I know you must think I'm awful. Please don't do anything to hurt yourself. Please, promise me that? You'll be ok."

With my eyes watering up but more zombie-like I lifted my head up and down. And then, with tears in her eyes, she abruptly left.

I sat there stunned. I actually suspected the night would end that way but not so quickly. I just wanted to be with her a few hours longer. A few more minutes.

I don't recall how long I sat there. It wasn't long. The shock – oh god, again? - wore off enough for me to stand up and then the sadness engulfed me. I had to leave and go have a good, long, uncontrollable cry. The big black hole opened up and swallowed me.

It was early in the evening and I didn't know where to go, what to do. I knew I was a danger to others on the road. Artie was home from Colgate so I went to his house. I think his mother answered the door and saw I was distraught and offered me a drink. Judi was there also. They all tried to cheer me up, to no avail. Maybe they were just trying to keep me off the road.

These are dark memories and, as such, few are clear. I'm sure I cried a lot but I seem to recall a numbness, a loss of feeling. Christmas was pointless. I didn't discuss any of this with my family. I also have the recollection of cutting my leave short and heading back early. Not sure if that actually happened but it is how I remember it. I just hated being there after that awful night. I wanted to close my eyes and never wake up. When I finally got on the plane I felt relief.

With my return to Ft. Polk, the incredible roller coaster year of 1970 came to an end. It began with such joy, so much happiness and pure fun. Life was great and would get greater, twice. I was deeply in love, twice. And my heart was broken, twice. My will to live wilted away, not once, but twice.

I found that the darkness of my high school years was just a shadow. I learned the meaning of depression. As with everything else, as the year ended, I hated 1970. And, to top off the whole year, I was still in the fucking Army, working for the fucking, lying US government.

Someone please put me out of my misery. I hate life!

Chapter 8 - THE Life Changer

I Want To Die, Again

January 1971. I had no hope that the new year would be any better than the last. I had no hope in anything. I walked around like a zombie. That's actually a good thing in the Army. You have a schedule, things to do and rules. No need to think. Just do what you have to do and then go back to sleep.

I slept a lot. I drank more, and I started smoking more pot with Michael. We were now working the same shift together. I also bought a combo record player/radio at the PX. When I came back from NY, I brought most of my singles and albums with me. Of course, I played mostly downers like James Taylor's 'Fire and Rain', the Ivey's single, 'Maybe Tomorrow (I Will Love Again)', and the Bee Gee's 'First of May'. Pathetic.

Michael started to talk about LSD and I was interested. I was back on track - looking for a way out of this life. When I poked my head out of my hole I saw nothing. When I let any feelings in they all turned to pain. I was considering volunteering for Nam. The description of an LSD trip sounded like it might be worth a try - there was a possibility that I wouldn't come back. Sign me up.

Thursday, January 21st, 1971. It all changed. I know, I have said that a couple of moments in the last few months had been life changing. Candidates for "Best Life Changing Event" had been the Pam saga and any number of decisions made during that timeframe, and the Jessica affair and heartbreak. They were worthy and, I suppose, did change my course, but, in retrospect, were just squiggles in the road compared to the big one.

Yes, this day stands alone as my sort of extinction event, like that asteroid some sixty-six million years ago where once the dinosaurs ruled, and then humanity evolved. (OK, so it took almost sixty-six million years for us to evolve. You get the idea, right?) I think of it as my own calendar dividing day, like BC/AD. It's not a term I use often, but I refer to it as BA/AA.

My life had been based around chasing happiness, love. I needed another to love me. I also needed to love me. My life was in the hands of others. With the devastating loss of love from Jessica, or at least, the potential for love, I was completely hopeless. In the space of six months I had given my heart and soul, twice.

Yes, Forrest, I too know what love is, but I had no more, just despair, and thus, life was meaningless. I wanted out yet again. And again I didn't have the courage to kill myself. Then Michael introduced me to an alternative.

Nineteen year old Michael T. Gross, Specialist 4th Class Kitchen Supervisor, otherwise known as head cook on a crew of two, the other being me, unbeknownst to him, turned my life around forever. He and I left the kitchen to the next crew at about 1PM, our twenty-four hour shift over and twenty-four hours of no responsibility beginning.

After showering off the smell of roast beef, I met Michael in his room. This moment is the dividing line between BA and AA. BA, Before Acid.

We each downed a tiny white pill which he called "White Lightning", and, if it was an Owsley manufactured dose, contained 270mg of pure LSD-

25, a whopper of a start to a new understanding of life.

So now it is AA, After Acid. Bye-bye old All-American boy.

Thoughts Per Second - That's All It Is

Let me pause a second here. This is the part you've been anxious to get to, right? No? Oh, you're the one waiting for the sex. Not yet. This is the LSD piece, the beginning. Hang in there.

So, you - you're ready for this? Maybe not anxious but curious? How does one describe an LSD trip? Even if you've done it, you know that it is completely personal and words that you use to explain the experience often are lacking. Very much like trying to put the details of a complicated dream into words.

Well, I'm going to fucking try. I've got at least fifty of these excursions under my belt, many in a very controlled, pleasant environment where the entire experience is examined and shared to try to understand what the fuck is happening to the brain! And, I know what happens. I'm dead serious.

If you've got any pre-conceived, negative notions including judgmental convictions about LSD, stuff them. Maybe you've got a relative or friend who burned out because that person fried their brain. Sorry, stop reading or drop your negatives right now. It's not the drug's fault. And if you don't believe that, go back to watching Fox news.

It's entirely true that the drug is not for everyone, just like peanuts, cat dander and opioids that cause reactions that can lead to death. You can't blame the peanuts. No known quantity of LSD will, by itself, kill you. It is not like heroine or alcohol. Your brain may not be able to handle what it does to you, but physically, in its pure state, it is harmless.

I'm not trying to glorify the drug here. I'm just relating my experience and what I learned along the way while trying to offer an explanation for the operation of LSD in the brain.

Even for you so experienced, if you can put aside what you think you know, or are just curious, come with me on this ride with a completely open mind. Try to understand not just the experience but what drives it. You need to understand what that chemical does to your thought process and that alteration is the only thing the drug does. All the other reported effects stem from this one main function.

You won't find this explanation in any scientific study, because there are no studies. In fact, no science exists when it comes to measuring – and this is the core concept – thoughts per second, or perhaps, conscious thoughts per second. What is a thought? Hang in there.

If I were trying to get this published in some psychological review I would designate the concept as CTPS. And if we have any serious researchers out there, don't go stealing my idea. CTPS is at least 45 years old so I own it – kind of like eminent domain. Don't fuck with me! But, I digress.

Consider that idea right now – conscious thoughts per second. I write, you read and understand what I'm writing. How? Your brain has been programmed to take the visual representation of language, an art form of communication, through our eyes and then through a mass of memory cells, deciphering my words, phraseology, and even intended intonation as if it were speech, seemingly instantaneously, yet a whole lot is going on in your head every second. Lots of thoughts, some conscious, many more subconscious, and even more apparently reflexive.

How much of that is conscious? That is, what is in the foreground of your brain when reading? Unless you are new to the language, very little. You go back to memory cells that learned letters, words, sentences and references to experiences, to finally provide you with an understanding of what it is I am saying. It doesn't matter if the thought process is linear or many thoughts happening at the same time.

How many? I don't know but let's just throw out an arbitrary number, say, ten. It's just a simple way to think about thinking (yes, that's circular and redundant – fuck you, get over yourself). It's a starting point – under normal circumstances we process ten conscious thoughts per second and I'm proposing that that number is fairly constant for all of us. And, yes, that dunce sitting next to you is probably only running at about eight, maybe nine on a good day (and you, jerkoff, the one over analyzing language, might be running at eleven but you're a bore and nobody likes you), but let's go with an arbitrary average, ten.

Introduce the chemical LSD-25. I propose, after over fifty first hand experiences, many to specifically analyze what it is that the brain is going through, that LSD simply increases your conscious number of thoughts per second. That's it! That is the only thing the drug does! Think about it, all you fucking geniuses!

All the reports of increased awareness, sensory enhancement and overlap, and mystical connections arise from a massive increase in conscious thoughts per second. You become aware of all the work your brain is doing behind the scenes in a split second. Regarding the mystical aspect and the associated ecstatic, religious and profoundly pleasant experiences – hang in there. I've got you covered and I'll explain later.

The overwhelming amount of data is confusing at first, and to some, terrifying trying to understand what is happening. But it is really simple. You are just thinking, that is, processing thoughts that are normally subconscious at a higher rate and as the hours pass, the effect is increased exponentially.

The brain is capable of so much more than it is programmed to do. LSD floods the synapses at an increasingly massive rate. Your conscious mind is now processing an enormous amount of data, not just from your senses, but from everything your brain has been exposed to since inception, and more! You're gonna love the "more".

It is also my contention that all psycho-active drugs do the same thing to lesser degrees though some are chemically arranged to also alter specific mood centers.

Marijuana is among those drugs and gives one an inkling of an LSD experience. Though jump-starting the thoughts per second aspect, smoking the Indica variation of pot can bring some calm to the seeming chaos of an LSD trip, while a few tokes of potent Sativa act a bit like a JATO – jet assisted take off. You so experienced know what I mean. I wonder how many of you reading this have had THE experience. As Jimi's album asked, 'Are You Experienced?' But, I digress.

Unless fully prepped and set in a familiar, comfortable environment before such an experience, a participant could easily be overwhelmed, not just by the current situation, but by one's own store of knowledge, beliefs, and fantasies, all reviewed in split seconds during the session.

So-called hallucinations, which usually don't start kicking in until the second or third hour, can be terrifying when focusing on a negative, or spectacularly beautiful when dwelling on a positive aspect of the experience, but are merely the visualizations of fear, joy, and other emotions mixed with the stimuli around. They must be understood as creations of the mind, like seeing a dream, and though it all seems out of control, you have to always remember how this adventure began. You took LSD! You are alive, living and breathing and taking it all in.

Much of our subconscious surfaces and contends with conscious control of thought processes. That's where it gets a little difficult – the sheer number of decisions you make that are normally below the surface are revealed and rather than automatically making the appropriate decision, you consider the pros and cons of such. You might get distracted by further examination of one aspect of the two, or many sides of that small decision. And on and on it goes until you snap back to the moment where only a split second has passed, yet you feel like you've been on a trip. Well, you're tripping!

For instance, you've got a billion things going on in your head when you identify a minor pain in your neck. You wonder what you can do about it. Then you realize, after recalling a similar discomfort, that simply turning your head could alleviate the pain. Before you turn, you consider pain. What exactly is pain? Why do I have this pain? Oh, I haven't changed my position in…how long? Time? Doesn't it seem time is going by so slowly? How can I be thinking all this in such little time? What is time? Can I stop time? What is that irritation in my neck? Oh yeah, I was considering moving. Ok, let's turn the head. Wow, that's better.

And that was another micro-second. You are aware of everything in minute detail. Your eyes dilate allowing you to see more. Bright light is bothersome which is why low light environments featuring candles and/or black lights are used in such sessions. You see more and think about it in detail. Your hearing is more sensitive. Music - we'll get to that later.

The meanings of words are considered in conversations and multiple internal reactions to a statement can leave you questioning the intent of the speaker, or writer. Your mind really starts wandering. You start to wonder what other people are thinking. Are they on the same page as you? What is with my fingers? Am I sweating? What was that flash of light? Trippers, are you with me? Again, almost no time has passed.

Under normal conditions, most conflicting thoughts are quickly discarded as not useful. Under the influence of acid, possible danger signals are amplified but also discarded as soon as the perceived threat is understood. It just appears to take longer because the sub-conscious thoughts that lead to understanding that no danger exists are also brought to the forefront, seemingly stretching out the time between actions and resolutions. More conscious thoughts per second digested in the same tiny time period. Your subconscious normally processes these little, internal decisions.

You may appear normal to another not doing acid but you know dealing with the enormous number of thoughts and internal conversations is exhausting and/or exhilarating!

It can feel like you are struggling to keep control of it all, if control is your thing. However, once you get that control, or conversely, release, that ability to be fully aware of what your brain can do, reports of enhanced creativity, universal understanding, and religious experience are common. I'm one of those reporting all of the above. Just beware. It is, as Harry Haller was warned, not for everyone. (Go read 'Steppenwolf' by Hermann Hesse.)

An average LSD dose lasts from six to ten hours. The intensity, that is, the number of extra conscious thoughts per second, increases from, say, multiple hundreds after about an hour, to thousands, and perhaps millions at the four to five hour peak, and then gradually decreases. Really? Millions, up from ten?

Counting is, of course, not possible, but when your brain seems to be exploding with questions, awareness, and resolutions in split seconds, you might be inclined to go with millions. In that peak timeframe, if you are not overwhelmed, the massive increase in thoughts per second can lead to a sense of understanding. Period! It is an ecstatic moment that is, I believe, the goal of the journey. That, of course, should be our daily goal.

Can I say that word one more time? Understanding. I don't mean intelligence. I mean understanding that dunce next to you. Understanding people. Please work at that. Remember Jackie DeShannon's song, 'Put A Little Love In Your Heart'? You might not feel that way about everyone, but try substituting "Understanding" for "Love" in those lyrics. Go ahead and Google that song and read the lyrics. Still got that old hippy idealism. Oh, I digress.

When that sense of understanding flushes through your being, all the overwhelming thoughts seem to merge into one and a sense of awe-struck ecstasy beyond any feeling of love leaves you peacefully satisfied. You are beyond hedonism. Remember that phrase, beyond hedonism.

Beyond Hedonism

Perhaps that sense of timeless oneness, that mystical sensation with religious overtones, has some science behind it. Wouldn't that be the ultimate bummer for all you spiritual holdouts? Here we go.

Now, let's consider another component of our chemical makeup that science is only beginning to understand, or shall I say, become aware of – Epigenetics. To dumb it down, this is the science of DNA containing memory. It has been proven in lower life forms. It certainly explains instinctual behavior in many species. Does it explain memories of past lives, the Shirley McClain Syndrome?

Hold on. There's too much out there to deny that some people remember past lives. I know, we're in UFO territory, but seriously, you need to do some research on people who recall other lives and their recall is verified. Google 'remember past lives', or just go to this link for starters: https://psi-encyclopedia.spr.ac.uk/articles/adult-past-life-memories-research. It's a fact. Some people have it. How is that? Could it be a genetic abnormality?

Seriously, if memories are stored in our DNA and those genes pass on some hint of prior life experience, even at a deep sub conscious level, if only to guide our decision making process for survival, does it not seem feasible that a mutant memory gene may allow some of its data to flow into conscious thought? And if we allow that, with our exponential advances in science, can we not imagine chemistry one day unlocking those memory genes? I know I'm taking this concept way out on a limb but opening your brain to possibilities is one "feature" of being exposed to psychedelics.

But, I'm still crawling out on that limb. Suppose that chemistry to unleash memories stored in DNA that has been passed from generation to generation exists and it is LSD? And suppose that DNA contains data from a thousand generations, from species that pre-date humans, from the original cellular life forms, from the carbon matter that exploded from the Big Bang – from that nothingness that was "there" before the Big Bang, before time or anything was a concept? Suppose we each have a DNA portal to the beginning?

Gotcha cranking? But don't think I'm going down the "I think, therefore I am" path that Descartes somehow twisted into proving God, by going way back and pulling the Mystic's bunny out of the hat. Suppose all the reports of mystical experience, being one with the universe, with "The All", or God, if you must, are merely the manifestations of that chemistry tapping into genetic memory – seeing back to the beginning? Boy, that would ruin every psychedelic's religious wet dream. But I'm not done. That only covers the past.

If you really want to cover all mystic bases, you need to experience the entire universe and all time, past and future. How does memory go forward? Well, I just offered the possibility of DNA memory all the way back to the Big Bang. All the way back to before the bang. And what was that?

We can't fathom that, can we? Or maybe some of us can.

Arthur C. Clarke proposed a collective memory of all mankind that spanned the entire lifetime of the species. The book was mainly about – no, my better editing sense just canned that spoiler. The concept of collective human memory proposed that an event in the future became so burned into human memory that it changed the path of human thinking for thousands of years. There, that explains it without giving anything away.

Clarke wrote that book, 'Childhood's End', in 1950. It starts with the US and Russia – in 1969 – about to launch men to the moon. Pretty cool, right? Anyway, his "collective memory" was always a bit outside my realm of getting it. I loved the book and owned and gave away at least three copies, one of the few books I read at least three times. Try it.

So I didn't buy the collective memory thing but I recently figured out how to pull memory into the future. We have to go back, all the way back, before the Big Bang. Our carbon-based "It" is now at that moment, the moment when time begins.

Now, suppose the universe is just a breath, an exhalation of a being beyond our imagination. The Big Bang is just a big cough. Before the cough is a big inhale – everything in reverse. You still with me? All that was spewed out as our expanding universe was originally inhaled. The universe in reverse. All that is our universe has already been here, a molecule in the lungs of another small being, and those DNA memory sequences store the ins and outs of the universe expanding and contracting. The time we experience and quantify is relative. And LSD unlocks the door to the room that constantly plays the video of existence.

That is some whacked out thinking, no? For PFC Carlin, such knowledge, or, shall I say, such imaginative thinking is light years away. It's obviously not knowledge (or is it?). However, I want to know why scientists come up with the Big Bang as the be all and end all (kind of curious that use of the word "all" – be and end?) of how this whole thing started while that boom still begets the question, "What caused the Big Bang in the first place?"

I can't quite fathom the idea of nothing, silly me, so what was there that caused such a massive explosion? How does nothing become everything? And don't just go giving up and surrendering to the God syndrome. Just because you don't understand something now and can't provide a reasonable explanation, there's no need to call it magic or some religious hocus pocus.

When you start considering the so-called beginning of the universe, you are left sort of speechless. No one has an explanation – and, sorry, Einstein plus Quantum Physics still means zip - except for the religious idiots. They've given up thinking through the problem and pretend that faith in a magical, supreme intelligence is the only way they can deal with the puzzle.

Cowards! And then they give this creator human traits like forgiveness, compassion and love, as if this divine entity who is all-knowing and all-powerful gave a shit looking down on the human ovens of Hitler and all the battlefields of the world, many in the name of such a super hero. God works in mysterious ways. Yeah, he doesn't give a shit about Earth.

Let me go back to my "Big Cough" concept – that suppose our entire universe is merely some short, old, bald guy with a lung disease reacting poorly to sucking on a cancer stick in another universe, far, far away. Consider that our solar system, our galaxy, the universe that we know, may just be a molecule, atoms, sub-atomic particles in the cells of a living and breathing entity – perhaps in the first millimeter of a pubic hair on the entity. Get it? Perhaps within our cells we house billions of universes. Perspective, right?

You think about this stuff when you get out there. When I say "out there", I don't necessarily mean while you are tripping. I mean thinking way out of the box. Certainly, doing psychedelics will get you thinking outside the box, but some people are just wired that way. Guys like Einstein have ideas many of us can't grasp, even after reading 'Einstein for Dummies' (not sure if that's a thing).

So, could it be that we have DNA with memories so far back that they bend into the time before time – the future. I know, sci-fi territory. Well, you just have to keep an open mind when exploring unknown territory before you surrender – your mind. And that's what you do, and dickheads like Descartes did, when the route leads you into areas too frightening to go further and somehow warp all those good ideas into proving the existence of god. Like God makes any sense and I insist that it all – all of this! EXISTENCE! – has a backbone of science and logic.

The LSD travelers often find themselves speeding through inexplicably ecstatic moments filled with the feeling of fulfillment and ultimately the contentment of total knowledge. Could those moments arise from the unleashing of memories originally designed to nudge the species to protect itself but instead, by the chemical LSD, provide a portal to the development of the species, all of it -

all that came before and after? Far out. Very, very, very far out.

You know I am testing the borders of normal, right? Well, so what else is new? Yeah, we went out there big time, but have you got a better explanation for those that claim to have reached that pinnacle of understanding? To have reached an ecstatic joy beyond any earthly pleasure? I contend that the drug does not create pleasure.

I still contend that it does only one thing directly and that is to open the veil to the sub-conscious, providing the user with more conscious thoughts than ever imagined. Harnessing that action and focusing on a deep line of thought, as if it were a ten thousand year old email thread, is what many a user experiences.

Finally, if you haven't already, do a little research – on LSD! Some studies have found increased activity between sections of the brain that transmit perception and internal processes that normally do not interact. That's what I'm saying! Your conscious brain now "sees" a lot more of what is going on – thoughts! Millions of them!

Science just can't quite grasp the concept of a thought being a thing. You know what a thought is, like, "This guy's nuts!", or, "I'm hungry, I want nuts", or a string of them – "toaster stopped working, lights over counter are out, is it a fuse?, a breaker?, pull the toaster plug out, smell for burnt wire, any other lights out? My nuts are itchy." Thoughts! Measure that, scientists!

If you're doing LSD now, into the third or fourth hour, put the book down, put some headphones on – with music you love, of course, and think about this stuff. Also, notice after reading, when you close your eyes how the insides of your eyelids produce a light show of letters. Retina burn, optical memory and LSD - very cool. Later for you high flyers. Back to the story:

Away We Go

...back to Fort Polk, Louisiana. Now, try to remember that this former All-American boy had little knowledge of the journey he was about to take. Thoughts Per Second was not in the vocabulary. Epigenetics? No. It was all just far out, very far out. This kid just knew he was going to get "high", really high. That's all he knew.

After swallowing that little white pill, I kissed my old life behind and then we walked over to the "Head" barracks.

The "Head" barracks refers to the main headquarters of the entire post where all the conscientious objectors and accused drug offenders were placed, pending review of their cases. Some were also awaiting court martial. All the hippies and war protestors in one place. They weren't prisoners, just guys who would never carry a gun, hanging out together, free to wander the post at will.

Remember, this is the Army. Someone with a lot of stripes thought that putting all these guys together was a good idea. At one end of their barracks, near a sun-drenched window, was a large pot plant.

We smoked a joint right there in the barracks with five or six of those guys, friends of Michael's. They had also dropped acid earlier. Michael had apparently planned this with the "heads". This was another world. And so, with a THC boost, and reality already a bit strange, a terrifying, wonderful journey began.

Within an hour, Michael started acting a little weird. He had one of those demonstrative personalities and he was trying to guide me a bit, but be was also goofing on me. "Things start getting strange and you go off on these little mind trips but you need to hold on or you might never come back". That "never come back" part was what I was intrigued by. I didn't want to come back.

What is the mindset of a twenty year old in 1970 who only believed that LSD was dangerous but intriguing? I mean, what literature did we have? A Newsweek article or two? Woodstock - do not take the brown acid? Music? Lucy in the Sky with Diamonds? Purple Haze? How about the 1967 Dragnet episode about "Blue Boy" overdosing on LSD (which is not possible)? By the way, that was the first color episode of the show. Far out!

But what did any of us really know about it? Take all of the above and mix with a Catholic upbringing, an underlying death wish, and away we go.

Well, off they went. The tripping boys from the head barracks were off to the movies. I was with them for about a block when I felt uncomfortable about it. I don't know why, I just didn't want to go. It was, as would every other decision this day be a difficult one, leaving the group and going it alone. I needed to do what I wanted to do.

That became an important theme, not only throughout the day, but for the rest of my life. The problem at that particular moment was that I didn't know what I wanted to do, so I headed back to my room. During that walk, I started thinking, "What do I want to do?" Besides breathing and taking the next step, I thought, "I want to go home." The thoughts per second are accelerating.

So, I altered my course and started walking toward the airport. I got as far as about a block or two from it when I worked out some of the realities of attempting to board a plane on an Army base. Wasn't going to happen. Disappointed about not being able to do what I wanted to do, I headed back to my room.

About two hours into the acid trip, the intensity of every moment and every decision started to circle around what I had done at one o'clock, swallowing that tiny white pill. This doom and gloom life that I had been living was not getting better. Something was awaiting me in that room and it wasn't good. What had I done?

When I arrived at the company area consisting of the four barracks, the mess hall, the small headquarters building, the rec hall, a garage and a storage unit, I decided, and all decisions required what seemed like hours of internal debate, to go into the mess hall and visit with the other cook team. They were headed by Sgt Johnnie Wilson.

Old Johnnie, yeah, he was probably in his late thirties, and reminded me a little of a taller Sammie Davis Jr., but very southern. I had smoked pot with him and Michael so I knew he was cool. He was so cool he nailed me.

Within about a minute – seemed like an hour - of talking to him he said, "Oooh, look at those big black eyes. You did some of that acid, didn't you?" Fact - acid dilates your pupils and I was obviously stoned.

"Oh, I did a lot of that a few years back. Everything gets real colorful and things start movin' and you start thinkin' 'bout what's real and what's not. Gets crazy. I don't do that no more. But it was fun for a while. How is it?"

I wasn't hearing much of what he was saying but I guess I did. What I was thinking was, "What did the white men do? Jesus, we fucked up generations of lives in slavery, fought a fucking civil war over owning black people. And it's still going on today." And I got really sad and felt guilty about slavery and now the bigotry I saw every day in the south.

I grabbed a soft drink, wished him a good day and shuffled off to my room. I didn't feel so bad about my own life when I thought about slavery, but, nevertheless, I was pretty sure that my life was about to end.

As a matter of fact, it dawned on me while taking that short walk that it had already happened. I was dead. This was the moment. I was reliving my last few hours in that moment of death. Trudging back to my room to face the inevitable was already history. It was a very dark realization. Very real. I had forgotten about that little white pill. Terror and dread flowed through me but more than anything, resignation reigned. I was dead. Let's get it over with.

Now it's after 4PM. Three hours into the trip and the tracers are blooming, hallucinations are beginning in earnest. Michael had prepared me a little bit for the stages of an acid trip - starts off slow, you start getting off, and in a couple of hours it gets crazy. You peak at four or five hours and then slowly come down. Whatever that means. That was all the preparation I had. This kid has no idea what to expect.

At 4:30 it is very intense. I'm sitting alone in my room looking at the lines in my hand move. The floor has faces in it. And this is it. The clock has run down and now I'm going to lie down and die. The moment is here. I share a bunk with Stan Sandler, the company clerk from Chattanooga, Tennessee who also was disqualified from helicopter training. My bunk is the lower one. I settle in and look at the bed above me.

Hallucinations are constant. Everything moves, wiggles, gyrates, and melts. The mattress I'm looking at is seeping down through the frame and it spreads around me. I close my eyes and feel myself being lifted up, up, and my body is dissolving, hearing something like "Human being number so-and-so now beaming up", and I was in a spaceship and suddenly whisked away. That was, most likely, my hope, an acidic daydream, but I opened my eyes and that bed was still above me.

Damn, I didn't die. Now what? I don't want to be high anymore, but what is high? What happened to me? Oh, that little white pill. I played with hallucinations for a while but I was also majorly freaked out. I'm losing my mind.

Stan got off work and walked in just after five. He knew I was going to try acid and wanted to know how it was. He smoked pot also, and actually lit up a joint right then and there, and the flame from his lighter was a bit frightening. That didn't stop me from taking a few hits which seemed to get me even higher. I tried telling him about the experience, but as I was talking I started hallucinating.

Stan's face started morphing and I remembered a conversation we had months ago where he bragged that he might have "got him one or two" when I asked if he had ever killed a black man - one of those ugly moments my brain has buried for decades. He started turning red and grew horns. I was sitting face to face with the devil. I had to get out of that room. I stopped the conversation and said, "Let's go to dinner". He suddenly became normal and looked worried about me.

At about five thirty, I'm now peaking, tripping my brains out. I'm trying to keep it together as we walk over to the mess hall. It's hard. This hallucination thing is tough to control. Faces keep changing into all kinds of shapes. People's words have so many meanings - need to filter out the paranoia, just go on experience. You know how the mess hall line works.

Johnnie Wilson is still there, running the show, serving the meat himself, and gives me a knowing look and a smile as I go through the line. I get seated with the few cadre guys attending dinner - most have rental houses off post and go home at five.

There's always one drill sergeant assigned to stay on post with the trainees every night and tonight it is Master Sergeant William White. Think of any gigantic football player with a voice like James Earl Jones. This man mountain commanded respect when he walked in a room and he didn't have to say a word. He was also one of the most reasonable and respectful of all the drill sergeants I have known. He was stern but fair and treated the trainees with dignity.

But tonight I'm sure he is all knowing and has seen my black, dilated eyes, which are now darting back and forth to see if he's looking at me, or maybe they are staring off into space, or maybe he has already called the MP's to take me away. I get over that conversation with myself by saying, "Oh, fuck it" out loud.

Lopie, sitting across from me says, "What?"

Lopie is Private Roberto Lopez. He works as a trainee with Stan in supply. He's got a thick Hispanic accent and he's about five foot nothing, one hundred pounds. Nice kid. I tell him I was just talking to myself. I look at the clock - five forty-five - and have a bad feeling. It's still happening. I'm still replaying the last moments of my life but it suddenly occurs to me what's really happening. Oh, and it's really happening!

It's not just me. It's the whole world coming to an end. The apocalypse! And I know when - six o'clock! This will all be over. It's either The Bomb - lots of them all over the world - or a meteor. For this sorry lot in Ft. Polk, it will end when the hands of the clock stand straight.

Lopie starts talking. He does that. A lot. He's excited. His wife back in New Mexico is minutes from having a baby. She just went into labor an hour ago and is at a hospital now. He's waiting for the call.

As he's telling me the story I feel sad. He has no idea that he'll never see his child, his wife, anyone back in New Mexico. I look around the room. They are all oblivious. In minutes we'll all be dead.

I feel terror but also some relief. A bit of gallows humor creeps in and I think, "Welcome to my world boys. Ten-hut! Let's give a big NY salute to Captain Doom." I imagine the whole room standing and giving the finger to Death as the room is engulfed in horrific fire. I'm smiling just as we are all about to die.

Stan keeps glancing over at me, wondering what the fuck I'm smiling about. Sgt. White is busily chewing his tough roast beef. He stopped looking at me. And Lopie continues to talk. He's been telling me about all his brothers and sisters, thirteen in all. Lucky number I think.

We Made It

And then I look at the clock. It's six-o-five. I interrupt Lopie, "Lopie, we made it!" He looks at me like I got four eyes. I go on, "It's all gonna be ok. Your wife's gonna have a beautiful baby. Everything is gonna be great!"

Stan is looking at me and wondering if it's time for the straight jacket. I calm down and tell him, "I'll tell you later".

At that moment I realized I had peaked from that little white pill and I was now getting control again. Life was going to continue. I'm still high as a kite, my senses are still bombarded, and my brain is processing it all at an incredible rate but I am back at the helm of spaceship Carlin, and what a ride it is!

In a few minutes I finish dinner and head over to the rec hall. The radio is playing some good music. Shooting pool seems like a cool thing to do. The tracers from the rolling colored balls are fabulous. I try not to think out my shots too long. The drug doesn't help me take the shot any better.

Ping pong is even more exciting. Somehow, as stoned as I am, my reflexes are up to the task. The tracers off the ping pong balls are just amazing. They should be colored. I'm almost laughing at the tracers. This is so much fun.

I try explaining to Stan what has been going on in my head. The terror of the first few hours has worn off and now I'm glowing, getting a grip on reality again while trying to understand what just happened.

Whatever just happened, wherever I went, I was thrilled to be back. Normal life was great. I loved it, but that crazy world had a fascination to it that drew me back. I wanted to be alive to understand what the brain was doing under the influence of LSD. The exhilaration I felt afterward was somewhat euphoric. Life! How lucky I am to be here. To feel alive.

After that day in January, 1971, I loved life again. The next morning I went to the post library to read everything I could about LSD. I still keep up with research. When I went back to work later that day I realized that I just had a shitty job in a shitty place with no love relationship and it was all great.

This situation wouldn't last forever and I was determined to make the best of it and of every day. I was in love again. Women? Later for that. No more regrets. No more pouting. Bring love with you. No need to look for it.

Now, come on life, show me what you got! Bring it on. It's a 'Brave New World". Right, Aldous?

Thank you, Michael T. Gross of Philadelphia, wherever you are. You saved my life. And, Jessica, I know it sounds crazy but thank you for breaking my heart again. You did it as gently as possible but it had the effect of closing the coffin. That guy is outa here!

Phase 3: Can You See The Real Me? Can ya?

Chapter 9 - Life Goes On – February 1971

Brave New World - What's Next Rube?

Aftermath of Thursday, January 21, 1971. Kind of hard to express how dramatically my approach to life changed. Maybe sort of a Rip Van Winkle thing. Suddenly I was awake. Now I know what they mean, "you can never go home anymore". Why would you want to?

Sleep came late that night and then I got up early Friday to go to the post library. I needed to find out what happened to me yesterday. With no internet, library research was quite tedious in those dark ages and with little more in print beyond the story of Albert Hofmann, the creator of LSD, trying it himself, I didn't learn much. Scientific research was very limited at the time.

Originally serious researchers, Timothy Leary and colleague Richard Alpert "tuned in, turned on, and dropped out" by 1971. The Army had done some experiments but it seemed that so many subjects "got religion" or experienced some form of mystic rejuvenation that objective research was impossible. And then they couldn't trust the subjects because many had become advocates of its use.

Reports say that at least one jumped out of a window to his death. I could understand that. Even at just the one-trip level I could see how the perceived loss of control, or perhaps, sense of immense power, could result in reckless behavior.

Alas, with the military finding it of little practical use, and with the rise of dissidents associating themselves with the drug as Nixon became such an anti-drug asshole, the freely distributed and legal mind expander of the 60's was classified as a schedule 1 drug in 1970, meaning it had no medical value, effectively ending research in the US and subjecting all in possession to criminal penalties. I was on my own.

Michael wasn't much help. He didn't seem to care what was going on between the ears, just that it was far out. That it was. I started to listen more intently to my records. 'Purple Haze' and 'Magic Carpet Ride' now had a kind of wink to them and 'Tomorrow Never Knows' was at the top of my list to play if I ever dared to try acid again. Even the cute little song by the Turtles, 'She's My Girl', turned out to be talking about acid. 'Eight Miles High', '5D' - the Byrds had been out there for quite a few years. Go look up the lyrics to '5D'. Right now. That is an acid trip no matter what McGuinn says. Late sixties music was laced with LSD.

Michael kept bringing over new albums and one day he comes into my room and says, "You gotta hear this. Total mind fucker. You never heard anything like it."

The album cover is a picture of a cow.

No title, no group name. I gotta know, "Who is this?"

"They're called Pink Floyd. The album is Atom Heart Mother. We played it at the head barracks earlier. Just listen."

With that he pulls out a joint and I crank up the vinyl player.

He's right. I never heard anything like it. And so my love of Pink Floyd music begins.

An idea pops into my head - eight hours of my favorite music - I have a lot more than that. I need the Pink Floyd record and I need headphones. The louder the better and I can't blast it as loud as I'd like through speakers so headphones are the way to go. January 31st is payday. Headphones and several new albums. Far out.

After reading every piece of reference material on LSD, other psychotropic drugs, and mystical experience at Ft. Polk's less-than-world-class library, I figure it's time for more serious research.

It's about three weeks later when we drop a couple more tabs. This time I want to start off in my room listening to music. Michael leaves after a couple of hours to get some dinner. I'm flying, watching the show inside my eyelids as blood vessels dance to the music.

Something remarkable is going on with my senses. I'm seeing colors and vivid shapes, letters dancing by, all choreographed with every note, the movements in the music creating intense mood changes and subtly unveiling an awareness of the interaction of the senses.

Atom Heart Mother is, except for the choir and, well, I don't know how you describe the Neanderthal chanting, an instrumental mish-mash stretching over an entire album side, twenty-one minutes and twenty seconds long. At three minutes and fifty-seven seconds, David Gilmour's twenty-eight second, softly toned guitar gently takes me to heaven. I'm on a rainbow pillow and every note pulls me to the sky.

Maqueezlebeck. I don't know what that is or what it means. It is a kind of mental sound I hear that is resonating from the music as that soft, angelic guitar surrounds me. I associate those seconds with the most intense pleasure, of the majesty of being, of just being. It is my auditory channel to infinity. It is inexplicable. To this day, I hear those twenty-eight seconds of heaven's entrance music and I feel Maqueezlebeck. I know what that word is now. My mind is exhaling from holding its breath through that light speed tour of the heavens.

As the hours pass and a billion thoughts explode to the surface, memories, experiences, facts, beliefs and imagination all blend as I surrender to the intensity and power of the drug. A true sense of peace washes over me. I am an insignificant spec in a universe of billions of galaxies - I see that space view - I am out there with the stars yet I am the most profound entity in all existence. I can bring it all together. I am bringing it all together. I am alive. I am life. I am THE ONE, the being, the creator, the beginning, the end, the ALL. I know this.

I KNOW. I am. And I love it. Life. It is me. It is all around me. It sears through me to the end of the universe, bounces back through me, takes me in its arms and spins me around. I take a breath, open my eyes and feel that buzz of being on that wild ride called tripping. It's been more than four hours since I dropped. I've peaked. Ride it down. My god, this is better than God. I have been God.

The magic slowly wears off. I go over to the rec hall and watch those ping pong tracers zoom-zoom-zoom off my racket. Michael shows up and we hash over our last few hours. His were far out. I haven't figured out how to articulate mine yet so I go with seeing music. A few beers slow things down but I'm left with a wonderful feeling. I need to do this again. And again.

When I started writing this, whatever this is, I knew that I would have to write about acid, how it became the great turning point of my life, why I did it. I thought I would have more to say about it but I don't right now. But, then again…

How do you put words and language into the sheer pleasure of being? I'll keep trying but explaining an acid trip is sort of like explaining the feeling of love. LSD truly did change my life, in a most positive way. It unleashed possibilities my brain had never seen or known before. It gave me a hunger for knowledge, to understand what this thing called life is. I thank LSD for saving my life.

We'll continue with the Army in a minute, and though it is not my last word about this amazing drug, I need to add a comment or two before talking about it casually. I mean, acid trips sort of became my menstrual cycle. About once a month for the next four years I would blast off to examine the effects and try to replicate those timeless moments when the music would unleash a magical (I wish a more appropriate word were possible) merge of visual sound behind my eyelids, the culmination of those moments - when the brain is churning through a billion thoughts per second and opening receptors to stimuli originating in past and, perhaps, future experiences, while the conscious reality intertwines with dreamlike imagination - redefining reality and leaving you in awe of being. Sentences like that, which really isn't one, don't come easy.

You try so hard to put the LSD experience into words and keep finding new ones to bring to the table - and they are all lacking in explaining it to the non-"experienced". If you babble on long enough and start talking about "the all" or timeless/infinite, your scientific credibility declines though religious folks might say you're on to something. Do some research for yourself.

Some interesting recent research has been done to explain, or at least, shed some light on the common experience of senses overlapping - like seeing sound. Google this: "April 11, 2016 David Nutt and LSD". Fascinating reading to all you who have closed your eyes listening to music and created the best light show ever behind your eyelids. Now you have some science behind the magic. Other recent research suggests that LSD is useful in curing alcoholism. Hey, FDA! There's a medical use.

LSD reveals all those thoughts per second that have been working behind the scenes. That awareness thing you hear so much about is more an awakening of the subconscious. All those behind the scenes decisions your brain makes, all the conversations you have with yourself, down to the most minute detail - they bombard you. Every input sensation of light, sound, touch, smell, taste, twisted around time bursting into your, now above ground, processor.

A billion thoughts per second. You get it. You feel it. You are overwhelmed by it. The words to describe it have not been invented. The Eastern religions claim to know it. You bow in reverence to the power of the brain.

OK, so I had a few more things to say about THE life changer. I'll probably have a few more things to say before we're done. I mean, if somebody saved humanity, you might write a Testament about him, if you believed your soul was at stake. And if somebody saved your life, you might be inclined to honor that person forever, if you valued life. Might not be a somebody, but my life was surely saved.

Back To Reality

"Extra-terrestrial Carlin, thank you for your visit. You are now back in Fort Polk, Lousyana, and it is February 10th, 1971, or as in your own new galaxy, 20 days AA. Good luck out there."

Well, a more bizarre reality might be hard to imagine, at least for a once näive, twenty-year old

All-American boy. But, you know, it ain't so bad anymore. Jessica? Oh, I don't know. I guess I'm still heartbroken but it's more like, that guy fell in love. That guy had his heart broken.

I'm an infant now in a big boy's body. I got a new brain to work with. It's innocent in the ways of the world. Love? I found a new kind of love. That hippy thing. Maybe she knew about it. I strongly suspect she did and that makes me love her more. I'd love to talk to her about it but I can't and I've got tomorrow to explore.

About that time, Stan - remember him? Company clerk and sometimes Beelzebub with the perforated eardrum? - decides that since he's now been in the Army six months, he's "regular" Army - that's a real term meaning you're not under the rules of the National Guard or Reserves and once you've served your six months you cannot be drafted - and he is going to apply for that unfulfilled enlistment commitment discharge.

I tell him that he's wasting his time. They're not going to let him out now. With nothing all that great to go home to, I don't have his enthusiasm. He's married. He goes down to the JAG office and applies.

I get high, drink beer, and buy more albums like 'Nantucket Sleigh Ride' by Mountain, 'If I Could Only Remember My Name' by David Crosby, 'The Yes Album' by, uh, Yes, and 'Ummagumma' by my new favorite group, Pink Floyd.

Michael brought that one over one day and said, "You gotta hear this. Total mind fucker."

Again?

It's a double album, one record live, one mostly forgettable studio disc - Oh, please, Floyd fanatics, it was good at the time, pre-Dark Side, but upon further review, eh - two long tracks on each side, each member of the group authoring a track. Now, the live disc was something else.

Michael's right about the live disc, total mind fucker. The live version of 'Astronomy Domine' from this 1969 release featuring the guitar of new band member, David Gilmour, who replaced original group leader, Syd Barrett, a brilliant musician-artist who succumbed to excessive use of LSD, is still, with all due respect to Jimi, one of the best electric guitar tracks in recorded history, live or studio. Talk amongst yourselves on that one.

If you have never heard it and are a fan of powerful electric guitar, find it and listen - crank it up, the 'Ummagumma' version. I've heard Gilmour do it live a few times but that recording might be the best. Well, we saw him at the LA Forum in March, 2016 and that was a mind fucker for its power and endurance, rather breathtaking in a way like one could appreciate a singer such as Streisand holding a perfect note on an extended finish.

Anyway, the 'Ummagumma' live vinyl was a true "space" album. The other live tracks are 'Saucerful of Secrets', 'Set The Controls For The Heart Of The Sun', and, the screaming hot, and while way out there, not particularly galactic,

'Careful With That Axe, Eugene'. Cool album cover too. Was that a huge digression?

Here I am going to outer space listening to the craziest music on the planet the same month that Andy Williams and Johnny Mathis release albums named 'Love Story'. The whole world is crying over the sappiest movie ever made and I'm learning about love in another galaxy. Music was always my feel-good fallback. Now it's my best bud, along with some decent buds.

Welcome To The Machine, Dave Jason

With the new year, 1971, a new basic training cycle began and with it, a new group of young men destined to die in Viet Nam, and a new group of kitchen police. I talk to these young dudes. Some are resentful of any authority and those assholes get the shit jobs. Lots of thugs from Chicago. Most just want to know how to get by.

Some have heard my music in the barracks and want to hang out. Some want to cry on my shoulder because their wives or girlfriends have left them already. One guy, Phil, just wanted to hear a Cat Stevens song over and over. It was he and his wife's song. Then he would break down and cry every time. She left him. I knew how he felt but I left that life behind.

There were always guys in the training cycles who went through the bullshit I did - signed up for helicopter training only to find they were medically rejected after getting accepted. One such guy this cycle was Dave Jason from Kearney, Nebraska. Dave had a degree in Psychology from the University of Nebraska. He was an excellent KP before he found out he was rejected from the warrant officer flight program.

Having drawn the short stick for KP duty so early in his eight weeks of basic training, he got stuck with it again near the end of his cycle, the end of February. By then, he was the most disgruntled soldier in the company. His second KP was welcome to him and me.

Michael and I had a field day with him. That is, recruiting him to becoming a cook. He saw like minds and joined the club. We had lost another cook to the call of war and he fit in perfectly. Dave was married and was, like the rest of us, very angry at the Army at first, then relieved that his odds of survival just increased dramatically. But, he now had an extreme distrust and hate of the Army. My kind of guy.

Michael just hated the Army because it sucked. Dave and I, and Stan, were lied to by the US government. It wasn't just the Army we distrusted. The whole damn military industrial complex just ate people up and spit or shit them out. Ike was right.

When Dave's training cycle graduated in early March, he went back to Nebraska to bring his wife down to the asshole of America. But before I get to this next period of fun, I must pull up this small story from the far reaches of my brain before it is lost forever. I think it is still soaked in alcohol.

At the end of February, Mardi Gras begins. This is Louisiana. New Orleans is about 225 miles away. I didn't think much about it but one of the trainees did. This guy Harry, from Chicago, had befriended Drill Sergeant Dan Hurtling from Buffalo, NY. Somehow Harry talks Dan into borrowing his monster, 1970 Hemi Dodge Charger that gets about eight miles a gallon, to take to New Orleans for Mardi Gras, under one condition - Harry goes with a member of the cadre, not a trainee. So he asks me to come along. We take another crazy trainee to share gas and hotel costs.

Here's where the story gets murky. When we arrive at our cheap hotel on the outskirts of the city at midnight that last Friday night of February, we buy a shitload of beer. That's why everything gets really fuzzy, so fuzzy,

I can honestly say I do not recall Mardi Gras in New Orleans. I know we went downtown, parked miles away and walked forever and drank non-stop. I know that happened. I just don't remember much of it. There were parades, there may even have been some bare titties. That's how bad it was. I can't remember any of the best parts, if there were best parts. Here's what I do remember - the Charger wouldn't start Sunday morning.

We took a Greyhound bus back to the post. Sgt Dan blew a gasket. He borrowed another car Monday night and we drove the five hours back with him, he got it started, and drove five hours back that night. That truly sucked. Somehow when you're twenty that loss of sleep doesn't matter. And that's all I have to say about New Orleans and Mardi Gras in 1971 because I don't remember shit about it. Here is a case where youth is totally wasted on the young. Totally wasted being the operative phrase.

Mid-March, 1971. I'm resigned to having a shitty job in a shitty place, but I'm not hurting. The pain from love lost has been numbed over so much that I don't really feel it anymore. How about love down the road? No. Not thinking too much about that. If and when love comes knocking, I'll be careful about opening that door.

Right now love is in the music, in the getting high, in learning about people, about life. I missed that in my obsession with being loved. Most of these guys in basic training at Fort Polk, Lousyana, the asshole of the world, have bigger problems than me. Let's make the best out of this shitty situation.

Between training cycles, our kitchen closes and I have to eat at other companies on the post where I meet lots of people and find lots of like minds - guys who get high. I talk to everybody. Of course, they're all guys in 1971. Any shyness I thought I had is history. When I get out I need to try this newfound me on girls. If I get out. Viet Nam is still raging.

Star Spangled Da-da-da-da-da-dah Choooo

Michael and I trip again and go to the movies. The movies are fun. As each show begins they play the same video with a gigantic flag blowing in the breeze as the US Army band plays the Star Spangled Banner. Play an instrumental version in your mind, ready? (Oh-oh say can you see) Dah-dah-dah-dah-dah-dah-cymbals-dah-dah-dah-dah-dah-dah-cymbals, etc.

Get the drift? Every pause is filled with cymbals. Sometimes the video switches to cymbals banging. Well, the head barracks crew and Michael and I and a few other sympathizers add our own cymbals. As the cymbals crash we emphasize the sound with our own hissy "chooo"

There's always some master sergeant there sort of as an usher making us stand up for the stupid anthem and he is also on the watch for guys smoking pot, which we did anyway. He's constantly telling us to knock it off. One day we got so carried away and were so loud they stopped the movie and he threatened to throw about twenty of us out. I think he was inwardly laughing.

Whenever I hear a band playing the national anthem I add the 'chooo' to any cymbals. Next time you hear it, feel free to join the 'chooo' brigade.

Anyway, this day in March we we're tripping and saw 'The Pursuit of Happiness', the 1971 version, a fairly ridiculous story about a guy convicted of vehicular manslaughter who breaks out of jail with a week left in his sentence and runs away to Canada with his hippy girlfriend.

Of course, the guy, Michael Sarrazin, reminds me of me, and the girl, a very young Barbara Hershey, reminds me so much of Jessica. New sensation - tripping and in love again. With hallucinations, she is Jessica.

Emotions on acid are intense. The movie ends with them happily jaunting around free in Canada and now we're peaking walking out of the theater. I want to go home and see Jessica.

We go back to the barracks, smoke some pot and listen to music. Thinking of Jessica is sad, so I don't.

I Can Hear Music, Sweet, Sweet Music

I had recently bought a King Crimson album, 'Lizard', because the cover art was really far out. Really. Go look it up.

Never mind. I did.

Far out, right?

My chance to tell Michael to listen to this mind fucker. The twenty-three minute title song is different than your average rock and roll ditty, but after 'Atom Heart Mother', our minds are open. This has a bigger jazz heart, more progressive rock than your Jimi or Janice. They borrowed Jon Anderson from Yes for the vocals. There are definitely moments of magic in that track. The album artwork looks a lot like the insides of my eyelids on acid in those days. Far, FUCKING out!

One more – the PX had a bunch of Moody Blues albums but besides the old, 'Go Now' and 'Knights in White Satin", both of which I had as singles, the only other song of theirs I was familiar with was 'Question'.

I loved the album cover:
'A Question of Balance'.

It reminded me of scenes
behind my eyelids during some
thrilling moments in an LSD experience.
Is it not another mind fucker?

'A Question of Balance' is one of the greatest albums of all time, consistently at my number two in my top five of all time. In fact, thirteen years later, one beautiful track, 'Dawning Is The Day', became my go-to lullaby to sing to our baby daughter to get her back to sleep in the middle of the night.

Ah, but I digress. Well, if ever there was a topic to digress about, music is it. I just hope you enjoy 'your' music as much as I do mine. Music often reminds me of a place and/or time, like the two songs in a row from the 'Watt' album by Ten Years After, 'My Baby Left Me' (pick a baby, Pam or Jessica) and the next track, 'Think About The Time's (a great tripping song to bring you down off the ledge). Both are definitely (in my most Rain Man voice) a Army era songs, though they remain on my top 1000 list to this day.

There will always be a group of singles I recall from the days and months after the Pam debacle. Sad songs. Songs that keep you depressed.

And, though I didn't do any drugs before the Army, I had my acid/pot singles I'd play when in a rockin' mood, 'Purple Haze' and 'All Along The Watchtower' by Jimi, 'Sunshine Of Your Love' and 'White Room' by Cream, 'I Had Too Much To Dream Last Night' by The Electric Prunes, and the one with the long guitar intro, the slow remake of The Supremes' hit, 'You Keep Me Hangin' On' by the Long Island acid rockers, Vanilla Fudge.

All of the above made it to my phone and can be organized into playlists but I kind of like the idea of something like the very electric Frigid Pink version of 'House of the Rising Son' being followed by Enya's 'Only Time'.

I suppose that's kind of a joke, a top 1000. So many songs strike such a resonant chord in me that I'm offended when some say I have severe musical tunnel vision. Yeah, bad metaphor but you know what I mean. True, most, though not all, country, jazz, hip hop, soul and classical stuff leaves me empty - does not grab my attention - so in that sense my taste is narrow. Even within rock I'm somewhat picky.

What do I like? What sounds good, to me. Having a lead guitar take you places is a plus. Big bass – plus. Keyboards of all kinds, plus. Drummer driving the show, plus.

How about '(I know) I'm Losing You' by Rare Earth? That long instrumental break takes you places. Just listen.

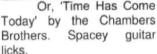

Or, 'Time Has Come Today' by the Chambers Brothers. Spacey guitar licks.

I love what I like and can listen to it time and again and it still sounds better than most shit I've heard on the radio since 1980. And don't send me suggestions on who I need to hear.

I like heavy rock with big guitar play. Now, I'm not going to suggest anything, but I am going to offer up a name for serious guitar freaks: Frank Marino. Google him and 'He's Calling'. Hook up to a good sound system and crank it.

From that I can sort of segue to a few weeks down the road - Michael and I drop some more White Lightning and go to the movies again, 'Woodstock'. As a matter of fact, nearly the entire "head" barracks goes tripping.

Four hours of hippies smoking pot, dropping acid - watch out for the brown stuff, and swimming naked. Oh, and some kick ass music. Talk about tracers. Check out Sly when high. And didn't Alvin Lee bring down the house, ugly faces and all?

Oh, I'm having too much fun in this shithole.

A little side note here – my memories of the Army after I did acid are so much clearer than those mired in the sadness of just months, even weeks before. The stories I tell here come with names that are mostly real. The events come back in extreme detail, especially those in that last month of the Army. I recall the conversations and the scenes as if they were yesterday. They re-run in my head. When you get to that part you may understand. And you'll understand if I cut some of those conversations short.

What I'm getting at is that though I believe LSD may allow you to dig up ancient artifacts of your memories, I also believe it is more likely that we remember more of the periods of our lives that are void of sadness.

You would think that being without friends and family in Fort Polk, Louisiana would be lonely and depressing. But it wasn't. I recall it as fun. And love was not involved at all, at least the kind of love that brought all that sadness. Making love? Well…

Chapter 10 - Life Keeps On Goin'

The Rube Rolls Spec 4

So where were we? Mid-March, 1971, and I get called in to report to the company commander, Captain Matthew Wall. Sgt Dealy, the head mess sergeant, is there. Oh shit, what did I do? Did I leave pot in my room?

Wall: "Private Carlin, Sgt Dealy has been keeping a close eye on you since we threw you in the fire, so to speak, at Thanksgiving. He has spoken very highly of you and we all have enjoyed your creativity in the kitchen. He has recommended, and I have whole heartedly approved, your promotion to Specialist, Kitchen Services, officially E-4."

Seriously? I hate the fucking Army.

"Sir, thank you, sir" I respond, robot-like.

Wall continues, "At ease, relax. This is a good day. Here's a new patch for your dress uniform to wear for that May leave I just approved. And here's another for good luck. Good job, son. You can buy another record a month now. I hear you play some good music over there."

"That's a good thing," I say.

Wall continues, "And one more thing - Private Jason is returning from leave with his wife tomorrow and moving into an off-post home. Perhaps you'd like to get to know him a little better and help him move in."

"Yes sir. Will do. I like Dave. Good guy," I offer.

Wall adds, "That's really good to know so I suspect you'll be happy to hear that he's going to be your new partner."

I interrupt, "That's great. Thank you, sir."

"Dealy recommended it. He'll need a good trainer," Wall goes on, "so I'm switching Gross to work with a new trainee, Rodney Clayton. Wilson is heading overseas."

"Nam?" I'm worried about Johnnie.

"No," says Wall, "Germany. He'll be fine. Good gig over there. Back to you. You have your own kitchen now. You've earned it. Now get out of here and go celebrate."

"Yes sir. Thank you sir." And with that and $10 more a month in my pocket, off I went to celebrate with a joint. Life is fucked up, in a good way today.

After he reports back in, I do indeed go with Dave to help him unload the U-Haul into his off-base housing. I meet his wife, June, and dog, Butch, and we drink a bunch of beers. June makes delicious burgers for dinner. Dave drives a '57 Chevy and also has a small motorcycle which he lets me borrow to go back to the base. This is going to be fun.

Stan Is Outa Here

Two days later, Stan comes running into the kitchen, "I'm going home!" His unfulfilled enlistment commitment discharge papers came through and were approved. He will be going home with an honorable discharge in hand in a week. Holy Shit!

We all went back out to Dave's place later and drank a lot of beer and smoked a lot of pot that night. Something really great to celebrate. Michael, who hates the Army more than any of us, it seems, parties pretty much every moment he isn't working, and this night was no different, but he seems restrained, not like him. The next day he admits he was jealous.

On Monday, March 22nd, before my first shift at noon as my own boss in my own kitchen with my new trainee cook, Dave, I went down to the AG's office, on Dave's motorcycle, and filled out the necessary paperwork to apply for my unfulfilled enlistment commitment discharge.

Based on Stan's experience, I'm expecting to be out by my cousin's wedding at the end of May. Life is looking up. Spring has sprung and with it, hope. There is light at the end of this tunnel, in the asshole of the world.

Cooking didn't come all that naturally to me, but once I got the hang of it and gained some confidence, I started trying things and stretched the boundaries of our very rigid menus. We had food deliveries every few days to keep us in synch with the scheduled meals.

I learned who was in charge of produce, meat, dairy, and bakery ingredients in the food warehouses, met them, drank with them, smoked pot with them, became friends with them and got little surprises in our delivery truck. No, they didn't give us drugs.

They'd give us the good tomatoes, ripe fruit, best cuts of meat, and some stinky cheeses that normally went to the general's kitchen. Paging through the big Army cookbook, I'd find a recipe that I wanted to eat and add it as a bonus dish to an evening meal. That was OK with Dealy. Extra is better.

You don't like roast beef three times a week? We gave them lasagna, chicken parmesan, beef stroganoff - all kinds of stuff that I liked. We'd make two hundred donuts for breakfast. None of this was on the menu. Drill sergeants got up early for breakfast and stayed for dinner.

Why did I do this? Because I was fucking stoned and had the munchies. I did what I wanted to do and Captain Wall loved it. Dealy would have preferred I stick to just the menu but, like I said, more food was good. And he knew about the food chain.

One day he had a couple of us over to his off-post house and when he got really drunk he showed me his two refrigerators full of food he stole. He was a dick but now I had something on him. And, if the company commander was happy, he was good with me wandering off menu.

Turns out the guys in the warehouse supply side had way too much stuff. The Army is fairly notorious for going overboard on purchases. The good guys managed to smuggle food out to charities. Among all the insane clowns were some normal people with morals and no hidden agendas just trying to make the best out of lemons.

Some schmucks sold it off post. Most of the excess went to us cooks who actually enjoyed what we were doing. We might just make extra salad or offer tomatoes and mozzarella as a "gourmet" side dish.

Or, we might just trade some baking potatoes for priority on the waiting list for dental work. Yeah, I took advantage of my position. Sorry, I ain't no saint and I ate too many Oreos as a kid. So, I got my teeth fixed before some guys without graft. That's one more tidbit of information that I rarely retrieve from those storage cells. I haven't thought about that shit in decades.

Cooking Is Fun?

Anyway, Dave and I get along great. He knows nothing about cooking but neither did I when I started. His intro into the kitchen coincides with a new basic training cycle. The new trainees have no clue that he doesn't have one about a kitchen, but he did two tours as a KP and he's smart, a degree in psychology, so he knows how to command respect. We make a good team.

This cycle of trainees is mostly draftees from the Chicago area and half of them are here because the other alternative was jail. There are some "toughs", wise guys, and total losers. We had to bring in MP's once in the first week to haul some asshole away when he refused to clean the grease trap and grabbed a meat cleaver. We gave those guys, the MP's, a couple of steaks and invited them for morning donuts (cliché but true) for future insurance. There's another incident I haven't thought of in forty-some odd years.

One cool thing about all those guys from the hood was the music. I got the company, thank you Cpt Wall, to put a big radio in the kitchen and I let the KP's pick the station for most of my shift. Not a lot of choices in Leesville but we picked up Shreveport, Lake Charles, and Alexandria stations so, for the most part, except for those rare instances when I let the hillbillies tune in country, we listened to Motown oriented stations and in 1971, Motown was fabulous.

I'd get my rock station time either at 4 in the morning or late afternoon but most of the day we had thugs dancing. It didn't take much convincing to explain how much better this job was than marching seven miles out to the firing range. Not long into the training cycle, we had gang members watching our backs.

Making nice with these guys helped everybody. They worked hard in the kitchen as we treated them with respect. They deferred to us in the rec room, allowing us to play the next game of pool or ping pong. And then they kicked our ass. Actually, they made us improve our game. Turns out making peace works much better than being an asshole.

After a few weeks, some of them started receiving packages from home and that's when we started smoking some really good pot. Anton was a big mother fucker with the gentlest soul and he'd rather get high than eat, but you don't get a linebacker build playing Gandi.

We'd often raid the kitchen for sandwiches at night. He asked me to store his pot and LSD during inspections. He liked my music too. Talk about an alliance. I was tripping with young crazy giants.

I was told that some guys started fucking up out in the field for the sole purpose of drawing extra KP duty. I doubt if that was entirely true.

In the meantime, Dave and I became pretty close. He was intent on getting out of the Army as soon as possible and knew that he needed to be in six months because, like me, he was also a draft lottery winner. That is, he drew a low number and would have been drafted after college graduation had he not signed up. With Stan's application taking about eight weeks, Dave figured he'd apply for the discharge in May as his entry date was January 5th. I was hoping to be home by the end of May.

On March 31st, Stan went home. That was both a very sad day and a day full of incredible hope. The guys at the Adjutant General's office assured me that my case was shut and dry. I just needed to show that my pre-induction physical had hay fever checked off in the medical history section. The paperwork I filled out had requested that original physical from whatever organization within the Army possessed my personal file. I thought about that every day - the day my discharge papers would come through.

I didn't think much about what I would do when I got out. I didn't think much about a love life. I did think about Jessica, and Pam who I blamed for getting me into this mess. But, I was doing a pretty good job of closing the door on life pre-January 21st – BA.

I became a regular at Dave's house after work when we got out at noon. His wife, June, was another college graduate who was sharp, funny, and totally accepting of me hanging with them. I turned them both on to their first acid trips. By then I had at least a half dozen under my belt.

When I did acid, I usually just liked to listen to music and get into the mind games, the internal hallucinations, the worlds behind your eyelids. That would make me, from an observer's point of view, a contemplative type.

With that mindset, I walked Dave and June through every stage with mellowness, putting their favorite records on, which were not so different from my taste, and explaining, as scientifically as possible, as if I knew, what was going on. Of course, the science then and today is rather subjective, but the important thing was offering a calm, reassuring, positive tilt on the observations of the totally fucked up, the chemically induced insanity.

Make It Fun!

Make it fun, add some humor, bring out some beauty and appreciation of your environment. Suppress any notion of anxiety and/or paranoia. Cat Stevens, James Taylor, Moody Blues for Dave and June. They did fine but it may have been more than they bargained for. I think it's that way for everyone. The first time is the most awesome.

By the end of April I'm going over to the AG every single day hoping to hear something. The young captain/lawyer handling my case assures me he will call our company clerk the minute he receives word.

Come on, Rube!

On May 12th the clerk comes into the kitchen and tells me Captain Sanchez called and asked me to come down to his office. Oh boy, this is it!

"Specialist Carlin, there's a problem. We've received the medical exam and history you filled out during that physical here at Fort Polk last August. We also received all the written tests, and psychological and medical results of the exams you took in Fort Hamilton last July," says the young lawyer.

"And the problem is?" I ask.

"Well, we did not receive the most important form of all, the medical history part of that Fort Hamilton physical, the part that states your history includes hay fever. It's not here. I am initiating an investigation. I'm not going to speculate on the reason that form was not included but I will get to the bottom of it. Hang in there."

Hope springs eternal. Not today. Those fuckers are out to screw me again. I'm going to buy a hundred hits of acid, climb up to the top of the water tower and drop them all in. Jimmy Cagney's got nothin' on me, "Top of the world, Ma!"

God, I was pissed. Instead of going back to my room or Dave's house, I went over to the headquarters barracks. I got totally stoned, bought a nickel bag, a hit of some new acid called Orange Sunshine - "only do a quarter at first, this shit is amazing", picked up a six pack at the PX and got wrecked. Isn't that what you're supposed to do?

I did not try the barrel acid that night. Remember that stuff? Looked like an orange beer barrel. One tablet had enough LSD to give you four full blown trips. Cutting it up was tricky. Somebody was going to get fucked up a lot longer than somebody else. Fucking tripping.

The Fort Polk Puke

OK, now the Army is my enemy. I start hanging out a lot more at the 'head' barracks. Their pot plants are thriving. Some guys there also started printing a newspaper, "The Fort Polk Puke". I have a copy somewhere, I think. The guys that put this together are mostly conscientious objectors and are very intelligent. They scrape up dirt on the more senior officers on post, the generals, colonels and anybody who has been involved in Viet Nam atrocities, or if they have a funny name. Nothing is off limits. Lots of targets here.

Fucking great! I volunteer to help distribute it. I start my off duty hours hanging outside the PX handing out copies to young guys who come out with beer and Cheetos. They don't want to be here. My life as a protester has begun.

Dave has a wife to report to after work so he doesn't join me in my anti-Army activities at the PX. But, we begin a campaign in the kitchen. Every day our basic training company provides us with six KP's to help clean up after us but who, in fact, are ordered to do "whatever the cooks tell you to do". These guys are very malleable. As a basic trainee you just want to get through this part of military life without too much extra shit on your plate.

The cycle of trainees coming through now are mostly draftees. They don't want any part of this bullshit, this bullshit meaning the Army. It becomes our job to help them get through as painlessly as possible and to tell them our story - how the Army and the US government lie to get you to give up your life to continue their agenda. We don't really know what that is except to give all these "lifer" morons jobs where they can exhibit their power, or like some of them, hide from the real world.

Our agenda is to make this group of six, impressionable young men hate authority and the Army - except Dave and I - and help us put out a decent meal. We know if we treat them right, like men, they will do a good job cleaning up (so we can get out early enough to get fucked up that night, or afternoon). We kind of leave out the last part of our plan.

It works well. Our KP's love us. We have one of the more efficient kitchens on post and get some dumb award - actually Dealy gets the award. The Clean Police come to inspect once in a while. I'd love to tell them about the wall of cockroaches at 4AM. All the while we now store cases of beer behind the gallons of milk in the fridge, because we can. But we got a Mr. Clean award.

There are more rumors of the trainees requesting KP duty. There's dancing in the kitchen. Tough guys are asking, "Specialist Carlin, what can I do next?" Respect is the one thing we drill into these kids heads - they will get it provided they offer it. If we did anything right in the Army, that was it.

We befriend all the drill sergeants and company personnel, except for a few asshole lifers. The hard-ass drill sergeants that we originally feared the first week or so were mostly draftees. They have all been to Nam and most have become a little unhinged.

They hang with us after work, smoke a doobie with us once in a while, and join the ever growing list of always-invited folks to Dave's house and June's now legendary hamburgers. These guys are counting down their days left too. Nobody wants to be in the Army in 1971, nobody with any fucking brains.

It's May. Gettin' warm in the asshole of the world. The smell of pine trees and the humidity is coming back. I want to get out of here. At the end of the month my oldest cousin is getting married, first of our generation. I got a lot of first cousins, pretty sure the number is twenty-three - it was in 1971, lost a couple since, maybe more but nobody seems to know what happened to Uncle Gene's kids. Ah, but that's today.

In mid-May, '71, I couldn't wait to go to Barbara's wedding. I thought I'd be going as citizen Carlin but those fuckers are screwing around with me. They can't find my medical history. The other form from Fort Hamilton was there. Why weren't they together? This is really pissing me off.

We're near the end of the current basic training cycle. One of the really cool kids (at twenty years old, with that advanced spec-4 rank, I think all of them are kids) is a short guy from West Virginia who seems to be on amphetamines all the time (you know, I never thought until right now that perhaps he was), Jerry.

I loved this guy after his dramatic introduction of a musical group to me. One day after work, I'm in my room and playing some music. Jerry and two or three other guys come in, close the door, light up a joint, and ask me for my headphones.

They make me sit down and put the headphones on, "Close your eyes", and they put on an album they brought in.

Speedy Jerry says, "You gotta hear this, you gotta hear this, you gotta hear this,..." about a million times.

Led Zepplin I

The pot is kicking in as the needle hits the vinyl and suddenly I hear this church-like organ music. Volume is high but I know it can be higher. This is very cool as the organ piece builds upon loud chords and then a few gentle single keys lead to - BOOM, they turn the volume way up to a dramatic drum beat, big bass line and gentle electric guitar lead, "Lyin', cheatin', hurtin', that's all you seem to do".

Well over a year after its release, I hear the first song, 'Your Time Is Gonna Come', on the debut Led Zeppelin album. It is breathtaking. And they wrote it for me to sing to Pam.

That was one hell of an album. Still my favorite Zeppelin. 'Dazed and Confused'. Fast-forward to my job at Sterling Optical, Woodbury, NY circa 1988. I remember that morning, still tipsy from the previous night out with our bowling team - I thought it appropriate to sing that song at the top of my lungs as I walked in the computer room. I have memories of air-Paging my way past the glass enclosed programmer cubicles and Myrna, our programmer momma figure, who on second thought thirty years later, was pretty hot, looking at me as though I needed sedation. Anyway, little Jerry made my day. Love that album.

Surfing at Galveston

Jerry also put me on a surfboard. Huh? Leesville, LA? Well, one Friday afternoon Jerry tells me he and a couple of other guys are driving to Galveston to go surfing. Do I wanna go? What the fuck? Why not? I'm on the late shift but they wait for me. The week before, Jerry's brother and his high school buddy drove down in two cars, one was Jerry's 1971 Pinto that he bought just after high school graduation. Freakin' Jerry the trainee has a car.

It's two hundred miles to Galveston. We get to the end of interstate 45 at about two in the morning, cruise down the beach while, no shit, Glen Campbell's 'Galveston' is playing on the radio. Absolutely true. We pull over to the curb near a closed surfboard shop and all fall asleep in the tiny Pinto.

On May 8th, I ride the only waves of my life on a surfboard. I grew up at the beach and I could ride waves before I could ride a bike. That's true - I didn't have a bike in the city, was ten before I learned. I was a bit skeptical of waves in the gulf. I thought of it like a bay in the NY area - no waves.

Well, shit, the Gulf of Mexico is like the ocean. That day the winds from the north were kicking up five to seven footers. None of us knew what we were doing, on the boards. I was sort of the guide - nobody else had ever seen an ocean - and led the group in the how-to-catch-a-wave part. This was way easier than using a canvas raft. Standing up? That was new. We all tried different techniques.

By the end of he day, Jerry from West Virginia, Robbie from Kansas, and Warren from Idaho had conquered the Gulf of Mexico. We all had stood up riding waves into the Galveston seawall. We didn't break the boards and the rental place didn't charge us extra for scratching them.

We couldn't find two cheap motel rooms so we headed up to Houston. What a shithole in 1971. Actually, Andrea and I lived about forty miles south of Houston from 2010-2012 and downtown Houston sucked forty years later. The baseball ballpark area was OK, within about a block of that ugly downtown, but that wasn't there in '71. It reminded me of the post apocalypse.

We found a cheap hotel on the outskirts, went to a cowboy bar, got drunk and with seemingly gallons of the Gulf of Mexico having passed through our lungs that day, passed out before midnight. Muscles we never knew existed had us whining the next day.

Not much to do in Houston on a Sunday afternoon but we found a cool tourist shop where I bought a four foot black light, a couple of day-glow/black light posters, a water pipe, day glow paints, and rolling papers. With that purchase, many a trainee and high minded drill sergeant would remember his colorful days in company A-1-2.

Tripping the Black Lights Fantastic

After I installed the black light, my room rarely saw a normal incandescent light. Every trainee in the company who didn't know I got high before, now knew they could offer me a few tokes so they could come in and hang out.

One night we had an acid party. Three trainees, one of which was Jerry, Michael, a drill sergeant, and I dropped acid, drank, smoked pot, listened to music and painted each other's faces with day-glow paint. That really happened. I remember Sgt Raymond Brown – think the comedian Jimmie Walker, tall, skinny, tough as hell, funny man – crying while telling a Viet Nam story and then laughing hysterically at all our glowing faces. What a fucking scene! It was one of the best nights of my Army life. One of. The fun was just beginning.

May 14th, the latest training cycle has ended. This was a good break - two weeks. Dave took leave and went back to Nebraska with his wife to see family. I had gone to the PX a few days before and bought a bright pink shirt and bright blue tie for my cousin's wedding. With my newfound appreciation of the arts of all kind, I was sure I had my finger on the nation's fashion pulse. Luckily, the rest of my civilian generation had no fashion sense either - anything goes.

When the trainees graduate, they get all dressed up for breakfast, march in a big ceremony near headquarters, get their little certificates, and the whole thing is over by 10.

Jerry and I start driving to West Virginia before noon. Now this was a road trip. Jerry was headed to advanced infantry training after basic. I hated to hear that but he was fearless. I hope he made it. He was very short, a small target.

Anyway, it was over nine hundred miles to Huntington, WV. Through Mississippi, a four hour nap in Tennessee, Kentucky and at about eleven Saturday morning, Jerry drops me off at the Tri-State Airport. I never saw or heard from him again. Great guy.

In my dress military duds I do that military stand-by thing with no reservations and hop on a plane to Pittsburgh and then La Guardia, NYC. I think my father picked me up.

There are no plans, no scheduled time for arrival, no cell phones. I called just before I got on the plane and asked if somebody could pick me up when it was supposed to land. It was nice to be home.

My father and I had a tenuous relationship by then but he was happy I hadn't gotten killed yet. And, as far as they knew, I was still the All-American boy, especially in my spiffy uniform with my sharpshooter medal. What a fucking joke!

Does Everybody Get High?

My brother, four years younger, was getting high then. Actually, he had been getting high for years, and, as I found out later that year, so had two of my younger sisters. They didn't know what to make of me the last couple of years. I wasn't home much except to sleep.

My life had been school, work, the bar, girls - in no particular order. They knew nothing of me. They knew I had arguments with my father. No one understood why I joined the Army. This might be their first honest explanation.

I didn't know how to approach my brother about getting high and my younger sisters were, in my mind, too young to even think they were getting off. I don't recall smoking those ten days home.

My good friend, Artie, was back from college to hear the stories about my crazy adventures including tripping. He had started getting high up at Colgate.

I drove by Jessica's house. I don't know what I expected. Love hurts. But, it felt good to be back in the real world.

Well, I came home for a wedding, first in our generation. I still have pictures, Polaroids. That's Barbara and me, probably a few days before the wedding. I'm the one looking like an idiot. She's the one with the legs and Cher look.

My cousin Barbara was/is highly regarded in the extended family. She was the oldest. She knew everything. I remember as a kid thinking how pretty she was.

And she had pretty friends. In fact, it was some of her friends who gave me confidence about my looks a few years earlier with some "bedroom eyes" comments.

Sheri

Now, at her Long Island wedding, on Saturday, the 29th, a true Irish affair, a few of us got drunk. Like everybody over 15. The younger ones were probably smoking pot. I was attracted to one of the bridesmaids and despite being younger, decided I had the balls to pursue.

She took me to an after-party with her into the Bronx. But, I only had a few pickup lines from my bar days and that part of this adventure had already been accomplished. Not quite sure who picked up who, really. At this point, I didn't know what to say to make it a complete one nighter and both of us seemed to lose interest.

Sheri sent me packing onto a subway to Penn Station. I fell asleep and was woken by a transit cop at the end of the line in Brooklyn. He directed me to the next return train to Penn. I was pretty drunk and fell out again, overshooting and waking up around 72nd St. I stood on the way back to Penn, which is on 34th St.

At about three AM I got on a Long Island Railroad train to Bellmore. I asked the conductor to please wake me. He did. About an hour later I was getting dressed to fly back to Lousyana.

Phase 4: Sex, Drugs, Rock and Roll (and Freedom)

Chapter 11 - June 1971 You're A Bad, Bad Boy

Dumpster Diving – Thanks, Rube, Good One

The day after I got back, the next training cycle came in. As usual, the first day's drill is to make these dudes deposit every personal belonging they came in with into a big garbage can. No deodorant, razors, shaving cream, combs, scissors, underwear, books, magazines, comic books, toothbrushes, toothpaste, soap - you name it.

You drop your life off when you enter, and if they're lucky you won't get it back. We all did it. Shitty. Unless you're in the cadre. After all the young dudes deposit their crap into pristine clean garbage cans, and they get marched off to get uniforms, towels, underwear and Army approved sanitary items, the cans are dumped into the parking lot and we, the cadre, pick it clean.

I feel a little dirty stealing their stuff but I see a book that grabs my attention, 'The Politics of Ecstasy' by Timothy Leary. That's all I want.

There's
the
book
and
my
new
moustache.

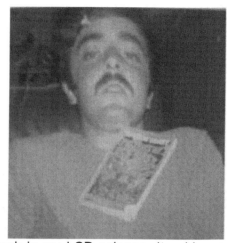

That book is my LSD science. It guides my thoughts regarding drugs for, well, it just might still be a reasonable assessment of my thoughts about psychotropic drugs, to this day, though, as you know, I KNOW what they affect – CTPS – Conscious Thoughts Per Second! The book's premise is almost religious in that it requires a leap of faith, but then, so does the Big Bang Theory in 1971, just about the time Stephen Hawking got involved.

There's no real, verifiable, objective science regarding the psychological effects of LSD other than the David Nutt brain scans and those studies focus more on the physical effects. But back then there was nothing. Nothing in the Fort Polk library, anyway. In June of 1971 I'm still trying to figure out what it does, but now I have a new bible.

I read every page in a day or two. I read it again. It all makes so much sense. It defines seven levels of consciousness and even allows the possibility of a God of sorts, the power of Karma, Love as the supreme being.

I had had it with the Catholic notion of God, but I wanted there to be something and I tried to find that something behind my eyelids on LSD. More often than not, I did. In a Pavlovian way, I was rewarded for believing.

"Our Thoughts and Prayers Are With The Families"

Isn't that the promise of faith? (Of course, watching the burials of twenty kids aged six and seven in Newtown, Connecticut will test your faith. What kind of fucking god would let that happen? "He works in mysterious ways." "They are in a better place." "God is taking care of them now." Jesus Fucking Christ! And those bastards still have their hands out for more money. Don't get me started, again. Fuck, too late. Pissed at the fucking Catholics again. Faith! Horseshit! But, I fucking digress!)

Shit, that really blew my train of thought. I get so angry when those assholes try to pretend they offer some comfort for the comfortlessly distraught. How do they continue to get away with it? I need to walk away a few minutes. Talk amongst yourselves. Your topic – faith.

OK. I'm better. As I was saying, back in 1971, I was still hoping for "something" out there. I wanted there to be a god. All that Catholic upbringing, or, as I call it today, brainwashing, still had a powerful influence on my thought processes, my end-game of logical thinking. We all wanted that life after death in heaven, eternal happiness, sucking God's dick. Sorry. Can't get Sandy Hook out of my head.

Anyway, yes, we had that whole scenario of going to heaven if we were good AND we

BELIEVED! The reward was a giant bubble bath with gramps and some angels. Something like that.

Describe Heaven

Well, after taking acid and getting mellow, listening to music, closing my eyes and letting those millions of thoughts per second take over, and overwhelm me, the reward was always unexpected and always awesome beyond words. I got into the words to describe it earlier.

There's always a new way - imagine concentrating on your heartbeat, thinking about the blood flow, and then being capable of realizing all the details of a heartbeat, slowing it all down to get to the cellular level, to the tiniest of atoms at work and their enormous universe while at the same time considering that our bodies are just tiny atoms in our known universe and this living, breathing entity is helping to keep the whole damn thing together, that we are each part of a single being and that being is the one, true entity worth acknowledging, but to name it is to defame it.

Those were the days. I no longer have much interest in a unifying entity with implications of intelligent guidance. I have become so pitifully grounded that I believe none of the magic anymore. Kind of hoping I'm wrong but if there is an intelligent being without a sense of humor, I'm fucked.

Back to the asshole of America, June, 1971. I never found out which trainee dumped that book. I asked all of the KP's. That's not all the trainees. The guys who volunteer to be squad leaders don't have to do KP. One of them? You never know. We walk among you. You ever look around at your fellow employees and wonder, you know, who did acid in the day? I did. And I asked a lot of them.

Lots of them tried LSD once, or so they say. Some claim a few times. Nobody volunteered that they did it fifty-plus times, not even me, though I would offer that it was more than a dozen. I don't count all the not so intense ones, nor the so-called mescaline and phencyclidine jaunts – and any over that fifty-count. I lost track. Throw those in and whoomp, there it is – nuts.

Anyway, after the first five months of the year, 1971, I've tripped seven or eight times so I'm now among the more experienced trippers in my world, so I think. How about by the end of my tripping career - could I be considered an expert? Hall of famer? Titles are cool – Spec-4, Sharpshooter, LSD Hall of Famer. At the time, I'd rather it just be – Civilian.

This new group of basic trainees consists mostly of draftees with a smattering of Warrant Officer Flight Candidates. As usual, a few guys hang around the door to the room of the cook playing the spacey music. Before long they offer joints to come in and hang out. How they have pot already is beyond me.

One of the new drill sergeants, Mooney, just turned twenty-one and a month ago returned from Viet Nam. He won't talk about it, hates the Army, and just wants to get high until he gets out in six months. He stops by to smoke a joint almost daily.

Biggest Boobs on Earth?

One of the new kids on the block is Daryl. Come on, no Daryl jokes please. Here's another short guy, kind of a blonde Klinger, who does Black Beauties (in 1971 it was speed) on occasion and drinks a lot of coffee - calm down, Daryl. He's like Jerry but brags a bit and tends to exaggerate.

On the positive side, he's all about making friends and doing something to pass the time. When we just sit and talk, he talks about his wife's breasts. Apparently she has the biggest breasts on the planet, "wait till you see". Sure, Daryl. Now, how are we going to confirm that? Yeah, he's a jerk, but likeable.

The first weekend he's allowed off post, and that usually doesn't happen until the third or fourth week for a basic trainee, he's going to bring her down from Gary, Indiana to Leesville and set her up in off-post housing. He pulls out a picture of Veronica and before I see it I envision a rather large woman with accompanying massive breasts. But Ronnie, as he calls her, is very petite, kind of cute, and wearing an Indiana sweatshirt so you can't tell how voluptuous she is, or not.

A couple of us nod, "she sure is pretty", assuming the boobie brag is BS. Another short guy trying to be big. I'm starting to take notice of guys' height. The Army seems to like little guys. I guess they are smaller targets and possibly quicker to dodge bullets. Just a thought.

Guess Who?

Daryl is always on the go. That first Saturday of the training cycle, June 5th, a bunch of us are in the rec hall shooting pool at about six. Dave and I are on the weekend brunch shifts and I had decided to stay back at the ranch. We're listening to the Shreveport radio station and they mention the Guess Who concert starting in a little while. Daryl talks Mooney into driving us.

Daryl is still in that early phase of basic where you are not permitted to leave the post. Mooney is Daryl's platoon's drill sergeant and he doesn't really give a shit. Like everyone else, he is, I guess you call it, charmed by Daryl. That and another chance to smoke pot without smelling up the barracks.

Two other guys jump into Mooney's '67 blah-Belair. A couple of us split a hit of acid. It's a hundred-twenty miles to Shreveport. (Research has found no Guess Who concert in Louisiana that June but I know four of us went as described – date? That's a good guess based on other related dates that I know are solid.)

Mooney is flying. We don't have tickets to the show. We split up and sneak in back exits near the stage just in time for the final encore, 'No Time'. How appropriate. One fucking song. I'm still on the way up – on the half hit of acid.

We go to a bar for one beer and then head back. Daryl drives because he doesn't seem capable of sleep. I watch the tracers of car lights passing in the opposite directions. Cool. I see stars in the dark sky between the evergreens. I see my own versions of constellations.

Those old Romans and Greeks must have been eating magic mushrooms. Weird night. I snuck into the kitchen for a handful of beers to get to sleep.

Every day I'm checking with Captain Sanchez at the AG's office, agonizing over each day that physical doesn't show up. Though it sounds like I spend a lot of time with the trainees, in fact, most of my off post time is at Dave and June's house.

Oh those burgers! They regularly have another couple or two or three over for dinner. It's a nice little community with folks having the same interest - getting this over without getting killed and returning back to a normal life. One couple that comes over often is Drill Sergeant Tim Clevenger and his wife, Rosita.

Clevenger is a racist asshole. He keeps his nastiest comments for Mexicans. Rosita is so Mexican she barely speaks English. Clevenger is about five-foot two, weighing in at about a hundred pounds. He is in incredible shape. He leads morning calisthenics, runs the troops five, ten miles, and then comes back and tries to get them to do fifty pushups with him.

Contrast him with Rosita, four-foot eight, maybe two hundred pounds, a near perfect medicine ball of a woman. Despite his nasty Mexican comments, this Texas boy with the blonde, handle-bar moustache loves her and treats her with the utmost of respect. Go figure.

Speaking of Mexicans, one of the cadre, Sergeant Major Luis Garza, is a lifer whose job seems to be hanging around the kitchen drinking coffee all day and reading "fuck" books. That's what he calls them. When new trainees are forced to give up their personal stuff and the cadre get to rifle through it, most rest of us grab soap, deodorant, comic books and the LSD bible. Garza grabs the trashiest books he can find.

Garza Is a Walking Fuck Book

As the month of June brings unbearable heat to this asshole of the planet, we cut back on making hot coffee. After breakfast we make an extra strong batch and make iced coffee. Garza is like all the other southern climate people who put winter clothes on when the thermometer drops under seventy. He wants hot coffee all day long. He promises to give me all the fuck books I want if we keep some coffee on.

I take one of his books and start reading it one night. The incomprehensible story line is about a couple of teenage runaways and it mainly involves them having sex in every imaginable way, in every orifice, with other teenagers and younger, and animals. That's not quite enough. They save their sexual, periodic, and normal body secretions and excretions in a jar, mix it up, slather themselves in it, lick it off each other and start all over again. It was, hands down, the most disgusting ten or fifteen pages I ever read. I threw it in a kitchen dumpster where no one would retrieve it again.

The next day Garza asked me how I liked it. I told him it was great and he gave me a few more. I think of myself as doing the world a favor by throwing them all out into a combination of grease and rotting food. This guy, Garza, is a world class pervert. My guess is the Army has stuffed him away here so he won't get in trouble again. Just a guess. I try to avoid him but he thinks I'm a friend now.

Fast Food Fun

In the kitchen, Dave and I are presented a challenge. The Army is trying to keep up the morale, and, with the times, wants to offer a fast food type lunch and even dinner that way sometimes. That means, for lunch, similar to breakfast, where bacon, eggs, waffles and pancakes are cooked to order after the first pre-cooked batch is gone, we're now cooking hamburgers, hot dogs, brats, fried chicken, and ribs to order. We don't just supervise serving lunch, we're making it on the spot. We've kind of been doing that for months anyway, so bring it on.

Fast food is a hit. Besides the burgers and dogs, our supply shipments include pre-cooked deli-like cuts of turkey, chicken, ham, roast beef, spam and that mysterious olive loaf which is among the favorite sandwich meats for those backwoods folks with the accents I can't understand.

It never ceases to amaze me the variety of tastes people acquire. We make Cajun cole slaw, bacon macaroni and cheese, and even learn to make pizza. The pizza is such a big favorite I have to negotiate with the supply guys and get Captain Wall to help out securing triple the normal delivery ingredients.

We start making Zeppoli's, basically fried dough with powdered sugar. That was a favorite back at the Jones Beach job. Somebody would drive up from the beach to Wantagh almost daily to get a batch. Sinfully good. When I found a recipe at the library, I couldn't resist. Yes, when the Army cook book didn't have something I liked, I'd try to find it in the library. And then I'd find another recipe, and another - sort of like Napster – oh, I like that song, and that one.

You would think that I might have ballooned in that environment. Well, I did go from about a hundred thirty plus pounds at induction, to about one fifty-five when I got out but most of that was just bulking up during basic. A non-air-conditioned kitchen in central Louisiana in June is a sauna. I lost five pounds a shift and gained it back in beer and Cheetos when I got off.

We had three huge fans blowing but I think all that did was to make every meal a little tastier. A bit of extra salt went into everything. Blowing sweat. I actually lost weight as the summer began, despite zeppoli's, cannoli's, donuts and any other fried food we could think of. I fell in love with the deep fat fryer. Hell, I didn't have to clean it.

Even as the temperature rose to the mid-nineties along with the humidity, I started to enjoy my job. I was able to ignore my boss and do what I wanted to do because I had his boss supporting me. I got respect. I had lots of friends. And I still had lots of guys that needed my shoulder to cry on. Good guys losing their wives and girlfriends just weeks after leaving home.

Come on, "Let's go listen to 'First of May', 'I'm a Loser', 'Fire and Rain', 'My Baby Left Me'" and then I throw on 'Your Time Is Gonna Come', to give them some balls. The music shifts the mood, Sly wants to take them higher and they don't kill themselves tonight. But we'll do it all again the next night I stay on post.

That was a good enough reason - babysitting grown men - for getting off post. Hanging with Dave and June was so relaxing after the grueling heat of the kitchen.

Hello Veronica

(Coincidentally, that is the last line of a movie we watched two nights ago in 2019, 'Veronica Mars'. – No relevance, just struck me as curious. This sub-chapter title has been there for months. Fun fact.)

Two weeks into the training cycle and little Daryl gets a pass to go off post for the weekend, kind of rare for a trainee but he's very likeable and talking at two hundred miles an hour, Captain Wall has little chance to protest.

Dave gives him a ride to meet his wife at the Alexandria airport and get her settled in the little community where our circle of friends call home.

The other wives help Veronica buy some furniture at the second hand store, stuff some other GI family used before.

The guys help move the furniture in but we don't get to see Veronica and her world class breasts. She was out food shopping with the wives. We've given up believing the breast boast because Daryl has proven to be a bit of an expert at exaggeration and downright BS, though he is a lot of fun. We laugh with him and at him.

Daryl and Ronnie come to Dave's house for dinner that Sunday night, June 13th. Daryl will have to go back to the post Monday and stay there until the whole company gets let out for a weekend. That's usually the four week point in basic.

We finally get to meet Ronnie and her mammoth mammaries, but, like the picture, she comes dressed in a baggy shirt that reveals nothing. As in her picture, she is kind of cute, sort of a baby face with those big blue eyes. During the course of the evening, she catches me looking at her a few times, though I am really just trying to verify Daryl's claims. Oh, and they have two kids! Seriously? He can't be more than eighteen.

In the course of conversations it comes out that she is seventeen! Holy shit! Yeah, she's kind of cute and may be built like a Playboy Bunny but keep me away from that! Don't look anymore. Avoid eye contact. That always gets you into trouble.

I borrowed Dave's car that night. Daryl and I made sure Ronnie and babies were secure in their new home and then I drove Daryl back to the base. He wouldn't be able to see her off post for two more weeks. It became three. Daryl got in a fight the next day with one of the acting sergeants who was, by all accounts, being a jerk. Still, Daryl lost a week of off-post privileges.

Ronnie gets rides to the post a few times a week with the babies to see Daryl at five PM, for like ten minutes. What a good, faithful wife. I happen to be at the kitchen door one day when she arrives. My discreet peak at the magnificent melons is soured – she's carrying both babies in her arms. She's got some muscles!

At the other side of the parking lot, appearing right behind Daryl out of the main office building is Sgt. Garza. He isn't subtle at all, visually undressing Ronnie, staring at her every movement. Captain Obvious! What a sleaze! Wonder what he did to get stuck in this shithole? He doesn't appear to do anything but drink coffee and read fuck books. And now stare at seventeen year olds. Maybe he got the memo that Daryl broadcast.

Now it's near the end of June. No physical in sight. I'm resigned to having a decent, oh, come on, it's still a shitty job, still in a shitty place.

Rube Goldberg Is a Peeping-Tom

The next Saturday night, June 19th, after Dave and I worked the first half of the easy weekend shift, a bunch of us are at Ronnie's house. It's a hassle taking the babies out so we bring dinner to her. She's only seventeen and with two infants has little time to cook or learn to cook.

After dinner she goes to the back door to take out some garbage and suddenly screams and collapses. Apparently, some guy was standing right by the back door when she opened it. Everybody rushes to the kitchen. The creepy guy runs away at the scream but a couple of the guys think they spot him and give chase. Great, she has a peeping-tom.

Someone calls the police who, in turn, call the Military Police because this entire area of homes is leased by the federal government for Fort Polk folks and they patrol the area. In minutes we're scrambling to hide the pot and aim the fans away from the front door. Like that matters. Every MP I know gets high. But, you never know, this is a serious matter.

In the meantime, Rosita is trying to revive Ronnie, who looks completely zoned out. I'm one of the last into the kitchen, mainly because a few people were a lot closer and rushed in there at the scream, but also because I was hiding all evidence of pot.

I feel guilty about being a bit slow to respond, but when I see she's still on the floor I hurry over to Rosita who is struggling to get Ronnie into a chair.

The MP's show up in a few minutes. Dave answers the door. Clevenger and Tommy, the company clerk, are still running blindly into the night after the silhouette jerk off, who, in fact, may have been jerking off.

Dave explains what happened - the scream, the two guys out there running after the creep at the back door, and finding Ronnie on the floor.

Everyone else is in the kitchen now, surrounding Ronnie, who seems to be in a state of shock. I guess whatever it was really freaked her out. But, I also kind of wonder if she's just a drama queen. Just a thought that runs through my head but, heck, I don't know her. I put that thought on hold as she seems to be shivering. She's not faking this.

Shit, the only person I've ever known who has needed medical attention, besides Jimmie Lee, whose arm I broke on the swings when I was about six, was me and my asthma – one night with the Jones Beach boys out in the Hamptons. Everybody is either drunk or stoned or both and kind of waiting for her to snap out of it.

I was too, but this shaking, zoned out thing is freaking me out. I get down on a knee to try to get her attention, "Ronnie, the MP's want to talk to you. Are you ok to talk to them?"

She's out there, no response. I wonder if she's not just stoned and loaded, but maybe having some kind of seizure What the hell happened? I can imagine getting really freaked out, but pass out? No. Well, she's pretty small. Maybe she was really loaded and ready to pass out anyway.

Now I try again, this time putting my hand on her wrist to try to get a pulse. I think sixty would be good, something like that. Fuck, I don't know squat about this medical stuff. "Ronnie, look at me. Please."

She responds to touch and raises her head to face me. OK, but she looks like she's seen a ghost, or something. What the fuck was it?

"What did you see, Ronnie?" I ask.

She's now focusing on me. The shaking subsides. Those big blue eyes are completely bloodshot and her makeup is all over the place, but she's coming back to us.

"Are you ok?" I still think she needs a minute to compose herself – maybe five hours sleep to sober up.

Now she sees me. Some recognition. Not sure I see anything. Is there anybody in there? I start to pull my hand away but she grabs it before I get very far. This is awkward. Or is it? I don't know. I never dealt with someone in shock before. Is this shock? Everybody is looking at her, us.

She speaks very softly, "He was holding it at me. I opened the door and he was there."

"What did he look like?" I pursue.

"Short, dark, scary. He was just there. It was awful." Uh-oh, she's drifting. "He was there. I saw it. Ugh." She starts shaking again and drops her head down, but grips my hand tighter. What in the wide, wide world of sports is going on here? Can't we just go back to being drunk and stoned?

"Somebody get a blanket," I say, "and make some coffee. And give her a hug." Somebody else, please, do something. Did I say, "Give her a hug"? Yeah. Dave gave me shit about that later on.

I have no idea what to do. This is what they do in the movies, right? So, I continue blabbering away, "I'll go talk to the MP's. She's in no shape to talk to them."

I try to loosen her grip on my hand and she resists. "Ronnie, I need to tell the MP's what happened. Are you ready to talk to them?"

She looks up at me with a really sad face and almost imperceptibly, her chin shakes a no, and, closing her eyes, very low, under her breath, and I know nobody else hears this as I am leaning my ear over to her mouth to hear words, she whispers, "Don't go."

What? I heard that but do not want anyone else to hear it. I say, "She says no". Then she lets my hand go.

Dealing with someone in shock is an experience, if that's what this is. From those last words, I'm not sure what this is but I'm going with shock. I think about all the guys I've met who were going on to medic training. Imagine the fucking shock victims they face, besides all the shocking wounds they see! That shit would put most of us in shock. I don't think I would have made much of a soldier. Maybe you get used to it. I don't know. I digress.

Anyway, no need to go out and tell the MP's. They had come into the kitchen. I had become so self conscious about Ronnie holding my hand that I purposefully zoned out, not wanting to see anyone else's faces.

I don't know, I was very uncomfortable with all those wives and a couple of guys looking on. It felt awkward but I also felt I had to concentrate on getting Ronnie to come out of whatever condition she was in. She seemed very scared.

Looking around I'm surprised to see everyone there in the kitchen – except the two ghost chasers. MP number one is taking notes.

"Did she say gun?" he asks.

Is he talking to me? "No, sir," though he was only a PFC, "she just said the guy was holding it at her."

MP number two says, "Gun for now. Can't take chances."

That is not what I think. I think she saw his dick in his hand but was too freaked out to say it. I think she would have said gun if he had one. But, what do I know? I'm no shrink. I mean, word is out by big mouth Daryl that the biggest boobs in the universe just moved into town and is living alone. Hey peeping tom's, you hear that? Maybe fucking Garza came out for a look.

Garza?!? You think it was him? Short, dark. Well, lots of short people, but he's dark. Son of a bitch! I wouldn't put it past that creep. He fucking stripped her down staring across that parking lot. I gotta find out.

MP number one turns his attention to me, "Here's my card. If your wife remembers anything more, contact me."

"Hold on," I protest, "I'm just a friend."

Fucking Dave can't hold it in, trying to stifle a chuckle. June kicks him. I think I hear a couple of more muffled sounds. I knew that hand holding thing would get me in trouble. I was just trying to get a pulse for Christ's sake.

"Her husband is in basic," I explain, "but everyone will be here for support. Right, guys?"

Heads nod up and down. Most of them are still pretty drunk and stoned. So am I but that acid training has come in handy. Acting straight is easier after you've tempered getting stoned with alcohol.

"OK," says the MP. Then he asks, "What's hubby's name and who is his CO?"

"He's Daryl Tillotson in company A-1-2 and the CO is Captain Wall," I respond.

"I'll call him and try to get the husband out here. Call me if she can provide any more details. If she's still out of it tomorrow, get her to a doctor. And see if you can get those two heroes back here. If that guy has a gun, he's dangerous."

With that they go looking around the neighborhood for a short guy. Every military guy who is not us is a suspect now. We're all fucking short guys in the Army.

Captain Wall gets the call and has someone drive Daryl out to the house. Daryl can stay the night but he had that fight recently and is on the shit list. Just one night.

By the time Daryl gets there it's nearly midnight. We fill him in. Only June, Dave and I remain from the party. Ronnie took the coffee after the MP's left and got it together to feed the babies. She still looks a mess and hasn't said much more than a quiet "thank you" but seems more alert.

I went back to drinking beer so I could sleep. We have to open the kitchen at six. Apparently, Wall checked the duty roster and told

Daryl to get a ride back with Dave in the morning. That will be two of us. I'm staying at Dave's tonight. I do that on most occasions that I get drunk, which is most occasions.

At five-thirty in the morning, June comes with us when we pick up Daryl. She figures Ronnie might need some help today. Daryl is very grateful to see her. He reports that Ronnie woke up when he did and seemed to be her old self but still doesn't remember anything more than what she said last night. She's pretty tired and could probably use some help with the kids. And, she doesn't want to be alone today. Good going, June.

The neighborhood wives think the same way and come over to spend the day with her. June invites her over for dinner. Later, they walk the two blocks back to the Jasons' house while the kids nap in the stroller.

Earlier, when Dave and I dropped Daryl off at 6AM, Daryl thanked me for helping out and asked if I could please check on Ronnie when I'm in the area, to be sure she's safe. I tell him sure. Why didn't he just ask Dave? I guess he knows and trusts me from hanging out in the barracks and getting high, and the Guess Who concert, and…ok, I get it.

I know what you're thinking. Well, maybe you're not, but I sure as damn hell was! What was that deal with her grabbing my hand? And, "Don't go"? Was she really whacked out or what? "Please check on her"? Check what, her heartbeat? No, come on. She's Daryl's wife. I like him, though he's proving to be a jerk. Yeah, she's kind of cute, got interesting, big eyes, big and blue, and maybe has the biggest tits on the planet, but, she's seventeen!

Come on! Give me a fucking break! With two kids? Who would do that?

No fucking way!

Rube, I'd Be Home If You Didn't Lose That One Paper

Dave assumes I'm coming back with him after work. That's pretty much become the norm when we don't have to be at work until about noon, though sometimes on Sunday evenings I leave June and Dave alone. He doesn't invite me anymore, I'm expected. Drill Sergeant Tim and the new office manager, Sergeant Tanner, are going to join them for dinner as well, so why not?

I was going to stay back today if Garza had come poking around. He didn't, it's Sunday. I wanted to talk to him. Not sure what I would have asked him. "Have you been looking through windows at young girls' breasts?" Kind of glad he wasn't around. I don't want to entertain homesick trainees tonight anyway.

We notice a Military Police car turning a corner down the block as we pull in front of Dave's house. Still looking for that short guy with his dick hanging out. I'm thinking, "Go talk to Garza."

As usual, we drink a lot and smoke a few joints. Ronnie is there and after avoiding her most of the night, while stoned I start wondering about those giant jugs. My good guy side shuts that down, for the most part. She catches me a couple of times.

The "party" breaks up as twilight darkens the neighborhood. This was Tanner's first time for dinner. He didn't drink much but he brought some good pot. I might like this guy. He heads back to his house on a scooter. As the Clevengers leave, Ronnie starts packing the kids' things.

Ronnie has a double barreled baby stroller (though it might have been a shopping cart) but I'm thinking maybe walking is a bad idea. It's dark now. She seemed to have been on a mission tonight – forget. Her eyes are bloodshot to the point of turning those big blues purple. She's wasted, again.

June is first to ask, "Ronnie, why don't you leave the shtroller here. We'll give you a ride home." Yes, she slurred stroller. She looks over at Dave who's catching flies with his head back on the couch. He's really fucked up.

She looks at me, "Can you..", hiccups and ends her sentence there, swaying. I guess we all tried to blur out last night.

On those nights when we don't have to come in until noon the next day, I prefer getting really stoned early, and then drink myself to sleep later. This is one of those nights. No shots, so far. I got ripped on three different kinds of pot. Tanner's was really tasty – skunky! I like that smell, in pot.

"Sure, I'm fine," I say, "let me help you with the kids, Ronnie."

We load the kids in the '57 Chevy and June gives me the keys. She holds on to them an extra second, struggling to stand up straight, gives me a smirky smile, tilts her head and eyes towards Ronnie, who is getting in the car, and says, "Shee you in na morning, hubby."

I tell her, "You're fucked up. Go to bed. I'll be back in a few minutes." I plan to put on headphones, play some Pink Floyd, smoke the remaining roaches, time-travel to Euphoria, and then drink myself to sleep. At least, that was the plan. Good plan, right? Sounds better as I think it out. Nothing I love more these days than getting stoned and putting on headphones. Of course, a new seed has been planted.

Was June fucking kidding? And don't you think it either. I'm very stoned so fucking a seventeen year old mother of two – how is that possible? (not the fucking part, the two kids at seventeen!) – is not really on my mind. I'm loving my high.

We had some eye contact tonight and Ronnie caught me staring at least once trying to verify Daryl's booby boast. I immediately lifted my eyes to hers.

Those eyes are kind of big relative to her head. Different. Makes those blues stand out. But she played the game, the eye game. Hold on, back off jack-off. She's really fucking seventeen? Jeez. Just don't! But what about those boobs?

Except for a few creepy ones in that 42nd Street bar we took Tom Semanski to last year, and maybe some in the lost weekend at Mardi Gras, I haven't seen any live boobs. I think I touched Pam's but those few moments were so drenched in alcohol, I can't really make that claim. Pretty sure I never saw them.

OK, I know what you're thinking. Every time I bring up that eye game thing, something happens. Well, it doesn't always happen. And think about this - that girl, and at seventeen, I don't care if Louisiana law says the age of consent is seventeen, she's still a girl, that girl is married. I still have some scruples, I think. Top it off – two kids! Now, seriously, getting involved with that whole situation? I am not going there. OK? Are we clear?

A Man of Scruples

I snap out of that two second mind conversation and kind of trot to the car. I hope June doesn't lock the door. Damn, she's toasted. Why do those guys do all those shots on top of good weed? It's like pissing into the wind.

"Thank you so much, Brian," says Ronnie as I hop in and turn the ignition. Love the sound of that old 283 engine. Purrs like a kitten.

"Oh," I say, constantly being reminded to get my shit together, from being so stoned, "my pleasure." Isn't that what you say in this situation? What is this situation anyway?

"Rosita and June were so good with the kids today," Ronnie breaks up my stone head as I put the automatic into gear. "I couldn't wait to get out of the house this morning. I didn't want to be there. June was so nice to come right over. She made a great breakfast. Rosita came over before lunch and entertained the kids for hours. The people here are really cool."

Seems to me she's talking nervously but then, again, I'm pretty stoned. Then again, again, she's pretty stoned. I get quiet when I get really high. I've seen other people talk a lot. Maybe she's one of them. Oh well, she's making this really short ride, really, really short. Keep talking, we're almost in front of the house.

What am I worried about? Am I too stoned? Too stoned? Then what, that something's going to happen? Like what, she's going to pop open that shirt and show me what she's packin'? Come on. But, that exchange seemed a bit strained. Anything going on here? My Yin and Yang are at it.

Did she really look back tonight when she caught me looking? Or am I just stoned? Well, that was the conversation, stone head. Or is it rock head?

I hesitate to shut the car off because I intend to drop her off and go, but I remember there are babies sleeping. Does it matter? They are out.

"You want me to take Maggie?" I ask as I turn off the car and open my door.

"Wait," Ronnie says, "I'm afraid to go in there now in the dark. Would you please go in first and make sure it's safe?"

Ding-ding-ding-ding-ding-ding…. Alarm bells going off. No wait, that's not an alarm. I've heard that noise on TV shows. That's a Las Vegas slot machine sound!

My stoned head just got real. I have no worries about running into some creep waiting for Miss American Boobies to come home. All I can think of is that I just got invited in.

"Sure," I say, "maybe I should take something with me." I go back to the trunk and find a long lug wrench. Yeah, I'm a force to be reckoned with.

Ronnie gives me the key to the house as she stays in the car with the kids. With a mighty lug wrench weapon, I fight off my stoned condition looking for a light switch. Got it.

Jeez, what if some asshole is in here? He's going to take this out of my hand and kill me. Oh, fuck, it's not going to happen. Just go through every room and then… What then? Yeah. Hurry! Upstairs too, Just in case.

OK, it's then.

"All clear," I say, walking back to the car. Both infants are still asleep so I pick up Maggie very gently.

Ronnie has the other baby and leads the way, "Follow me."

We head to the babies room, upstairs next to her bedroom. I tuck Maggie in and say, "I turned the back door's outside light on. Keep it on but turn off the kitchen light when you go to bed. You can see out. They can't see in." I remember something like that from when I was a kid.

"Also," I add, "I made sure all the downstairs windows are closed and latched. I know it's hot. Keep that fan on and the kids will be fine. And lock the door behind me. Stay cool. Goodnight."

With that sage advice I think I convinced myself to do the right thing – leave!

I'm halfway down the stairs when, "Wait," she says, "don't go so fast." One of the babies starts crying. "I don't want to be alone just yet."

More casino bells ringing.

She continues, "I have to change Janey's diaper. There's beer in the refrigerator. Get yourself one and open one for me."

The bells are deafening. The light on the top of the slot machine starts flashing. Standing on the stairs I sense serendipitous sirens screaming. Jackpot!

I'm pinching myself. If this Karma shit is real, I'm owed one and here it comes.

I get a feeling I'm about to.... Don't you? To a married seventeen year old with two kids? I'm a moral scumbag, and thinking I need a real one.

Really? Did you really think I would?

Moment of Truth

Well, suppose you are a twenty year old heterosexual male, only been laid once - and that was in the dark and too awkward to count, and the biggest boobs on the planet just invited you to have a beer in her house, just you and her?

My once stoned and slightly drunk head is now completely clear. Am I really going to do this? My head is spinning. Straighten out, man!

I used to have that tedious conversation with myself about trying to advance my sexual horizons by attempting to touch a girl's breast and, whether that would diminish her respect for me. Now it's respect for myself or - The Whole Enchilada.

Damn! This is not so hard. Come on, morals! Are you really going to do this?

Are you kidding? Of course!

I almost sprint to the kitchen to open those beers, leaving those morals far behind!

I settle into a large, comfortable chair in the small living room. Ronnie is taking a few minutes with the babies. Some crying. Maybe I shouldn't have opened her beer. Now it's quiet. Maybe she fell asleep with the babies. Maybe I completely misread this. Where is she?

I'm almost finished my beer. Nervous? Maybe she's just getting me a blanket. Too hot for that. What's going on? She's taking a long time. Maybe…oh shit, I don't know. What am I doing here? Wait, creaking from the stairs. Here she comes.

Ronnie tip-toes into the living room in a sheer negligee. You can't make this stuff up. Well, sure you can, but I'm not. And she's got on fresh lipstick and eyeliner, mascara, The Whole Enchilada, with all the toppings! Holy, Fucking, Shit!

The last year and a half have had so much drama, an emotional roller coaster – and now I am back on that ride, flying in the first car with my arms reaching for the sky. And tip-toeing slowly around me is a Playboy model. Well, she looks like one. Boing!

She walks slowly, letting me get a good look, pulls me close and kisses me like I've never been kissed before.

If ever a kiss could talk, this one does, and it says, "Do me". I was waiting, not too long, for my better self to say, "Don't do this", but Ronnie is unbuttoning my jeans.

This somewhat shy, young kitten is really a tiger. What have I gotten myself into? This is exactly what I've always thought those little eye games would result in. Hah! Never, in my wildest dreams did I really think that this would happen. Maybe in my dreams. Well, here we are. Top of the world, ma!

The sheer negligee is opening as she draws back from leaning over for that kiss, revealing the truth to Daryl's claim – he wasn't lying, biggest breasts on the planet. She sort of climbs onto me and sits up. I'm leaning back in the chair and my eyelids seem to be opened by toothpicks. And then I'm blind!

All that nervous conversation in the car and now she is like a silent cat on the prowl. This girl is only seventeen? No wonder she has two kids already. I don't have a rubber. Do I give a shit?

The thoughts that go through your head when your face is between two gigantic, firm breasts! This can't be real. God is fucking with me. Did I do acid tonight?

I can't deal with this. Well, I can if we stop with the teasing. I'm a babe in these woods. I'm gonna 'splode!

"Ronnie," I say, almost gasping for air as my peripheral vision creates a comical scene in my head – I'm pushing her large nipples into my ears, they're earplugs, "you are…I can't think of a better word than breathtaking."

Her first words, "Are you ready?"

I'm thinking I'm probably good for about thirty seconds. She stands up, removing the little bit of the negligee not already falling off. Make that ten seconds.

"Yeah, where to?" I ask.

"Right here, right now. But, one thing," she says.

"What's that?" I'm hoping it's not too kinky.

"Please don't ask me to put it in my mouth. That's all Daryl wants anymore and then I'm left horny. But, would you do that to me?"

Would You Do That To Me?

I know. I was speechless too. Well, I'm about to come on first touch so maybe this will slow me down. I'll be useless after about ten seconds of fucking anyway.

I nodded my head, lowered it some more, and took directions. Nuff said about that. Let your imagination fill in the rest.

The image of myself as the All-American boy is completely shattered. Life taught me a new lesson - sometimes it's ok to get fucked. Scruples? Hah!

Not sure how long Cunnilingus 101 lasted but I believe passing the clitoral discovery quiz satisfied the core requirements. Such was the response. We moved on. Finally, some fully naked sex, over and over. We must have gone at it for four or five hours. I needed practice. I was too quick on the draw, the first five or six times.

Who knew all Daryl's bragging was real? I'm sure he knew his wife had some nymphomaniac tendencies but that she had a master's in sex education?

Now, all you morality judges out there, you're right. But tell that to a horny twenty-year-old when a voluptuous, nearly naked nymph noodles your noodle.

God is going to strike me dead, but not for making up one word of this. If you had such an experience, would you forget? In truth, I did, for years. You move on, new life. But if you go back to that timeline in your head, those moments are pretty easy to recall – in such detail. Whoo!

Anyway, all that honor I thought I had was gone. The recklessness of youth.

"Mama always told me not to look into the eye's of the sun

But mama, that's where the fun is" (Springsteen's 'Blinded By The Light' performed by Manfred Mann).

Yes, I was a dick, and ruled by it.

Chapter 12 - July 1971 – The Last Few Weeks

On our country's Independence Day, Daryl gets a dispensation to go off post. He and Ronnie and kids come over to Dave's house with a whole bunch of people. We all get wasted and light off fireworks. That day with Daryl was a bit weird. If he had heard any rumors, and I probably started all of them, he didn't let on.

Short-Timer

The next day, Monday, July 5th, I get a call from Captain Sanchez in the AG's office. My physical was found in Hampton, Virginia. He has been told that the paper is on its way. "Specialist Carlin, you're a short-timer".

Finally! I'm getting out of the Army, and a nymphomaniac loves me. More proof that God doesn't exist. You don't get rewarded for what I've been doing the last two weeks – every fucking (you can reverse those two words) night. Or, perhaps God is getting me out for my own good. He knows it wasn't my idea. The devil made me do it.

For months I've been considering deep philosophical questions. Now this? Well, the fact is, I don't want to die anymore and I suspect that continuing this insanity would get me killed. Maybe I was going to get my original wish after all.

There was one negative to the affair, Ronnie's complaint that her sex life with Daryl had devolved to oral sex, but just one way. His method of contraception, I suppose. Two babies before seventeen? He might have had a point. So she wanted to be on the receiving end. None for me. The positive, I learned a lot.

Enough of that. I'm not going to write about that education. Nope. Not going to talk about it. I never liked the sex part in movies either. Just kiss and go to black.

I don't want to see other people doing it. If it ain't me babe, it ain't important. I get it. Next scene. Never really was that big a fan of x-movies either. Even worse, watching a porn movie with a bunch of guys at a bachelor party is just creepy.

Wait, creepier yet - at a bachelor party with a Catholic priest. Yep. A few years later I was there at just such an event with just such an espoused guest. Absolutely true. I swear to his God I am not making this shit up. That ruined porn for me. Strike me down with lightning if I'm lying. Why would I for one lousy paragraph? Think about it though. Oooh.

The same day that I'm told I'm going home, Dave gets word that his discharge papers are coming through also. We are scheduled to get out the same day, Thursday, July 22nd. How great is that?

Poor Michael

This is an amazing day. The company has to scramble to find two cooks to take our place. Who gives a flying fuck? Poor Michael - remember him? He throws a shit fit. He is scheduled to get out August 6th. We're getting out before him? Sorry Michael. I'm with a nymph every night and getting out of here in two weeks. Life is not fair.

The next day, Michael gets in a fist fight with Sgt Dealy, gets court martialed, loses two stripes, and gets two weeks in the brig, that part suspended because of the sudden cook shortage but tagged on to his duty time, now making his discharge date August 20th. Dealy has a huge shiner, Michael is stuck in Fort Polk for two extra weeks, and, oh, a nymphomaniac won't let me sleep. That part is all I think about. We laugh and cry together. Life is definitely not fair. Or is it?

The next weekend, the 10th and 11th of July, Dave and I are working. Daryl's extra week suspension of off-post privileges is over and he's with Ronnie getting his..., he's practicing birth control. I'm jealous. I want that.

Dave and I are not into working this weekend at all. We bring some vodka in and drink Bloody Mary's all weekend and, when we get tired of drinking, switch to Ballantine, a horrible NY beer they were introducing in the south for 2.99 a case. It was like water. Twenty-four beers for three bucks. You get what you pay for.

We are so far away in our minds, we break all the rules. We put all the bacon on huge baking sheets and throw them in the oven. Same with toast. No eggs cooked to order. We make a giant batch of scrambled eggs in a giant soup bowl. We teach the KP's how to make pancakes and let them do it. Fuck this.

We get through Saturday and then go back to Dave's house. Everybody comes over, the first big gathering of all the friends, and even some of the cooler trainees, since we heard we're getting out. Daryl, Ronnie and kids are there also. Smirks everywhere but he still seems to be in the dark.

I won't kiss Ronnie hello because I know where those lips have been. We have to be at work at 6am Sunday so the night is short for us.

Just as we take the bacon out of the oven before serving at about 8, Dealy shows up, black eye and all. He sees the bacon on cookie sheets and blows up. Regulations say we have to cook them on the grill. The KP's have pancakes going on the grill, I tell him. Another KP starts spooning the sloppy scrambled eggs to a trainee.

Dealy is out of his mind. He wants to lock us up. He's jealous too. And he doesn't know, well, maybe he does, that I'm having the time of my life after hours. I think everybody knows by now.

After breakfast is served and the KP's are cleaning up, he tells us to come outside. By now he has composed himself. He's come to grips with the fact that we don't give a shit anymore. But he feels compelled to give us some of his sage advice by way of a story.

"You know, I came from a small town in Maine. My father worked in a factory that made shoes. He worked hard to make a living. We didn't have much, but we had pride. We had pride in what we did. When I got older, I was about to drop out of school to join him in the factory, but I heard about the Viet Nam war and I had to make a decision. You know, I could have made a good living making shoes. I already knew how to repair them. I could have opened my own shop fixing shoes, making shoes, selling shoes. But I didn't. I joined the army. You know why I'm not making shoes and doing this today?" He's getting excited and worked up again. He repeats loudly, "You know why?"

Because You're Stupid!!!

Dave doesn't miss a beat and has no intention of taking Dealy's shit. In a split second, he yells back, "Because you're stupid!"

Dealy was not expecting that. The top of his head exploded. His eyeballs popped out. Blood came pouring out of his ears and nose. All his teeth fell out. His skin burst into flames and his skeleton rattled as it ran over to company headquarters. It was Sunday. No one was home.

Dave and I laughed our asses off. That was one of the funniest scenes I had ever witnessed. From that day on, whenever I heard someone start to explain why they did something against the grain – ok, dumb, if I could squeeze it in without getting punched, I'd offer the Dave response - "Because you're stupid!" You hear it more often than you think, "Why would I do that?" Remember to answer, "Because you're stupid!"

We went back to Dave's place that night and repeated the conversation to just about everyone who worked in the company and a half dozen trainees. We were not too worried about repercussions. If we had to, we'd lie. It was our word against his. My scruples had already been corrupted beyond repair.

Our Monday shift began at about noon, but Captain Wall wanted to see us in his office at 11. He first met with Dealy. Ten minutes later he called the two of us in.

After the "At ease", he asks us our side of the story. After Dave is done, word for word, he laughs and says Dealy told him the exact same thing.

He's still chuckling when he says, "That was pretty damn funny. But, you showed disrespect for your immediate superior, even if he is a horse's ass. With a week to go, can you try to be nice to him?"

He then asked us about how the recruiters screwed us and expressed genuine disgust with their tactics. He actually sounded apologetic when he said that he realized we had volunteered for the most dangerous job in the world and were treated with such disrespect.

I had never thought of it that way. Holy shit, an intelligent lifer. He added that he knew we were going back to the real world and would probably paint a bad picture of the Army. He hoped we would consider that those recruiters don't represent the Army as a whole and, at the very least, please have some kind words for the friends we've made here. He also hoped we'd consider him a friend.

On that note we did and shook hands. He called Dealy back in, made us shake hands, and agree that we just get through the next week of our service in harmony. Something like that. Dave and I were smiling, Dealy was scowling, his fading shiner glowing red, and the real Captain Wall was hiding behind a very straight face, our new friend.

The horrible, no good, very bad year in the Army was coming to an end. And good things kept happening. Poor Michael. He fights with Dealy and gets screwed. We use words to fight with Dealy and come out smelling like a rose - Dave deserves all the credit for saying in very clear and loud words, "Because you're stupid!"

I will remember that moment for the rest of my life. I can see a movie built around just that moment. I try to see an actor taking Dealy's part and I try to envision a Dave, but I only see their real faces in 1971 - Dealy's thick black glasses almost falling off his blonde, crew cut head as he can't find words to respond. Dave standing up with his thick, wavy black hair and beard-stubbled face, standing up and roaring at the Master Sergeant, "Because you're stupid", barely restraining himself from chest thumping Dealy but almost knocking him down with the ferocity of his shout. Remember it. Never let stupidity win.

Ten Days To Go

We take over the kitchen at the lunch shift and poison the minds of another six KP's. It's my turn at the radio dial so we listen to the new Alexandria station playing 'album tracks'. Wow, six, seven, ten minute versions of those three minute AM songs.

Dave and I sneak off to my room one at a time, purportedly to pee, but we smuggle out beers hidden deep in the fridge, chug them in the room, take a few hits off a joint, really pee, then pass the baton. That was one, fucked up, happy day.

Dave drove back to his house totally shitfaced. We did that a lot back then. Nothing to be proud about. I crashed in my room, a hundred yards away. Then we were back at it at 4AM. Fuck!

Ten days to go. I'm now using Dave's motorcycle most of the time. It was a small one, maybe 250cc's. At the beginning of June I had gone to a Honda dealer in Alexandria to try to buy a beautiful, new model, the 750. When I showed them my $105 monthly pay stub they laughed. Good thing, I would have gotten myself killed.

That little 250 scared the shit out of me. Well, that might have been because I was stoned all the time and 50mph seemed like 150. Of course, when I was drunk, 100 seemed like 50.

And there you have a perfect example of the concept behind the seven levels of consciousness, and my adaptation, the concept of thoughts per second. Remember that? Here's a direct connect to the seven levels of consciousness in Timothy Leary's "The Politics of Ecstasy". I made everybody I tripped with read that, or at least get familiar with the seven levels.

The Politics of Ecstasy

I don't know what happened to my copy of the book and I'm not going to buy another one. I'll let you verify my memory but it goes something like this - the levels are based on drugs. Let's see if I can list them:

1. Heroin (and now fentanyl, etc)
2. Alcohol/downers
3. Normal - no drugs
4. Speed/amphetamines/cocaine
5. Marijuana
6. Mescaline, lower level psychedelics
7. LSD

Something like that. Pretty sure that was it. My thoughts per second concept was based on that hierarchy. The pot and speed levels may be flipped. However, I'm not so sure the speed and coke level even belongs. I felt they were physically oriented, not so much of an effect on the thought process, and I'll argue with Timmy on this. I did a lot of speed and cocaine later. Body only. Not mind.

Anyway, drinking slows your brain down so that your perception of speed is decreased. Hallucinogens speed up the thought process increasing the perception of speed. With so many thoughts going on when high, like being ultra-aware of the dangers of moving faster than a walk, one tends to slow down. When drunk, and only considering a few consequences of moving quickly, one can be emboldened to go faster than prudence or local laws dictate.

On a much simpler level – did you ever catch yourself speeding after two or three drinks? And, if you smoke pot, did you ever catch yourself doing 40 in a 55 after getting high? If you don't get high, next time you start yelling at that dufus in the right lane slowing everything down, take a look and see if it looks like a stoner. Oh, good luck with that ID. We walk among you. Anyway, driving that little 250 motorcycle was exciting most of the time because I was higher on pot more than I was lower on beer.

That, dear friends, was one hell of a side-track! Whatever! The mind is not linear, but language is. That's why we edit. Where were we? Oh yeah, ten days left in the Army.

I drove very fast to Ronnie's house when I got off work that day. Actually, I parked the motorcycle at Dave's house and walked the block and a half, just in case somebody who wasn't in the know wanted to make an association.

On hindsight, perhaps it would have been better to have a getaway vehicle if Daryl showed up with a gun. That was a constant worry but common sense was not getting a lot of playing time then. I spend every day and night I can with Ronnie. She is, as am I, I suppose, insatiable. Catch a breath. Make sure the babies are ok. Do it again.

Sergeant Garza, World Class Sleezeball

Thursday, July 15th. I had spent the night in Ronnie's bed. The morning light provides one more opportunity while the babies still sleep, but before we get too far, the doorbell rings. Shit! I gotta get outa here. The bedroom upstairs faces the street.

I peek out the window while trying to get dressed and see a guy in a military uniform. Ronnie puts on a bathrobe and runs downstairs. She opens the door a crack and there's that voice, "Meesus Teelotson. Can I come in?" It's Sergeant Garza, the sleezeball.

She says, "No, what do you want?"

"I know your husband is at work and I thought you might be lonely. I can make you happy, you know what I mean? I've been watching you. You are a beautiful woman." I can't believe what I'm hearing. This is the peeping tom!

There's a commotion. "Stop. Get out. Go away or I'll call the police" and she slams the door. She runs upstairs and is freaked out. He had actually tried to grab her.

My first instinct is to get the hell out of there but she needs some tender care. As much as I'd prefer to resurrect my carnal urge, I resort to being a comforting, nice person. The babies are now crying. No sex this morning.

Now Garza is on my shit list. I can't exactly report him but the coffee I made for him that last week was inspired by those nasty books he loved. Let me be clear about that - I spit and mixed boogers into his coffee. He probably thought it was good. I was so tempted to spike it with acid.

The End Is Near

Ronnie and I have a couple of more nights together and she is now begging me to take her with me. She's in love with me. This wasn't supposed to happen. I'm the one that falls in love and gets hurt. It doesn't feel so good on this side either. I bet Jessica felt like this. I bet Pam didn't.

That last week I ship my records, stereo, clothes and precious black light back home. Everything arrives safe and sound, except the black light.

Rodney, the replacement cook, owes me fifty bucks. I lend him money every month and he offers me twice as much back. I'd be happy just getting my money back but he sends me twenty bucks a month for five months. A man of his word.

Michael is trying not to kill Dealy. They really don't like each other. Michael is going home in a few weeks and antagonizes Dealy every chance he gets. The lifer has not been having a great time lately.

I help Dave pack up for the trip back to Nebraska. We make some strategic plans for our Army exit – like where they are going to drop me off so I can get a decent flight back home. It will be Dallas where I'll wing it. Ha.

I spend the last night with Ronnie. The hot sex is rather anti-climaxic. Something like that. She cries a lot. The babies cry a lot. I'm going to miss those babies. The breasts, that is. And that education. Looking forward to applying that lab work to real world situations. Imagine that? Having a sexual relationship that isn't doomed?

Good bye, Ronnie.

I drive into the post with Dave and June in the early morning. We are all packed and all that awaits is our exit ceremony.

July 22, 1971: Honorably Discharged - Unfulfilled Enlistment Commitment

Thursday, July 22nd, 1971. Eleven months and eighteen days. That's what my discharge papers say, my Unfulfilled Enlistment Commitment, Honorable Discharge. It's a code on the official DD-214. I try to remember what Captain Wall said, "You guys volunteered for the most dangerous job in the Army". And they fucked us over.

Dave remembers that as we drive out the main gate at about 8AM. I have my camera and take a picture of the MP saluting us. I take one more of Dave's left hand outside the window of his '57 Chevy, returning the salute with his clenched fist and middle finger standing proudly at attention as if it were a dick offering itself to a horny seventeen year old with massive breasts, a tiny waist, and double-wide hips. Dave's venting.

I'm still thinking about the only thing I'm going to miss about the Army. But, I'm also relieved. I was told that Daryl found out this morning. Whew! Drive faster.

Up to Shreveport, onto I-20 west through Tyler, Tx and at the Dallas airport by about 1PM. Goodbyes to my life support the last few months, the Jason's. We all agree we couldn't have done it without each other. We'll remember all the crazy goings-ons, the acid trips - and finally, we'll be in touch with phone numbers and addresses. I walk away with my duffel bag.

That's it. It's really over. What a fucking year! It all seems so surreal – the way I got in the Army, the pain that led up to taking LSD, the amazing journeys I've had doing it, the Ronnie affair, and now I'm standing in an airport a free man. I'm bursting with happiness.

I also come back to the thought of driving out the gate. That was perfect - that the MP's didn't chase us for flipping the bird upon our exit. And now the first task of my new civilian life - I'm finding a flight that works. First to Atlanta and then on to JFK. In my spiffy military uniform, some old vet pays for my two drinks on the first flight.

During the Atlanta layover, the bartender bought one of my drinks. I got lucky on the ATL-JFK flight and got bumped up to first class. Four more screwdrivers. I should have been slobbering drunk but the adrenaline was flowing like, uh, like I was expecting a young Playmate model in a negligee to unbutton my pants. I gotta forget all that.

Finally, at 7:43PM, I remember the time because they were standing under a clock - my sister Susan and Jack, her fiancé, are waiting for me at gate 19 with a large brown bag. In the bag is a large bottle of champagne and three flutes. There are no security gates back then. Anything goes, though we have to brown-bag it. Keep the party going.

Driving back to Bellmore I can't believe it is over. I'm so happy. It's over. Now what? Who cares?

Chapter 13 - Freedom: July 22, 1971

Now What?

Now what? Well, the celebration that began with a bottle of champagne at JFK continues back at 400 Washington Avenue in Bellmore. Artie and Judi stop by to welcome me home.

My brother now has to share that room again, and his pot until I can find a dealer - oh, that would be the late Frank Gurgi. He was a character. OD'd a few years later, I think. Or was he the one blown away in a drug deal gone bad? Lots of dead young people back then.

Anyway, about 11PM, after a few beers and sneaking a few hits of pot outside, offered by 15-year-old sister Debbie, Susie and Jack load Debbie and I into Jack's car and we take off for his mother's home in West Gilgo Beach. Debbie rolls another doobie that we smoke on the drive. Upon arrival, we put yet another parent to bed, and then continue to drink and smoke until the sun comes up over the ocean.

And so it went for a week or so. Five days after the sun came up on my first day of civilian life, I turned twenty-one. Not that big a deal back then. Drinking and dying for your country was the same, eighteen, in New York State, but I think if you wanted to get killed at seventeen they'd let you. Except for fifteen days, my twentieth year was in the army. What a fucking year!

I was unemployed for the first time in two years. The couple of hundred I had was enough to get my Cyclone on the road again. It also covered my first ounce of pot as a civilian, a whole bunch of new albums, and the paints required for a makeover of my room, the little room I shared with Michael right over our dining room.

About that dining room - sometime in the next year we procured an old, five gallon, glass milk container into which we fitted a big rubber stopper, into which we inserted a chemistry class thistle tube to make a giant bowl, and another glass tube onto which we attached a long rubber intake tube. This was the mother of water pipes!

When you sucked on that baby the chandelier in the dining room below shook with the ceiling. The first toker always inhaled too much and coughed for five minutes. Excess smoke wafted through the room and would have triggered a smoke detector. Visitors didn't need to use the bowl after the first hit. The space above the water was loaded with THC laced smoke. Just inhale, man. We didn't use the term dude yet.

The paints? I negotiated with my mother who allowed a dark blue, as opposed to the black I wanted, to cover the walls and ceiling. The broken, four foot black light bulb was replaced and with the very dark background, the day glow stars and other oddities I painted on the ceiling and walls burst with color.

During one of my acid trips in the army, I had a god-like vision, tainted by my Catholic background, something like that. I really wanted to believe that there was more than this. On acid, there is. How you envision it is entirely dependent on your expectations of what such a deity or an all powerful "it" might be.

Anyway, during one spaced out session I had painted the internal white paper jacket, you know - the sleeve that covers the vinyl of an album, in this case it was the Atom Heart Mother sleeve, with all kinds of designs, including a drawing that turned out to be pretty similar to the cover of the Moody Blues' album, 'In Search of The Lost Chord'! Now there's an album cover!

As I said, that sleeve was sort of like the album cover which I bought, by the way, on that first trip to the record store. I merged the two ideas for the mural. I drew sort of a crucifix with the top part trying to look like two arms outstretched and, where the head should be, a diffusing of all colors into the heavens. Something like that. I had no confidence in drawing a human head. On the dark blue wall next to my bed was this four foot tall mish-mash of day glow colors.

My parents never commented on it. I think they got the idea that something was different with me. The mural was a sight. All those day glow colors lit up the room. Black light posters were

227

added and my old WWII airplane models went psychedelic.

It would do until I figured out...I don't know, who I was, what I was doing here, and where I was going...that is, the basics of Philosophy 101. I never thought much about that before doing acid – just "somebody love me". In the meantime, when you walked into that room with the black light on you felt a little awestruck. Or, maybe, your reaction might be, what the fuck? Black lights are cool.

Ronnie?

I wasn't home more than a few days when I get a call from Ronnie. Are you kidding me? I was not very good at our big secret and it seemed like the whole base knew about our affair. She just wanted to get out of there and wanted to know when she could come to Long Island.

Great. NOT! I talked her down. We would talk next week. She loved me. That's two. At least two who said they did. So I guess that balances my love account with Karma, or, back then it was still God. I might not have told Jessica I loved her, directly, but she knew I did. I'm sure. That counts.

Pregnant? It Ain't Me Babe

A week later she called again from Indiana. She went home. She's pregnant! Ahhhhhhhhhh! "Don't worry, it's not yours. I was already pregnant when I was with you." Whew! Gotta go. Bye. I avoided the next two calls. My mother answered and told her I was not home. I had to explain a little about her to my mother, but, of course, not everything. I assume she told my father.

I wonder if that made him smile. There wasn't much I had done in the last year and a half that would have made him smile. Anyway, never heard from Ronnie again and put her out of my mind for years – except for her training!

Last Try With Jessica

I'm a creep. But, I've been on the losing end before. Speaking of, as soon as I got my car on the road I went down to Jones Beach to look for Jessica. My old friends were still managers and directed me to where she was working. She was out in parking field 4 picking up trash.

We talked for five or ten minutes. I asked specifically if there was any chance we could get back together. She was nice about it but the answer was no. I never looked for her again.

That was over and I wasn't all that devastated anymore. I was excited about life. But, I went away sad. It was confirmed, I had loved her. Still did. In a way, still do. Kind of like the Titanic movie thing. Short, sweet, intense, bad ending. You move on, but you don't forget love if it was real.

Dating Again

My army money was running out. All I did for a couple of weeks was go to the beach in the day and go to the Tabard Ale House at night. I needed beer and pot money so I got my old job back at the drug store, this time full time, ten to six, Monday to Friday, weekends off. A regular job. It was too late in the season to get the Jones Beach job back. One thing I did not do, starting on

Freedom Day, was shave or cut my hair. Hey hippies! Here I come.

I didn't know what I wanted to do the rest of my life so before I went back to school I decided to think about it - for a year. I figured I got a free year by getting that discharge – only eleven months and eighteen days! Never forgot that. For me, there was no rush, no real need to get out of my parents' house. The drug store job was brainless. I just needed some time to figure out what direction to take and I needed to save some money if I wanted to go to college.

Mostly, that direction I was looking for was up. I got high a lot. I learned how to act straight among straight people, though I never got high at work.

Getting high at bars took some getting used to. Social skills need to be recalled constantly until it became normal. Just relearning the same skills under new conditions, hundreds of thoughts per second faster than usual. Things you said and did naturally are questioned (by yourself) in the process of doing them. Thoughts between those seconds of action need to be reigned in but also examined.

Before approaching a girl, I might have a few dozen more conversations with myself about why I should. But, for the most part, I realized I was more socially adept with a couple of beers under my belt rather than a joint, and eventually avoided getting high going to bars, for now. It was slim pickin's for a while as I was still mourning Jessica and because of her, had set a very high bar. I also had this feeling that I was so much older than these "kids" – having done acid with moments of understanding everything. Being kind of a hippy now also changed my thoughts about some of the girls.

And so, one night in late August I'm at the bar with a couple of guys from the old gang. Paul, one of the founding Bellmore Drinking Club members, starts talking to a girl and a few minutes later calls me over to meet her, and her not-identical, but better looking, twin sister.

I haven't shaved since the last day in the Army so I'm not sure how the eye-to-eye trick is going to work. Never had a beard before.

This is a few weeks later, obviously, Halloween. "100 days" (I wrote that on the back of the picture) without coming near to a blade.

Guess having a beard and hair in your eyes doesn't matter. Zoe Kohl and I hit it off immediately. She's cute, slim (no breasts – Ronnie raised that bar so high that I'm not even looking there), and athletic – got some muscles. I make her laugh. We get drunk at the bar - what else is new? – and start getting touchy-feely.

Zoe

We're close to closing the place. We walk outside and I can tell this is not going to be a peck on the cheek goodbye. She's not aggressive, but I am pretty toasted and feeling my oats, and, in anticipation of the kiss, quite horny.

She's leaning against the outside wall of the bar as I plant that kiss which gets very sloppy. It goes on and on and my button-fly bell bottoms feel awfully tight. I finally just move my hips up to hers and press that bulge in my pants to the bull's-eye.

There was a noticeable relaxation of any tenseness in her muscles and an audible, but gentle, "oh", yet the kiss response was strong. Wow, got away with that. I never had done anything like that before. We made a date for a couple of nights later. We both knew where this was headed.

As much as I tried to convince myself at first, I wasn't in love. I was definitely in lust, having had a good taste (oh, please) with Ronnie. Zoe was a virgin but after a few weeks she was ready, with help from her sister, who was now dating Paul, and he didn't beat around the bush with sex.

This next story is weird but true. This whole fucking book is true. I keep saying that because it all seemed so unlikely. Do we really expect life to proceed like a 50's TV show? Nothing ever seems to go as planned. Life keeps throwing shit at us. You can only take so much shit before you start throwing it back. But, I digress.

What's so weird now? How about this - the twins planned Zoe's cherry popping? But wait, the plan was even weirder. She can put this story in her book for her grandchildren.

Zoe's sister, with Paul, drove us out to Montauk one weekend at the end of September in their parents' big old station wagon. There were no SUV's then. We had a picnic, ran around on the beach, went to the lighthouse, and then headed back to their home in Seaford, two towns east of Bellmore.

The other twin is driving the old wagon. Paul is right next to her on the bench seat and I think one of his hands has been missing for a while. Zoe and I are making out in the back seat most of the time.

Every once in a while there is some mysterious communication between the twins, with an occasional, "Stop that," followed by giggles from the front seat. We reach the Long Island Expressway and Zoe tells me it's time - to do IT!

Yep, the twins cooked up the idea of doing it on the LIE. Zoe wanted her sister nearby. Something like that. You got me. All I know to do is, pull out the lambskin - remember, I work in a drug store, no cheap rubbers for me.

I Did It...On The Highway

Anyway, my pants are coming down faster than I can spell hard-on, the prophylactic is employed, and we're working on Zoe's pants. Far, fucking, out! Billy Joel was still nobody in 1971 but this could have been a line from one of his songs - "It was cherry poppin' glee on the L-I-E", or perhaps, it could have been inserted into Frank's 'My Way', "I did it... on the highway".

You can't make this stuff up – well, yeah, the song stuff, but wanting to do it the first time near your twin sister, and, of all places, on the Long Island Expressway? Well, fuck! And so we did.

I'm not going into the relationship and why it didn't work out, but, it didn't. We had a nice three months or so but I had to end it. You won't believe why.

First, there were two highlights that make fun stories, the first of which I've never told. It was a bit personal but we're old fuckers now so WTF. Both stories involve sex so fast forward to the next chapter if you've had enough tawdry lunacy for now. Yeah, right. Like you'd do that.

After the LIE awkwardness, sex became pretty regular, if only in the old '55 Dodge. Oh, I screwed up the Cyclone. This is not one of the stories I was talking about but it has its moments.

One night we were out at a bar and got really drunk. Uh-huh. You mean like most nights? We pulled up in front of her house and we both fell asleep. At about 3AM she wakes and tells me to go home. I go about two blocks, turn down another and fall asleep.

Boom! I'm woken by a crash. Yeah, me into the rear of a brand new Mustang that was now up on a curb. Shit! I gotta get out of here. I pull away and speed home. I would have gotten jailed if I stayed around. Yeah, I'm a shit! But not so fast.

Next day we have tickets to go to the opera (WTF?) with her sister and mother. I have the worst hangover of all time and my car is fucked up. When I wake up in the morning I think, at first, that I had a bad dream about the car. But then I look outside to see the damage. The front end is smashed and the radiator drained. And I have massive guilt.

Zoe and her mom pick me up. The opera is like sticking darning needles through your eyes to the back of your skull. As soon as I get home I take the old Dodge out and retrace my route. I have no idea where the accident happened.

Near Zoe's house I see a police car in a driveway and behind the cop car is a Mustang with its rear end all mangled. I wait until the cop leaves and then knock on the door.

"Sir, was your car rear-ended last night? That was me." I tell him I fell asleep and was in shock when I woke and just drove off. He calls the police to drop the complaint and we go through insurance. Whew! My hangover just improved dramatically. There, I'm not such a shit.

But that wasn't one of the two sex stories. Skip to next chapter if you can't handle it. It's more comedy than sex. Your choice…. I knew you wouldn't skip this stuff. Shame on you. "But, Mama, that's where the fun is!" Come on.

First story - back to sex in a '55 Dodge. It had huge bench seats so front or back would do, twin or king. It, the joy of sex, didn't go so great for her at first - until we perfected the do-it-then-do-it-again-in-fifteen-minutes technique. You might say I was a bit quick on the draw, even with all that Ronnie training. That technique delayed my second climax enough for her to achieve one. The plus – two home runs each session. This was very new for her so it was all very hands-off. She wouldn't touch my penis. That was about to change.

You Can't Make This Stuff Up

One day Zoe meets me in the parking lot at the bar after I worked an odd evening shift at the drugstore. She had just gone to the movies with a friend - an x-rated movie, 'Deep Throat' - and she professed to be very horny.

"I want to touch Charlie."

Oh, yeah. She had somehow felt the need to personalize my penis. I preferred Sir Charles, but she wanted to be less formal.

"How do I make Charlie feel good?"

I explain in great detail and she practices up to the point where I have to stop her because I'm about to explode.

"Can I kiss Charlie?"

Whoa, I wasn't expecting that. Well, not exactly "whoa". Be my guest and be creative. French kissing is encouraged.

Then finally, "I want to put Charlie in my mouth. Tell me what to do then."

I was not going to get into this much detail and I'll stop at this point but decided that the way she approached giving her first blow job was just so precious I had to tell you.

Remember Ronnie from the Army? How she trained me in the art of oral sex? Well, Zoe became the most eager of performing students. Absolute truth. You can't make this stuff up. Thinking God is not in on this one, I just figure life - Karma? - is evening up the oral sex score. Who says life isn't fair? Just give it time. Shit happens.

One more story with Zoe and then we'll say adieu. Shortly after the sex went oral, it went dual oral, the beloved sixty-nine, or eighty-eight for some, though I would argue that number looks like a foursome. Anyway, one night we get drunk - what else is new? - and rather than drop her off in front of the house, we park around the block, hop in the backseat and indulge in this new activity.

A little while later, the rear passenger door opens. I'm on my back. My head is on the driver's side, doing things Ronnie taught me. Zoe is doing what I taught her. The door-opening sound is quite disturbing. A cop would knock first.

I hear a 'smack', and then Zoe's mother's voice, "Zoe, get in the house, NOW".

The door slams. This is not good - I'm not getting off tonight. Damn! Just lost my woody. Absolutely true! Lucky I didn't get bitten.

I had to have a man-to-man with Mr. Kohl the next weekend. That was rather awkward. Her dad worked construction jobs in upstate NY and only came home on weekends. He was pretty rugged and could have kicked the shit out of me, and pretty much threatened to, but I got a sense from his minimal rage that he was no innocent choir boy.

After something resembling an apology and the law being laid down about a two week ban, I knew I was done with this family. But, that's a memory that doesn't ever fade - getting caught with a mouthful. I wonder if her mother wasn't a little turned on. Not sure what Zoe did with me at that moment – go deep or point me at mom? Hey Mrs. Kohl, if you're still alive, remember that? Oh, come on, you made it into the book. Chill.

Damn, I'm a sick fuck.

By December, the Zoe fling is over. I ended it because, well, a few things. One, of course, was the relationship with her parents. Her mother was always going to have that sight in her head. Tough one to get over.

And then, there was this, and this is just one example – we were watching TV with my family one Saturday night before going out. It was an 'All In The Family' episode and it was very funny. Even my youngest sister, Marilou, at 13, understood all the jokes. Granted, she's pretty smart. But, after laughing hysterically at them, Zoe seemed to think the jokes needed to be explained. I kept getting looks from my siblings that said, "Is she for real?"

I said you wouldn't believe why I broke it off. Well, her being a little slow on the uptake wasn't it. It really was because all we had was sex, and I recognized that. I still wanted to find "the one". She wasn't that girl.

Now, walking away was hard, as I was when I saw her. When I picked her up, she unzipped my pants as soon as she got in the car. I did most of the talking because she had her mouth full. Truth. It was bizarre but how could I complain? And that wasn't enough for me!?! I know, I'm a fucking idiot. Couldn't I have just gone along? Well, no. She was in love. Here we go again. I couldn't. So I'm stupid but still a bit of a romantic, at heart. Give me that. I did the noble thing, so says my conscience.

So now it's time for some serious getting high. Relationships and getting really whacked don't seem to blend well. You don't think too much about the future when you are completely stoned and I was very much interested in a relationship with one person that would last a lifetime.

Finding such a person while blasted didn't appear to be a likely scenario but I went out to bars every night nonetheless, looking for her, totally ripped.

1971 - The year that changed everything is over. It had started out in despair, sadness, and hopelessness. I was alone again but this time it was my doing. This past year life taught me many lessons, the most important of which was that I was stronger than despair and sadness and there would always be hope. Love lost would always be painful but life lost was not an option anymore.

238

Phase 5: The Philosophy of Rock Concerts

Chapter 14 - Early 1972 – Super Freaky

After my fling with Zoe, I kind of retreated from the girl scene for a while. I wondered what was wrong with me. I was having incredible sex every day and just cut it off. There was something missing. I'd look at Jessica's high school picture once in a while and knew what it was. I missed love, the heart kind. There had been a lot of damage in there and reconstruction was still in process. I really wasn't ready to open up completely.

In the meantime, I was wondering what this whole life thing was all about. How 'bout that Alphie? Any answers there? What the hell are we doing here? Why do people act so cruelly? Pam? Why? What was your problem? Have I been cruel?

Many philosophical questions, though I had no idea what a philosophical issue entailed, and many heart wrenching questions. I was no longer the impetuous, act-and-ask-questions-later asshole who had little value for life, but while waiting for that heart to heal, went full bore looking for answers to all those questions.

As the new year began, I continued my examination of the brain on LSD. My brother, Michael, and sister, Debbie, had connections to keep feeding my brain. It was a little weird getting high with them, but then, the last year was more than a little weird.

I was working ten to six every day at the drug store, putting enough money aside to start college again in the fall and pay for my Tabard Ale House tab, as well as support my marijuana and acid requirements.

A few months went by like that. Work every day, sometimes weekend too, trip every few weeks, get high and go to the bar every night. I love the music when I'm high. Several months without a date and I am OK with it. Being really stoned is replacing being "in love". My hair is getting pretty long. I'm starting to look like every other hippy in 1972.

It's A Freak!

One night in March, I'm at the Tabard Ale House, as usual, stoned, with very red eyes, hanging out next to the ladies room (you see them all if you hang there long enough), when a girl walks up to me and says, "It's a freak!"

"Excuse me?"

"It's a freak!", and she had the biggest smile. That was another term for hippies back then. She was using it in an endearing way and sort of dragged me onto the dance floor.

Donna Super, yeah, that last name (real) always got me too, was super cute, a bundle of energy, high as a kite, a kindred spirit, and wanted me. Just like that. Some people see what they like and wonder what they have to do to get it. Some people take it.

Donna grabbed my hand and took me outside, lit up a joint, and kissed me. I was a little blown off my feet but I knew what I wanted. She lit a fire in my pants but instead we went back to her car and smoked another doobie. Pot was pretty mild back then. Today, two joints would get me so high I wouldn't be able to converse, especially when you consider the size of the stogies we rolled.

"Can we take this slow?", says me. Really? This is, like, too easy, if you just want to get laid. I'm hanging out at a bar for months, no action, and then this? (Patience really is a virtue.) How does shit like this happen?

Donna wants me to meet her friends, so we get in separate cars and drive back to her home, a shared house with three other people, one of which is an off-and-on boyfriend. That won't work for me.

After meeting them all, we're alone in her room. "Sorry", I say, "I don't want to start this off with sex. I'm coming off a relationship where that's all we had at the end."

Am I fucking nuts or what? What is wrong with me? She wants to fuck me. But she agrees - same with her. Her last relationship ended with the only thing in common being sex.

Is this what happens once you start fucking? (You know, sometimes you say things that sound awful after you say them. Same thing happens when you write, the difference is, of course, your ability to correct yourself after the cat is out of the bag. I'll try to do that if I write something that sounds awful.)

I have this feeling that the sex will ruin the getting-to-know-you part. We talk about just that and she seems to be on board. The thrill of our alcohol and marijuana laced meeting with a quick sex finale has been tempered by a sobering hope for love. We love the idea that this isn't a one night stand. Hope springs eternal, in spring.

Now suppose I don't like her but the sex is great? One of the many deep philosophical questions a twenty-one-year-old must deal with. Or, suppose I really like her but the sex is awful, or she doesn't get the jokes on 'All In The Family'?

Biggest On The Planet

That purity stance lasted about a week. Remember Ronnie, the girl from the Army with the biggest breasts on the planet? Not anymore. Underneath Donna's floppy, hippy garb is a Dolly Parton body. I had no idea what was hiding under those sweatshirts. Holy shit!

Young love is quite a balancing act. That is, you're as horny as you ever will be and need to relieve that pressure cooker once in a while, yet you want to be "in love" and treat that with the utmost of respect. At least, that's how this twenty-one-year-old felt.

I wanted love. I also wanted sex. I wanted them to be the same but had already learned that they certainly weren't. I wasn't sure I could mix them though I knew, or believed that eventually, such chemistry would occur.

The balance with Donna suddenly tipped to the sex side. I always thought that a beautiful face was enough for me, but as my experiences below the neck grew more plentiful, I found other feminine attractions were becoming important. Beautiful, smart, and caring, and now, I want her to be voluptuous and horny. Sure, why not? I don't know if I'm just another pig but I know what happens when I see curves. You might call it a tingle in the dingle.

On the other side of the equation, this is a girl that thinks like me, and perhaps in my same inappropriate way, acts like me. We are very much alike and I'm beginning to think this might go somewhere. She's got a lot to like.

Sometime in early spring, sister Debbie introduces me to an album by John McLaughlin and the Mahavishnu Orchestra, 'The Inner Mounting Flame'. Talk about some wired rock! Whoo! She also informs me that the group will be performing in New York City soon.

On April 9th - the date I had to look up, but forty-five years later I remembered it was a Sunday night, Donna and I drop acid and hop in the car with Debbie and a friend, headed to Manhattan. The band is playing at Philharmonic Hall (since renamed Avery Fisher) that night. What a magnificent venue! It will be my first concert tripping and first experience with Donna tripping.

We arrive in mid-town about an hour later, just as the acid is kicking in. Circling the block around Lincoln Center, the only parking I see is right in front of the place. Must be no parking, but that massive buzz is really coming on, so I park.

A dozen other zoned out long hairs park in front of and behind me. We don't bother to check for no parking signs. Screw it. We're tripping.

Tripping Through the Mid-Town Tunnel

The music was so loud we barely talked. The light show under my eyelids far surpassed anything on the stage. What a fantastic experience.

With no parking ticket, I managed to drive back to Long Island at about the five hour point of intense acid, through the Mid-Town Tunnel. This ain't so hard.

Just keep those hallucinations in check and drive the speed limit. Those lights in the tunnel create such tracers - zoom, zoom, zoom as they go by - stay in the lane, dude.

Visibility at night is fine with pupils dilated, open like dimes, but the tunnel is like going through a wormhole. As if we even heard of wormholes then. Not that I recommend driving on LSD but it's safer than driving on a bottle of Jack.

Pink Floyd – Carnegie Hall, May 1st, 1972...

Next day I'm searching the newspapers and listening to the radio for news of upcoming concerts. I want to do that again.
And then, wham!

An ad for Pink Floyd at Carnegie Hall, the first of May. Are you kidding? (No, the ad was not in color.)

I scrape together the $18 for two tickets, mail cash and a self-addressed, stamped envelope to the Carnegie Hall box office and two weeks later

I have tickets for great seats in hand. That's how it worked back then.

There was no Ticketmaster and certainly no internet. And I wasn't spending all that money going into Manhattan for tickets unless a pound of pot was involved. A year later I scored the biggest ticket coup of a lifetime. Later for that.

Donna and I are doing fine. Sex is becoming more frequent but I might be getting my heart into this a little quicker than expected. I'm not ready to say love yet but I stopped going to the bar alone. This is becoming serious.

In the meantime, I went back to the state park commission to try to get my Jones Beach summer job back. My veteran status gave me a leg up on all the college kids, so much so that they offered me a job at Bethpage State Park, where I could manicure their beloved golf course. You might have heard about the famous "Black" course. Doesn't matter. Not important – golf name-dropping.

I switched to the night shift at the drugstore and started the full time state job in the middle of April. It sucked. I didn't know anybody and the work seemed a bit demeaning for someone of my stature. That was a joke. I had no stature. It was a shitty job. I got ticks every day. Bad move.

A few days later, Donna told me she thought we were moving too fast. She was going out with her old boyfriend on Friday night. I was crushed. Friday morning I got in the Cyclone and drove up to Hamilton, N.Y. to visit Artie at Colgate. I needed a friend. Fuck the state park job. Fuck the drugstore. I made one of those irrational, young adult decisions. Screw responsibility! I'm hurting.

That little road trip, maybe six hours, kind of planted the nomad seed. I had always liked taking the car out for a drive to think, relax. This was taking it to a new level. I had enough time to cry, get mad, understand, reflect on all that life had presented so far, and contemplate the future.

So I got dumped again, but this time I didn't plan on dying - just run away for a few days. So much for the state job. I'll figure that out Monday. My sister Denise will cover me at the drugstore when I don't show up. My mother will worry.

This turned out to be a big weekend. Artie had been wallowing in lost love for two months and had decided, like the rest of us in the league of broken hearts, that it was time to leave the constraints of this awful world behind and explore the universe.

Artie's first space trip had a similarly, exhilaratingly, liberating sensation as the real world came back into focus after he had wandered out on a hill to watch the sun rise. We talked about it.

Quite frankly, much of that weekend was, for me, a haze of pot, beer, and that "joint" acid adventure. The only clear memory I have was a warning issued by one of Artie's dorm friends. We were hanging out in someone's room drinking, smoking pot, probably playing Hearts, when I told of my driving to Lincoln Center on acid and seeing the John McLaughlin concert with Donna.

One guy pipes up, "Whatever you do, do not see Pink Floyd tripping!" I smiled with great amusement as he went on, "They have explosions, flames bursting up from the stage, a mind blowing light show. It will freak you out."

I don't think I had even mentioned I was a fan. Artie responded, "That's exactly what he's going to do next week."

Well, I blew the Bethpage State Park job and with it a chance at working at Jones Beach that summer. My irresponsibility prompted the guys at Kee-Zac to offer Denise more of my hours. Things with Donna evened out. I was extremely disappointed that she was not going to be the one.

So it devolved to sex. Is this how relationships go when you get past puppy love? The good news there - it was good sex. She was so cute and had that body to kill for. Well, maybe not kill for, but I it was sure nice enough, as was she, to come back for more.

...On Window Pane

On or about 6 PM on May 1st, Donna and I were waiting for the next Long Island Railroad commuter train into "the city" when we each put a hit of Window Pane acid on our tongues. Window Pane was about a three-sixteenth square inch (I made the size up) piece of thick cellophane that melted on contact and allowed the LSD in it to be absorbed into your bloodstream much quicker than a tiny tablet.

Thus, when that next train deposited us at Penn Station, we were fairly disoriented trying to find the Seventh Avenue subway up to Carnegie Hall. We entered the hall just after the lights went down and couldn't locate our seats after the usher kind of waved us to our row. So, we sat in the aisle for the first ten minutes or so. Like time had any significance. I had never heard any of this music before and got lost trying to identify it.

'The Dark Side Of The Moon' was how this tour was billed. Back in the day, Pink Floyd perfected new music on tour, then recorded it. This tour had started in the fall of '71. The album was not completed until early '73 and released on March 1, 1973.

Donna and I sat there in the aisle mesmerized until we got shooed into our seats by ushers trying to get around us. Oh, this is better, I can sit back and relax. It was pretty far out but I had no idea what I was listening to and I owned all their albums by now.

This was quite a bit different from the studio recording the whole world would know years later. No 'Great Gig In The Sky', some weird bible reading instead, and the finale, 'Eclipse' was rather anti-climactic. But, unless you followed them around the world and had heard this concert before, it was all new, and wonderful.

That whole album made up their first set and then you had an intermission to get your breath, and make you realize you are tripping heavily. The second set was mostly from 'Ummagumma' and the twenty-five minute, 'Echoes'. Fantastic!

When the lights came on the show had been so long that the acid trip was on the downhill leg. We walked the twenty-three blocks back to Penn Station. It was thrilling.

The next day I got up around noon. My father had been up early and as one did back then, read the morning papers. We subscribed to at least one of them, Newsday, the Long Island edition, though I recall The NY Times, NY Post, and NY Daily News also in the house quite often.

Waiting for me on the dining room table was a column torn from the Times, a review of the Pink Floyd concert by Robert Christgau. It described a drugged up crowd and a show consisting of more fire, lights and sound than music.

My father and I never talked about it.

Christgau is an Idiot

I saved the review and a few years ago posted it on, perhaps, the biggest Pink Floyd fan website on the planet, A Fleeting Glimpse, hosted by a guy who refers to himself as The Colonel, out of Australia. I included another review Christgau wrote in 1979 of Pink Floyd's 'The Wall' show at the Nassau Coliseum.

If Mr. Christgau is entitled to his opinion, then I suppose I am too. His ear doesn't hear what I hear. That's much nicer than saying he's a fucking idiot, right? Oh, I don't really give a shit about being nice. Christgau is a fucking idiot who is as qualified to be a music critic as he is to judge your masturbation technique. But I digress!

John McGlaughlin's band added a show at the Capitol Theater in Passaic, NJ and I couldn't resist. This time, my sister Debbie and two of her friends joined us. She and her friends were about 16. Everybody dropped acid. Harry Chapin opened the show. Years later "he blew his mind out in a car". His song, 'Taxi', always rang a bell, "...and I was gonna learn to fly", and then the last line, "I go flying so high, when I'm stoned".

My only true memory from that concert was the ride home, driving through the Lincoln tunnel thinking that this was very far out, stay focused, it's tight in here. The lights flashing by in the tunnel tempted hallucinations but the thing about pot, acid, any hallucinogen, is that you can control it. That is, you can keep your sanity and seem as straight as the next guy. It's just a lot of work. Drinking? Good fucking luck with that!

Concerts are perfect for tripping. You don't have to talk. You don't have to act "normal". You can just let it all happen, let it go. Of course, you can do it straight too. Also, if you're not drinking, you don't need to pee.

I saw Donna once more after that concert, though I tried to see her twice more to get back my 'Winwood' import album. She wasn't home and I finally gave up. That was a damn good collection of his work to that point with Spencer Davis, Blind Faith, and Traffic.

I had tripped four times in six weeks and was getting more interested in the internal search than finding a female partner. I started reading more, trying to find more in the local library about psychedelics. Summer came. Artie came back from Colgate. Life was good, sans a woman.

Casual dating just wasn't my thing anymore. The bar kept getting raised. I had dated pretty women, smart women, hot bodied women, including a nymphomaniac, and women that loved me. I wanted one woman who was all of that. Mostly, I still wanted to be loved. How am I going to find her? Casual dating seemed too tedious, but, I went back to the bar.

Chapter 15 - A Joy Ride to The Dark Side

Summer of '72

A bunch of us went up to Roslyn, a north shore Long Island town, home of My Father's Place, to see Harry Chapin in early June. We went to a bunch of folksy concerts at colleges and bars around Long Island. Hey you Long Islanders, remember The Good Rats? They seemed to play everywhere.

The summer of '72 is kind of a blur. I was at a bar every night, usually the Tabard Ale House or Jones Beach Hotel, also in Wantagh, but, we expanded our horizons.

Artie's brother, Lt. Joe, was back for good from Viet Nam. He had met a woman in Viet Nam with whom he had fallen in love. While the rest of us were getting our hearts broken here, he went to the other side of the globe to get fucked. He went back, after his ROTC commitment was over, to bring back his future wife. Sorry Charlie. She had moved on to another Joe.

So, the Three Musketeers do what all recently shunned lovers do - get fucked up, like a Beach Boys song, 'All Summer Long'!

We went to a very hoppin' bar in Rockville Centre, Solomon and Grundy's, at least one night a week, as well as a weekly visit out east, to Mama Leone's in Deer Park. They both had great rock bands. Mama Leone's was especially memorable, a hippie heaven, stoners everywhere. It was a bit of a drive on the LIE.

I clearly remember rolling a dozen joints for at least one trip out there - as well as anyone who smoked a dozen joints in a night could clearly remember anything. We would smoke a couple before going out, stop at Gruber's, a local old man's pub in Bellmore where Joe tended bar, for a couple of beers, smoke maybe three more on the drive, drink a whole load of beer at the bar, as well as stepping outside for two or three more joints, three more on the ride back to Gruber's, more beer and then one more doobie for the couple of blocks back home.

And we wondered why we weren't meeting girls. We even made a trip or two out to The Boardy Barn in Hampton Bays, but, though I was looking, never saw Pam again. It really was an enormously fun, bonding time.

I think some of my family had suspicions about my sexuality then because Artie and I hung out all the time. I mean, if one of us wasn't working, we'd be at the other's house or out a park. All we did, and not necessarily in this order, was play chess, talk about the meaning of life, smoke pot, and go to bars. We started tripping together and treated each session like a science experiment, discussing how our brains were digesting the experience.

It didn't take long to bring Joe along on our journeys. Those were wonderful times. The three of us started doing a whistling routine, but only for beers at Gruber's. Our routine consisted of military branch theme songs along with the big finale, 'Stars and Stripes Forever' in which I whistled the melody, Joe handled the bass, and Artie brought it all down with a rousing piccolo solo. All the old WWII dudes bought us beers. We were beer whores.

In the meantime, we were looking for female companionship but, I know for me this is true, losing at love was taking a toll. Getting high, really high, with music and chess - yeah, we played chess all the time, the summer of Fischer-Spaasky, reported by Shelby Lymon - was fine. OK, we had a small case of Nerdia, fuck off!

Life was good. We talked about it a lot – life. What is this thing we've been thrust into? What's the deal with God? What happens when you die? Is there more?

One serious thing I had to get done over the summer was enroll at Nassau Community College for the fall. That included applying for my GI Bill education benefits, and trying to find some grant or scholarship money.

I was on my own for funding. I took some tests and got a couple of bucks from some grant for children of NYC fireman and a few more dollars from a NY State scholarship for vets. Nothing else I did all summer was serious, though my hair got seriously long.

September came and I was excited to go back to school. It was time to move on with my life. Not really knowing what I wanted to do, I thought a career as a pharmacist looked pretty easy. I watched Al and Pete count pills all day long. Well, shit, I'm good at math, 1, 2, 3.

Unfortunately, when I transferred my credits from the Ag and Tech school at Farmingdale, they only accepted the basic English and Math course credits. Airport Operations, Dynamics of Flight, and Welding were worth zilch.

They gave me nineteen credits so it was like starting the second semester of freshman year. I'd need to do three semesters before moving on to a four year school.

Artie was trying to get back into Judi's life so he transferred to Long Island's Adelphi University as a visiting student for his final year.

His brother, Joe, also went back to school. They had a younger brother, George, who I would later claim to be the best chess player of them all. Did I mention that we played a lot of chess? Always stoned.

Their family bought a three dimensional chess board which created marathon sessions. You know that thing about hallucinogens increasing your thoughts per second? Well, we put that concept to work with three dimensional chess, and then took it to the ultimate level - playing chess through an entire acid trip. Chess is a game of war. You might think that's a bit of an exaggeration. Try it on LSD. You're playing with foam swords until you do. It was intense!

Artie's sister, Martha, eventually joined our lot getting high. She and Joe became my good friends for many years. Actually, I became part of the family. Their mom, Gert, who I mentioned earlier was my Sunday school teacher, and also a fifth grade teacher at Winthrop Ave Grammar School in Bellmore, always welcomed me into their home. I spent more time at their house than my own.

Fall: Back To School

My first semester's class list at Nassau included chemistry, for the pharmaceutical major, counting pills – maybe it was a math class, sociology, poetry, and philosophy. Artie had suggested philosophy. I really didn't know what it was about.

He explained to me, "You know, all the bullshit you've been spewing, like, what life is all about, since you came back from the Army? That's philosophy!" Cool. They have a class about that stuff?

And poetry? I had been a big fan of reading lyrics when they were included in albums and started writing my own poems. I thought of them as songs but I could never remember the original tune in my head and I couldn't read or write music. So they were just poems.

They started out as lamentations and sorrowful crap about Pam and Jessica, but then I turned a bit more inspirational after memorizing all the lyrics to The Moody Blues' 'A Question of Balance'. They were poems.

My new student ID:

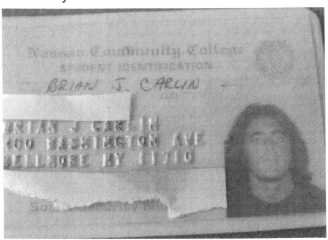

They were big on using Social Security numbers in those days. Today, even Medicare stopped using them. I hid mine here. Nice hair though, right?

Anyway, day one at Nassau Community College, my first philosophy class. I was excited. In walks this middle aged guy who looks like a cross between gruff Mr. Friedman, my HS driver ed instructor, and the horribly intimidating and nasty, HS football coach and my physics teacher, Mr. Rockstroh. He was an asshole.

My worries were put aside when the professor opened his mouth, "Anybody here like beer? Good. We're gonna learn all about beer this semester and maybe you'll learn some answers to a few questions. Better still, maybe you'll come out of here with some new questions."

Philosophy 101: The Mesopotamians Drink Gablinger's

Ken Bennet was cool. He made philosophy fun. He said, and it's one of those things that always stuck with me, "Philosophy - what is it? Well, it basically attempts to answer three questions. One, who am I? Two, what am I doing here? Three, where am I going? That's it! Every philosophical thought revolves around one or all of those three questions."

I loved this guy. He slipped in some comments about the Mesopotamians drinking Gablinger's beer. That got the attention of most of us. I loved everything I was reading. Those PHI101 books covering a dozen different philosophers were great.

These were the things I'd been thinking about for years. This is what I really care about. I couldn't get enough of this stuff. Within weeks I went down to the registrar and changed my major from chemistry to philosophy.

Mixed with the poetry and sociology class scribbles, the margins in my notebooks began to fill with ideas and comments - mostly about Love, the big Love, and poems. Lots of poems, mostly about Love and life and death. I was rather consumed with the great question of, "What happens when you die?" There was still a lot of that Catholic upbringing that needed to be purged, or at least, cleaned up dramatically.

Gina?

One glorious day in late September, I had just finished some morning classes and went to the cafeteria. I headed for a table to do some reading, and perhaps some girl watching. A girl with long brown hair was sitting there with her head down, but she looked very familiar.

I say "Excuse me", she looks up and NO! Yes, it was, Gina Leary, my secret love from the bus to Seton Hall. "I can't believe it's you."

"Brian?" asks one of the prettiest faces on the planet. "Wow, that hair threw me. How are you doing?"

I had run into her a couple of times over the years after ninth grade. I saw her at a football game in eleventh grade, and talked to her a couple of times at the Tabard Ale House the exact week that I was falling in love with Pam. My hair had gone from faggy (calm down, gays, it used to mean nerdy) to short Beatles cut to the shoulder length shot on my college ID.

So, we knew each other, if just barely, since those bus days. But now I was all confident, sat down across from her and we shared our life stories, to a point. I did tell her what a crush I had had on her in ninth grade and that she looked exactly the same. She was still beautiful. What happened next just felt like the most logical thing to do, the most natural thing to do - I asked her out on a real date.

Oddly, I was not really surprised that she accepted but I was still blown away for days that I had talked for a wonderful hour with Gina Leary.

THE Gina Leary! This is THE girl who raised the bar of beauty so high for me that not one girl in my high school came close enough to her pretty face for me to come out of my shell to approach. And now, she still has that Helen of Troy face. And now, I'm going to love her.

After being high, drunk, and without a woman's touch all summer, I was ready to bear down on my studies and be the new me, scholastically. I can take a break from women. And then along comes Gina. The first one, my first love, though only I knew that. Really? Nobody told her.

All the heartbreak in the last few years and here is the girl I was destined to be with. The world kept amazing me. How does this shit happen to me? This is good shit.

I'm actually rather ecstatic and really thinking that fate is involved here – I hadn't kicked that belief yet, fate. Eight years ago she was my dream girl. Now I'm dating her. No what-if's. This is happening.

We took it slow, both of us wary from multiple failures at love. I so wanted to say the word, love. But, we stayed at arm's length, emotionally and physically. Well, hugs and serious kisses but that was it. I did not want to lose her respect. Remember that part? Here we go again.

All seemed to be going well, though very slow. I just didn't want to screw this up. It just seemed that so much destiny, Karma, was on my side. I think I love her, all over again, if there was a first time. Oh, I really wanted to. But, I really wanted her to love me. I couldn't go into this alone, again.

In September, I had missed out on Moody Blues tickets for an October 23rd concert at Madison Square Garden. Then in mid-October, it was announced that they had added a matinee show for that Monday, at which point I did whatever was necessary to scoop up four tickets.

Artie's plan to stay on Long Island to finish his last year of college so that he could win back Judi worked. We were going on a double date to see the Moody Blues.

The Moody Blues, October 23, 1972 at Madison Square Garden

"Monday Afternoon, I'm just beginning to see, now I'm on my way." OK, so the lyrics are "Tuesday", not Monday. It was the third song in the set list. By then we were on to at least the third bowl of hash. We didn't have any pot, no joints, so we kept lighting matches to heat up our only THC source, Moroccan Hash. Gina had done LSD but didn't like it and wouldn't do it again. I understood, clearly.

Back then, smoking indoors was ok – well, maybe it wasn't but everybody did, so no one knew if you were lighting a cigarette or a joint. Of course, passing a glowing stogie was a bit of a tip off but everyone did it at concerts. The Man sort of left you alone (until The Grateful Dead Nassau Coliseum concert busts the following March). Continually lighting a bowl of hash required some subterfuge, but not much.

Anyway, it was a fabulous concert. I was a full-fledged fan by then. After buying 'A Question of Balance', I had bought all the previous albums in chronological release, all sort of "concept" albums with each song flowing into the next, no silence between tracks.

The lyrics, the stories, the music – just beautiful. And, these guys seemed to know something. Like, they figured it out. They talked directly to you. Their music made you feel good.

Perfect music for coming down after or during an intense LSD experience. "Now you know that you are real, show your friends that you and me, belong to the same world, turned on to the same word. Have you heard?" (From 'Threshold of a Dream')

Gina loved it. She kept remarking about how beautiful their voices were. True. Justin Hayward and John Lodge were amazing in their heyday. Ray Thomas and Mike Pinder could hold their own as well. Any edge (drummer was Graham Edge) you were on was smoothed out by those voices. You get that? Like being talked down from a bridge.

A few days later, I wrote a fairly lengthy poem to Gina and, against my better judgement, presented it on her birthday. The poem was a very structured piece of work. It consisted of three parts, titled, "Salutation", "Request Of The First Order", and "Thought Of The First Order". The "first order" was a clue. It meant, read the first letter of each line in the groupings of the entire poem. The first letters resulted in this: To RL (Regina rather than Gina); Listen To My Mind; To Be One With Your Love. The last section is a line from the Moody Blues song 'Isn't Life Strange?'

I Love You, Gina Leary

There it was. And here we are. I laid it out on the line. It was, in a way, obtuse, but it was, in my mind, a clear profession of love. I couldn't say the word, so, in fear of rejection, I did my best to express how I felt in writing. The immediate reaction was, sort of, "I don't know what to say". It wasn't the loving, "Oh my God, I feel the same way" reaction I had hoped for. I had opened up, finally, in my way. She stayed in her shell.

Apparently, this was going nowhere. We went out once or twice more. She had discussed the poem with her sister, who sounded like she got me, but Gina never gave me an inkling that she was ready to let her heart go.

I was deflated. What went wrong? Was anything wrong? Was it me? Was it her? Why did I let Gina Leary go? Why didn't I just come out and tell her with clear words that I was falling in love with her? That damn fear of rejection. That would have hurt too much. Did Pam and Jessica do that much damage?

How many beautiful relationships have never made it past this stage? Who takes the next step? Maybe it's just a one-way thought process. Maybe we just imagine a genuine shared feeling. We want it to be something we both feel. And if that's true, don't be afraid. Yeah, rejection hurts. Of course, you could make the case that experience guides you.

So, anyway, Gina Leary, how'd your life go? I know you're out there somewhere. Gina? I did love you. Or, at least, I tried. Even if it was only a thing in my head, love, in that poem, was directed your way. I hope you've had a lot of love in your life. You were my third "Titanic" love, though an argument could be made that you were the first.

Three strikes. Loved and lost three times. Strangely, I shed few tears. It wasn't meant to be, as much as I wanted fate to make that life work out. I guess it wasn't really love. Then again, it stuck with me. I began to question whether any of it had been love. What is love? I believed I knew but, what is wrong with me? Why won't the ones I love, love me back?

God wasn't giving me any clues. Back to the bars. My beer loves me. Speaking of the bar, a new guy started at Gruber's, the old man's bar that Joe works in now as a cook. His name is Lenny. Don't recall his last name. Just Lenny.

Lenny was one of the true characters on the planet, you know what I mean? He was the most normal guy while at the same time being the strangest dude you ever met. He was a wise guy extraordinaire, unless you didn't get him.

A short, mustachioed, wise ass, but a perfect, old-fashioned, bow-tied gentleman behind the bar who could handle the change-stealing, Mr. Tully, the bull-shitting owner's brother, Friedel, and a host of other characters you'll find in every old man's bar in the country. And, Lenny did every drug he could get his hands on.

One day the two of us took the Long Island Railroad into the city to buy a pound of pot from one of his dealers. We smoked a joint or two to make sure it worked, then got back onto the commuter train near rush hour with all those suited businessmen and our brown paper bag wreaking of the smell of marijuana. Holy shit. Oh, thank the GI Bill for that one.

GI Bill: $200/mo for Education

The GI Bill gave me $200 a month for college. Not much, you say. Well, in 1972, Nassau Community College cost $210 per semester. I had a job and lived with my parents and therefore, I didn't need much. So, after the first month of each semester, those $200 checks paid for a pound of pot a month. In those days you had three grades of pot - Mexican, $200 a pound; Jamaican, $250-300; Columbian, $350-400.

Sometimes, if we could get my brother and others to contribute, we'd get a pound of Columbian. We got hash when available, the best being that black, gooey stuff, marketed as "opiated hash". Who knows what the hell was in anything we smoked or ingested in those days.

Anyway, Lenny also gave me my only hit of heroin. I snorted it - after blowing half of it away. I don't recall any reaction. Opiates and downers never did shit for me except put me to sleep. To each his own drug.

The day after Thanksgiving, Lenny comes over to my house with a girl he wants me to meet, Joy. I never understood what Joy and Lenny's relationship was but I was glad to have a girl to talk to. We hit it off via eyes right away, and, now having an interest in what lies below the neckline, I was immediately aware of her tight, knit blouse.

Joy Trotter was smart, quick witted, pretty, very nicely curved, and loved getting high. We blew a lot of smoke in the gigantic water pipe that night under the black light and listened to some music. Her favorite was John Lennon, whose philosophy I embraced, though I thought George was a better songwriter, singer, and musician than either John or Paul. Oh, Lenny was there too but he suddenly became background.

Anyway, after getting stoned, we then had a beer or two at Gruber's. We dropped Lenny off and then I drove Joy home to her parent's house in Merrick, the next town to the west of Bellmore. We exchanged phone numbers and discussed seeing each other again when she returned for winter break from college, Alfred University, in, of all places, Alfred, NY.

In the next couple of weeks, we talked a few times on the phone and, at some point, I volunteered to drive up to Alfred and bring her back to Long Island for the holidays. What is wrong with me? It's a fucking six hour drive! Do I just want to get laid? I don't know. She's nice. I like her. What am I doing? This could go very badly, then imagine the ride home!

That long drive, with those thoughts circling in my head, to western New York state, means I will be staying the night. Joy assured me that her roommate would be gone by the time I got there so I would have a place to sleep. What could go wrong? In the back of my head I hear a Beatles' song. That damn 'Rubber Soul' album haunting me again. I see myself as the guy from 'Norwegian Wood' who "crawled off to sleep in the bath. And when I awoke, I was alone".

Before cell phones, you had to find a pay phone along the way to keep people up to speed with your progress on long trips. Quite frankly, I don't remember calling before I showed up at Alfred. With no phone, I went right to her room.

I was welcomed with a hug, a good sign, though I thought it might be for the sake of her roommate whose ride home was delayed a day. Shit! This could get very complicated. Where's the bath?

Joy and I, sans roommate, went out to dinner at the college Rathskeller - didn't every college have one? - got a bit toasted, smoked a joint outside, and went back to her room. The roommate was still out but had put up a bed sheet curtain. Good sign.

We drank some wine, smoked another joint, and then it was time to call it a night. By this time, we had gotten quite cozy but to this point hadn't even kissed. Things were going well. I hadn't said anything really stupid yet – no stories of past loves. The alcohol and pot had loosened us both up. What could go wrong now? I know, any second the roommate is going to burst in, completely shit-faced, wanting to party. Or worse, I'm reading this all wrong and I'll have to find someplace else to sleep tonight.

I go to the bathroom to size it up. Yeah, I guess I can sleep in here. I also brush my teeth and, with enough alcohol bolstering my courage, come back out wearing just my boxers. What the fuck! Here goes!

Oh Joy! Spectacular!!!

Joy was sitting up straight, cross legged on her bed in her birthday suit!

For an instant, my brain pulled out that question - "How did all that is my life lead me to this moment?" Just when life seemed to give me the finger, it presents me with Joy.

You know that phrase, "They're spectacular!"? Joy looked at me with a coy expression, completely lacking in innocence, a look that screamed, "Look at me. Are they not spectacular?"

No argument. Here we go again. What is it with me and big breasts? Yes, they are spectacular!

So what went wrong?

Nothing! Gotcha!

Actually, after an hour of, uh, you know, the roommate came back but didn't say a word. We were quieter for the next few hours but our activity produced unmistakable sounds. I wonder if the roommate has a story to tell about that night.

Joy and I were a couple for around two years, off and on. Mostly on. We tripped together a few times. We went to a few concerts together but for reasons I don't recall, she missed the best concert of all time.

Early in 1973, the New York Times entertainment section had an ad for an upcoming Pink Floyd concert at Radio City.

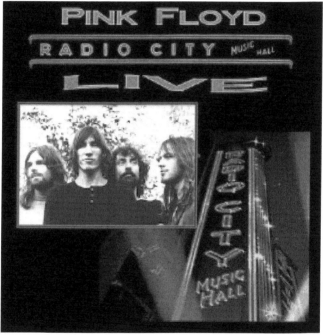

I gathered up money from interested friends and sent $150 in cash to the Radio City box office with a note asking them to use the money for as many of the best seats available when the tickets actually go on sale.

On March 1st, 1973, Pink Floyd released the album, 'The Dark Side of the Moon'. I bought it a day later and wore it out in a month. The mind fucker of all mind fucking albums! What do you think, Michael T Gross?

Here's a little, "but I digress". That album entered the billboard top 200 chart on the date of that Radio City concert (March 17) at number 95. It eventually made it to number 1 for just one week. But, it stayed on that top 200 for 736 weeks! Later in 1988 it popped back on and as of March, 2018, it's 937 weeks is a record no other album has come close to. Wait! Billboard came up with a new category, Catalog Albums, that ranks older albums that still continue to sell well. Make that over 1,500 weeks on the charts, and still counting! So, bunky, you say you never heard the album in its entirety? Why do you think it is that this album has survived disco, punk, whatever that shit music was in the 90's, and hip-hop? Go find out. Use headphones or crank up a big system. Then, "I'll see you on the dark side of the moon."

A few weeks later, I received an envelope from Radio City containing a dozen tickets for reserved seats in row A in the first balcony, centered. Turns out the floor seats were general admission. Let Jerry Garcia and the Dead, Andy Warhol, and other New York glitterati fight for those seats. The concert was scheduled for midnight, March 17th. Far, fucking out.

I don't remember everyone who was with our group. Artie was there, maybe with Judi, but for sure with two or three friends from Colgate. Joy was not there. My sister Debbie, 16, came with us with her friend, Anne. That only accounts for half the tickets. The rest of you know who you are. Hope you still remember it. Debbie says it was, and still remains, the best concert she ever saw.

Pink Floyd – Radio City, Midnight March 17th, 1973 (really 1AM 18th)

We all dropped acid sometime after 10 or 11PM. I'm thinking early rather than later because I recall being very fucked up while waiting on line. The Long Islanders in the group took the train into the city and met up with Artie's college friends at an apartment in Manhattan where we smoked a load of dope and took our LSD hits.

We walked to the show from there and I recall getting off on the way. As the midnight starting time passed while waiting on line, I began freaking out about missing the start of the show. I asked a security guard twice about being on the right line for the Pink Floyd show. Turns out we were on the wrong line. We were in the General Admission line holding reserved seat tickets.

They finally let us in at around 12:30. We were all zombies, as it appeared was everyone else on line. Of course, that may just have been this zombie's perspective.

I had brought balloons and a felt marker with me, knowing we had those first row seats looking down on general admission. Blowing up balloons on acid was its own trip. Hard enough without thinking you're going to blow the top of your head off. Then I wrote little messages on them, like, "How is it?", "Close your eyes", "Breathe!". Stuff an acid tripper might get lost in.

Then, at about 1AM the lights dimmed, the stage filled with smoke, a bass synthesizer note droned, and from the bowels of Radio City the front part of the stage rose up as a bass guitar started thumping with an accompanying drumbeat and then David Gilmour's fierce guitar pierced the night.

What a fucking entrance! The first half of the show contained a variety of old material.

By intermission, most of us were peaking. We smoked more pot. The second half of the show was the entire, refined, album version of 'Dark Side of The Moon', done to perfection. The 'Echoes' encore sent everyone home as the light of day broke.

It was, by accounts of all who were there, one of the most profound concert experiences of a lifetime. Breathtaking! Debbie and friend, Anne, went to a park in Bellmore and took another hit of acid. Troopers!

Time has a way of blurring memories. I don't recall many specifics because I totally immersed myself in the music but I do recall that it was spectacular. Look it up.

OK. What else is there? I've seen God. I've loved and been loved. I've seen Pink Floyd do 'The Dark Side of the Moon' live at Radio City.

Well, I had something to say, something to add to this thing called life, besides defining the action of LSD on the brain - CTPS, my contribution to being human, something called "Metahedonism!"

Chapter 16 - Metahedonism

Start Your Own Religion

You know - no, you don't know, not about Metahedonism, unless you're one of the couple of hundred people I have gotten close enough to for the schpeil. You may recall that I used a term "beyond hedonism" to describe the ultimate state of consciousness.

Metahedonism is my religion, if you call a couple of rules that guide your entire system of values and by adhering to them allows you to trip to the heavens without guilt (and that's the only way), then you can call it a religion.

The concept being that every acid trip I took that led to that ecstatic, timeless, eternal moment wherein the entire universe was at my fingertips had to be entered with a clear conscience. On acid, your conscience will come after you. You cannot get THERE without a clear path. The Eastern religions know this. Being a westerner with no patience, instant karma worked. How does one clear their conscience? Well, that takes some work, and time, so, not so instant.

The deal is, I was a big fan of Timothy Leary, even if I also thought he was off his gourd. Certifiable! But his books on LSD were spot on, if not tending a bit much to the spiritual side. And didn't many of us trippers lean that way? Upward?

Well, I was not all that enamored with the "Tune In, Turn On, Drop Out" thing. Once you drop out, it seemed more like cop out. I just didn't get it. What I did get was his other big mantra, "Start Your Own Religion". That clicked because I was already running down that path.

When I first got out of the Army, I grabbed the family Bible and read every piece of the New Testament that supposedly contained quotes by Jesus. Then I compared his words with the Ten Commandments. No wonder the Jews distanced themselves from him. He said "do this", "do that", not a whole lot of "Thou Shalt Not's". Positive stuff.

I think the most profound thing he said was, "Do unto others, as YOU would have them do unto you!" That's pretty much Metahedonism, but I spell it out with two and a half rules, basically, Jesus For Dummies.

But the word itself? Meta, from the Greek, beyond. Hedonism - seeking physical pleasure, sensual gratification. For me, Metahedonism means pleasure beyond the physical. And I mean really beyond.

Some of those early psychedelic experiences were so magically pleasant, ecstatic, and also related to religious experience that I felt compelled to tell people how to get to that moment. It was overwhelmingly apparent to me that to get beyond your fear and paranoia you should rid yourself of just that - all the things that western religions scare you about.

In 1973, which is most likely the year that the term Metahedonism was coined, 2 years after I first read Timothy Leary and identified with many of his concepts, I thought it time to start my own religion. Joe, Artie's brother, dubbed me the God of Odd. I was proud of that name for a while.

We Got Rules

When the description of my state of mind in this ecstatic state was achieved and was put into the words "beyond hedonism", it was time to tell my friends that I have indeed started my own religion. Before I did that, I figured I needed some rules like all the others.

At the time, I was using my GI Bill to finance my philosophy/religious studies degree (and buy a pound of cheap pot a month). After studying rules of religions all over the world it became apparent that the religions of the world, the ones that don't include clauses about justifiable killing (you know who you are) are pretty much the same. I took all their crap and put it into a blender and came up with my 2 and a half commandments (and this was a decade before George Carlin did it). The half? That's because the last one starts with "if".

Rule #1: Don't hurt anyone.
Rule #2: Have a good time.
Rule #2-1/2: If you can help someone else along the way, do it.

If that sounds right to you, then besides a few laughs, you got your money's worth with this book. Tell your friends to buy it. Buy more copies and give it away. Or, contact me via email so you can send a big check. Isn't that what those fucking, cock-sucking, lying, shithead evangelists do?

Do you get the sense I hate those pricks, or any religion that asks for money? Look at the fucking Catholic church. They've been sucking poor people dry and suckering the rich with their bullshit since they figured out how to turn morality into a business.

Once I had read about a dozen or so religions, I realized they were all the same. They provide children with stories to help them through their growth into adulthood where questions like "Why?" - "Why Me?" "Why Anything?", need to be answered. Adults don't know the answers so they let the powerful tell them what to believe. And for a few bucks a week you can buy your way into everlasting peace. All you have to do is believe. (And keep throwing that gold in the basket.)

By the end of the spring semester in 1973, I had had enough of the pedophile religion, Catholicism, all of Christianity, it's mommy, Judaism, and that other horrendous offshoot, the maker of killers, Islam. You can take that bullshit that these are peaceful religions and shove it up your collective asses. Look at all the dead people these religions have killed! If you still follow any of these, you are wasting your time and all that energy that could be put to productive use.

Praying? Give me a fucking break. You want to waste time yet do something productive? Nap. You'll be saving the world some energy. Think about it. Suppose there is no light at the end of the tunnel. Suppose that this is all there is. No heaven. No after life. You die and that's it.

Praying! After every mass murder – our prayers are with the families! What good will that do? Make you feel like you're doing something? Bullshit! You want to do something? Take their fucking guns away. Write your congressman to support or write a bill that, in the very least, bans any automatic weapon. No quick fire bullshit either. Get every AK-47 and similar assault rifles off the streets. It's no different than banning recreational drugs that can kill.

Stop the killing. Do something or your kids could be next. You could be next.

Stop fucking praying. It's a complete waste of energy.

Why can't you deal with that? Do you think you are that important that some big old guy with a beard has got a special place in eternity for you where everlasting love will surround you? Well, I got news for you, Sunshine, if God put Cardinal Law of Boston in charge of your infinite love, expect a good butt-fucking to go along with all that love.

It just sickens me that the true believers are that ignorant. They deserve all the butt fucking they get. You just can't fix that kind of stupid. The rest of you Christians? Don't get me started on the Billy Graham idiots, and all the other soft-shoe-shufflers that followed in his footsteps. Religion as a private business. Circus hustlers, swindlers! They are all nothing but low life thieves. You voted one President!

But, I digress. How did I get that far off track? Oh yeah, I asked you to send me money if you liked my idea. Now that was a bad idea. Sorry. I could use the bucks but I hate putting myself into the same boat as a common thief. So don't send me bucks and believe what you want if it makes you happy. Of course, if it makes you happy to spread the wealth and you have Jeff Bezos kind of money....

Let's get back to Metahedonism. Let me try to explain in some detail what the vagueness means to me.

Don't hurt anyone: That means physically, which few human beings do (except for the billions who fight wars and husbands and wives who star on 48 Hours), or emotionally. Relationships and wounds go hand in hand. Just get a grip on your feelings. Try your very best not to inflict pain. You know it's going to happen at times. Be gentle.

The rule is vague on purpose. If something you do comes back to make you feel guilty, you will never get to that timeless moment. Be nice. Pretty simple.

Freak outs on acid generally arise from paranoia and paranoia is a derivative of conscience. If you will never do or never have done acid, same deal. Review your life. Bring the guilt to the surface and make it right.

Fix whatever it is that you drag along with you like an anchor. You won't fly with it. Maybe just an apology is all that's needed. Simple things like that can let you soar beyond imagination.

The rule is just a giant compression of what most religions attempt to do, promote civility. Not so remarkable, just simplified.

Of course, you may, at some point in your life be forced to inflict pain on another in self-defense or in defense of another. Don't get all PTSD about it. Deal with it.

And you defenders of the republic and localities within - that's a tough spot you got yourself into and must be very hard on your psyche. If you're reading this I suspect you are among the good guys who try hard to do the right thing. Kudos to you. Somebody has to keep the lunatics on the path.

Now, rule #2, Have a good time. That kind of covers the hedonism thing. The deal is HERE. It is NOW! You can't do a good job here and attain that ecstatic moment that is the goal of Metahedonism if you're worried about life after death or some conception of God that is an "other".

Yes, it's seemingly selfish but not so much as believing that you are going to live forever. However, we got rules about our rules in this house. Before you go hog-ass wild on Rule #2, Have a Good Time, you must first get rule #1 covered. No guilt. You will know that 3 hours into the acid trip.

So, follow rule 1, then rule 2 will provide heaven on earth. Must we wait until we die? Do you have to do acid? I don't know. I do know that I never got out there straight. Got pretty close on good Mary Jane a few times, maybe because I knew where I was going. Sorry, yoga and meditation buffs, I never got your schtick.

Maybe the one line that the nuns drilled into my head created this concept of Metahedonism. It was a line I had to memorize from the Catechism: "God made me to be happy with him in heaven." I questioned that from about 7 years old. Why can't I be happy now?

Well, the ecstasy of the sense that you have touched the center of the universe, that you feel the energy of keeping the whole thing going, that if there is a God, you are part of that entity, not bowing down to it and that you are a part of the on-going consciousness - a mammoth ego trip that brings you down to earth in awe of being. That's the problem with getting out there and feeling it. Words cannot describe fully that fleeting glimpse. How do you put that moment into words? We've been through this before, haven't we?

I was thinking about analogies to that ecstatic, split-second, eternal moment. And I thought of the early seventies Yes album, 'Close to the Edge'. The title song, 18 minutes long, an entire vinyl side, really says it and musically brings you there. You need to have the lyrics in front of you, though their poetic meaning requires several readings and even then the meaning may still lie with the author. If the lyrics are too distracting, just go with the music. There are several movements but you will feel it build to this incredible crescendo, this height that the lyrics and the music bring you to. Breathtaking if you let yourself go.

Music like that gets me there. My first such experience, as mentioned earlier, was under headphones, listening to Pink Floyd's 'Atom Heart Mother', specifically, that angelic guitar solo. The electronics producing the sound are toned way down with a very soft and gentle timber by David Gilmour. Thinking about that, I still see the rainbow of colors swirling around. Heaven.

Rule 2 and a half: If you can help someone along the way, then do it. Half a rule because it starts with "if". You may be physically or emotionally unable to help the poor bastard crawling at your feet with no legs begging for help. If you can help it's the rule that you do. But you can use any excuse not to. I get it.

It would be nice if you could get by your fear of some kind of loss. Me too. Not being able to help a fellow traveler doesn't disqualify you. The rule is to remind you to help when you can. If you do, it will make you feel good and isn't that the goal?

Why? To Get THERE!

The whole point, originally, was to achieve that MOMENT. I had to be guilt free, or pretty damn close, meaning I was feeling guilty about shit over which I had little control - stuff that would be resolved in my head before peaking. Soon it just became my way of getting through this world.

That's it. If this "religion" and its simple rules appeals to you just do it and if you ever get the chance to contemplate your existence and you've cleared your conscience, enjoy. If you like what you've read and feel like these simple rules will make the world a tiny bit better, spread the word. You got three lines to remember.

This blooming idiot figured it out. Thus, I give you Metahedonism!

Chapter 17 - Dec 1973, Early '74

The State University of New York at Stony Brook

This was the middle of my concert era, almost every one of which I attended on acid. I've tried to put a list (see appendix) together using memory and whatever I can dig up on the web. I'm sure I missed a few and some of the dates are likely off but – it was just fun doing it. I loved going to concerts. The bombardment of sound and light on top of a brain soaked in psychedelics, now in the midst of processing a million thoughts per second, is just fantastic beyond words (though I've tried). Whoever I was with was usually tripping as well. We went to many concerts. Besides all the big name bands, we went to see lots of the folky groups playing colleges and small, local theaters and clubs. Of course, there was usually one night a week to see a really good bar band. Standing right in front of some speaker grouping would vibrate your backbone. Maybe that's what caused my disc deterioration.

Then there's the tinnitus. See the appendix listing for the John McLaughlin-Frank Zappa concert. First row on the floor at the Nassau Coliseum, right in front of the left side (facing the stage) speaker column. A glutton for punishment, nearly forty years later I ate a 40mg THC Cheba Chew and saw the Trans-Siberian Orchestra, or, as I dubbed them, Heavy Metal Christmas, the loudest concert ever, an ear-ringer for sure. But, I digress. Going off on a tangent.

My love life was with Joy during these times, but it was off and on. She was very artistic and dramatic, and that drama followed us around. I was on that philosophical journey searching for truth, not bullshit, and I was beginning to hear too much of it.

In December, 1973, I finished my time at Nassau Community College, getting my Associates Degree in Philosophy, and had been accepted at the State University of New York at Stony Brook, out in northern Suffolk County on Long Island.

It was about an hour from my parent's home in Bellmore or fifty minutes from the room in the house that Joy was now sharing with Artie's girlfriend, Judi, and the third housemate, Peggy. Peggy was dating Neil, a guy from my high school class. Small world.

That was in Mineola, in Nassau County on Long Island. In the prior six months or so, when we weren't fighting, I stayed with Joy. I had really wanted to get away again, but SUNY at Binghamton turned me down. So, I rented a room in an off-campus apartment in Stony Brook.

Uh-Oh, This Can't Be Good

That place was a disaster waiting to happen. My cousin, Richard, who had become my main source of psychedelic drugs, was a budding big dealer in the area. The room I was in had been his. He moved to a place in Sound Beach. A roommate on my floor, Doug, was a local, small time drug dealer. The guy in the room upstairs was a straight (no drugs) senior at the college, another philosophy major.

With Richard stopping by regularly and loads of locals running in and out buying nickel bags from Doug, there was a constant haze of marijuana smoke throughout the place. It's a wonder nobody got busted. Oh, wait – everybody got busted, but that story might embarrass some people, like me. I know, could any of this be less embarrassing for an old coot closing in on 70? Skipping that saga for now. Sorry. Maybe I'll include it in the upcoming fiction.

One nice aspect of my room was my acoustics. When I got out of the Army, one of my first orders of business was to obtain a kick-ass music system, albeit with a beggar's wage. I bought things piece by piece. First were a pair of three-way Pioneer speakers with booming twelve inch woofers from the P.C. Richard's on Sunrise Highway in Bellmore.

Next, from a specialty audio store in Levittown, I nabbed a classic Marantz receiver/amp. Only thirty-five watts per channel but it was perfectly matched with the speakers.

The Dual turntable completed the original functionality. About a year later I added a top loading Akai GCX-something cassette recorder. It let me manipulate the recording level for each channel so I could do my own 'Lucky Man' shit. (You gotta hear that ELP tune on headphones. 'Starship Trooper' by Yes is another from that era. A decade or so later, 'It's a Kind of Magic' by Queen. Get some real headphones, not those buds.)

That tape-deck also had the capability to allow you to overlap the last couple of seconds of one song with the beginning of another so that there were no silent passages between songs. Some of us appreciate that feature. Makes for some smooth mixes.

Making your own tapes also put an end to listening to some of the shitty filler songs that some groups thought worthy of recording that weren't. Now I could create my own mixes – like putting a stack of singles from different groups on a spindle. But best of all – I could put the entire 'Dark Side of

The Moon' on one side of a tape. I almost never bought albums on tape. Buy the vinyl, play it once while recording on tape, and preserve the album.

But, I digress. I was talking about the acoustics in the Stony Brook apartment. Those huge speakers were positioned on each side of the head of my bed providing a multi-dimensional effect when turned inward, headphones with a vertical aspect, tweeters high, mid-range lower and big bass at the bottom. The beginning of my tinnitus.

In the meantime, Joy and I were devolving into, you guessed it, a sex relationship. We knew that part was good and we were both mature enough to agree that it was enough until the other found another soul mate. I wasn't looking elsewhere too hard.

Reminiscing

I started to reminisce about Jessica. Yes, I fell hard for Pam but her disregard for my heart made closing the door on any lingering feelings somewhat easy. OK, perhaps I went through the wrong door at first, the one that said "50% Chance of Life". I know, trying to get killed wasn't exactly the best "easy" way to numb those feelings.

Now, Jessica. She was genuinely sorry it didn't work out. Her understanding of feelings, the heart, love, was her greatest quality, as beautiful as she was to me. That tenderness she showed at the end gave me a sliver of hope – if her new relationship didn't work out, she still had a place in her heart for me.

That hope emerged one lonely night in my room. I wrote her a carefully composed letter, you know, snail mail. I told her about the Army, not so much Ronnie, and I told her about acid, how it pulled me out of my darkest void. And I told her that I must have really been in love with her to fall that low, and now, to still have those feelings.

There was no obtuse expression of love. I said I loved her, plain and simple. Please write back.

I'll never know if she read it. After a few weeks I wrote another one but addressed it to her mother. The first page asked mom to give the rest to Jessica. The rest, shorter than the first, simply stated that I had loved our time together, appreciated the way she handled the break-up, and that I did, and still do now, love her. And, please write back. Anything.

Never got a response.

Phencyclidine

I had plenty of dope and, when not attending classes, I was partying all the time. My cousin had come by a massive quantity of a small yellow tablet marketed as low dose mescaline. This stuff was cheap and gave you a tremendous high but quite short of a tripping experience. Perfect for getting really ripped without the lung damage from smoking a lot of pot.

The "mescaline", we learned a few months later, turned out to be phencyclidine, thirty years later known as PCP and Angel Dust. I don't know how it got such a bad rap. It's just a horse tranquilizer that produces an amazing high in the human brain. I suppose that it being so good is the problem. You want to do more. I loved it – got you right on the edge of tripping but with a mellowing quality. And, no. I'm not glorifying that drug either. Apparently you can do too much of that and get yourself killed. I know about that. More, shortly.

We, the locals and myself, started crushing it into powder and snorting it. Quick big high. Snort a couple and out to the rock band bars.

Fire Drill

One night, a carload of us got pulled over. First we pulled a fire drill on the way to the bar at a traffic light. The police officers a couple of cars back were not amused. Tom, one of the locals and a now a good friend, decided that he wanted to alert the car full of girls riding parallel to us that we were a car full of guys.

The Dark Side of Mooning

As the cop car pulled up behind us, Tom, not a little man, dropped trow, opened the window, and mooned the ladies. That nauseating exhibition was immediately followed by flashing lights and a quick siren burst.

Bye girls. See you at the bar. I was driving. Not sure if it was Toody or Muldoon but one of them yells in my window, "What the hell are you guys doing?"

Tom pipes in, "We saw the girls in the car next to us."

Officer Muldoon replies, "You sure know how to impress the women! Have you been drinking?"

"Not yet", came the chorus from the back seat. Muldoon holds back a chuckle, tells us to keep our pants on and not get into any trouble.

My straight character assures him that I will keep the boys in line tonight as I'm really getting off on a couple of those little yellow pills. He wishes us luck with the women. I'm impressed at how the college town cops handle goof balls.

Dirty Dancing

At the bar, a huge place with occasional big name acts, things are already cranking with a great rock band doing James Gang and Byrds stuff. I am high as a kite and grooving (WTF does that mean? Ok, eyes closed watching the music, body swaying) off to the side of the stage when the cutest girl in the place grabs me and pulls me onto the dance floor and in seconds is engaging me in very dirty dancing.

She was a very hands-on dancer. I suppose those tight bell bottoms I wore didn't help as they left little to the imagination with some stimulation. She was working me like Jim Morrison did on stage in Miami. Yeah, a hand job right there on the dance floor. You can't make this shit up.

She's laughing, dancing, and rubbing the boner going down my leg when she introduces herself, "Hi, I'm Chris. I think you're cute and," looking down at her hand she adds, "that's cute too."

"I'm Brian. Would you stop that for now?" I ask, but really not wanting her to, "or go outside?"

She responds, "You want to get high?"

"I'm way high," is my honest response. Those crushed up little yellow pills have me on the edge of tripping but I agree, "Let's go."

As soon as we get out the door she lights up a joint and we head to her car so she can swig a half pint of Southern Comfort. I'm thinking blow job. She's not. Come on. Her fingers were so precise, she could get me off in seconds. Ugh.

Chris wants to know if I have anything stronger than pot. OK, if that's what it takes. I go back into the bar, hand off the car keys to Tom, and go with Chris to the apartment.

I had some Orange Sunshine. I cut it into two pieces – double what I'd normally take, and I'm already flying on the two phencyclidine hits. We drop and stay up all night playing. Fade to black. Sex, like most physical aspects of an intense acid experience, is not all that memorable. Acid does seem to have Viagra-like qualities but it also just might be a little of that time distortion making you feel like Superman. Yeah, I'm Donovan, Sunshine Superman.

Chris was one weird coot. Cute as a button with extremely short, like crew cut, blonde hair. Turns out she had recently been released from a sort of mental rehab place. Her parents committed her after she shaved her head on a wild acid trip. She claimed that she only felt normal on acid. Uh-huh.

Well, I really liked her and she was willing to immediately say she loved me, but not to the exclusion of anyone else. Ah, another Pam. But Chris was vulnerable and smart as a whip. Both her parents were professors at Stony Brook, astrophysicist and psychologist. No wonder she was fucked up.

When she was in the nut house, her doctors found that her brain was wired tighter than her butt. That was saying something. Those ninety pounds were all muscle and a good percentage of that was in those beautifully rounded, yet tight-as-honeydews, gluteus maximus muscles. But it was her face first – she was cute. No breasts to speak of, if you were wondering.

Anyway, as part of her rehab, they sent her home with a machine that could sense alpha waves emitted from the brain. She was wired without too many of those calming alpha waves. They taught her in the hospital how to chill out and to use that machine to measure and create alpha waves – to chill.

She hooked me up to it one day. Apparently forty-some-odd acid trips will unlock your alphas. Or, maybe focusing on what makes one happy helps? Or, good, recent sex? Multiple losses at love? I don't know but she said my alpha waves were off the chart. Never saw anyone as calm as me.

I volunteered that the sex did it and I needed to get calmer but she thought it was all the acid. The more you're able to handle the real world when tripping, the more calm you are when straight. Such is the logic of insane people, and I count my many cumulative hours under the influence of LSD and other strong hallucinogens, as time insane, based on accepted reality, or saneness.

Whatever, pretty sure I was always very calm. I'm going with mostly genetic makeup, some conditioning. Age old argument about how one develops. Did Bruce's parents make him that way or was he born a fuck up? That's not fair. Was I born a slow developer or was it environment? Do you have the genes to get through 300 pages of this or have you learned the behavior?

Sometime in our short fling, Chris and I saw Joe Cocker in a basement bar in the town of Stony Brook, maybe it was called The Basement, or The Cellar, something clever like that. It was a tiny venue. His reputation was in the toilet, for good reason. He was terrible. He had kicked heroin by then, but in early 1974 he was a falling down drunk. You could look it up.

Just a few months later he released 'You Are So Beautiful', to me, one of the most touching vocals of all time. If he sang it at the show it did not impress. And it did not bring Chris and I closer together.

We both knew and acknowledged our relationship was a short term thing. I was somewhat sad because she was so cute and smart. The magic just wasn't there. She was so hyper that the sex part was kind of mechanical, so it seemed. Focus was not her strong suit. She disappeared in a couple of months.

In the meantime, school was great. I was taking a poetry class on Emily Dickenson. One year, Emmy decided she would write a poem a day. I decided I would do the same. My notebook was filled with them. For my term grade, I wrote a well-received paper about her "Sea".

We both went to "The Sea", that place where heaven and earth came together, where we could hide away from the world, where we were at peace. I got her. She knew what I knew. Or was it the other way around? Emily Dickenson went to the same places I did. She was out there. I loved her.

Is God Dead? No. He Never Was a Thing

That first semester at Stony Brook, I took three philosophy classes though all of them also qualified for credits in the religious studies major. One of them was in Tibetan language. Who thinks that's a useful class? OK, it sounded like a good idea at the time.

Another class was with Dr. Thomas Altizer. He and a colleague, while at Emory College, were quoted quite frequently in the 1966 Time magazine featured article with the breakthrough, words only cover, "Is God Dead?"

I wondered if he was an atheist, though he was now head of Stony Brook's Religious Studies program. I, and others, pressed him about it in classes. He gave every indication he was an atheist until he hinted that perhaps more thought should be given. He wanted everyone to work through their own issues with belief. Philosophy professors could be annoying that way. "Good question, young man. Think about it!"

One of his favorites was Nietzsche, who quickly became one of mine as well. We were given a choice of assignments for our first grading. I chose to analyze Nietzsche's 'Thus Spoke Zarathustra' in a ten page report.

I really struggled with my paper as I was struggling with the book. This guy was despicable. But about 80% through the book and my paper, I got it. Fucking Nietzsche had strung me along, as did his character, Zarathustra, strung along his followers. I had to restructure, slightly, what I had written, more specifically, focus on the irony of being led astray, only to arrive at the truth at the last moment. It was a metaphor of one's spiritual search. I felt so enlightened, believing I really understood this old, insane geezer. Nietzsche did end up in an asylum, institutionalized before the book was published.

Altizer loved the paper and had me come see him after class. He wanted to know how I figured it out. I told him I was, quite frankly, stumped at first, but after smoking a dozen bongs it came to me.

I wish I had really told him that but instead, just said, "It was obvious, no?" I knew the paper was good and was being an asshole, smug. But, in fact, I really did smoke a lot of pot reading the book and writing the report. From there on, I got high before and during the writing of every paper in philosophy. True. Many artistic people find inspiration when high. I totally get it. You just have to filter out the sublime from the ridiculous.

So when I hear people say that pot makes you stupid, I think that those who make the statement are the stupid ones. Pot just emphasizes who you are. Don't tell me pot makes you stupid, stupid! There are a lot of stupid people out there in disguise and many will expose themselves daily. Check out the person next to you. Case in point, W was president!

This was the most productive period of my scholastic career. I was full bore into every class that interested me. The ill-chosen ones that I took to fill in credits, the ones that lost my attention in a few weeks, I dropped. I could not stand being bored.

To Cut Or Not Cut: Idealism vs Reality

In mid-March of '74, I had a big decision to make. My hair had been growing for over two years and I had to make an appearance before the NY State Parks commission to try to get my Jones Beach summer job back. Let it grow or cut it? It became a philosophical issue that became the focus, in a fictional, conversational form, of another philosophy class paper. Idealism or pragmatism? The paper got an A. In real life, pragmatism won. I got the haircut. My approach to life was changing ever so slightly.

Pot Thief

One night while out at the bars, my apartment was broken into. The only things stolen we're a couple of pipes, rolling papers and my pot. My stereo was still there, my bong and its stinky water was untouched, and ten thousand phencyclidine tablets were still hidden in one of the Pioneer speakers.

Richard had asked me to hold onto them when he thought he was going to be busted a week or two earlier. He took them back after the break in. It was rather unsettling and a bit puzzling. They just took my pot?

Too Much Will Kill Ya

A week later, Tom fell off his motorcycle and died. Autopsy said he had a massive amount of phencyclidine in his system.

Chapter 18 - The ONE!

Spring, 1974. Crazy Chris had drifted away. Hanging out with the local yokels was getting tired and my favorite local, Tom, was dead. I was lonely. Stony Brook was a pretty decent sized school but it seemed like high school – I hadn't seen one girl I was all that attracted to. I was also very tired of the chase.

Then, one day between classes, I'm walking into the student union, who do I run into? No, not Gina.

Jessica!

There on the steps near the bridge to nowhere (there really was a footbridge that had been started over the road but funds had run out to complete it) was Jessica. She looked as beautiful as ever. She had matured a bit in three years, still adorably cute but more exotic.

The awkward small talk that followed was sad for me, most likely extremely uncomfortable for her. That was the last time I saw Jessica. If I wasn't at the bottom of one of life's low points before that meeting, I hit one that night. That being said, rock bottom was no longer a bottomless hole. I knew by then that life was a roller coaster and I was now just on a particularly deep bottom of a hill. No doubt I cried that night, even with a dozen or so bongs.

Having gotten the state job back and finishing the semester, I started working at Jones Beach again, but now in the umbrella crew. What a great job, renting umbrellas at the beach. There were as many girls, if not more, than guys in the group. Our manager had been a philosophy major in college and got high with everyone he visited on his daily tour of the umbrella stands.

We had a softball team in the state park league. We usually got creamed because of our heavily weighted female contingent. Hmm. I didn't say that right. We had six or seven women in the lineup, none of whom were overweight, though one could have been considered top heavy. Katie was our pitcher.

The word spectacular comes to mind. A cute, bespectacled blonde, with a slightly wandering eye, she had a sort-of librarian look. But, when you put that skinny girl and those bra-less double-D's into a tight, softball team t-shirt, she became an opposing team's favorite player to watch run.

A terrible hitter, she was given the easiest pitches to hit just so that they could see her do a Pamela Anderson running imitation, twenty years before Baywatch. I can honestly say the male members on our team were on the dugout steps to watch as well. Dare I say we feared for her bruising her chin at times?

I was not on my game – the girl-chase game - that summer and just enjoyed watching Katie run. It had been my history that large breasted women were attracted to me. Maybe my karma exuded bad vibes. No sparks flew between us.

Summer came to an end as did my time with Joy. I was not thrilled with going back to school. The robbery at the apartment out at Stony Brook convinced me to go back to commuting.

The ONE

Then on September 4th, 1974, the crème de la crème of all life changers came into my life. Artie and Judi invited me over to the house in Mineola. Joy had moved into an apartment in Staten Island and a new girl had moved in. They thought the new girl and I might get along.

A fucking blind date! It had been years since I went on one of those. Never heard of one working out. But, I'm going to meet this girl eventually if she lives here. Artie is still my best friend so I'll be visiting often.

When introduced to Andrea I was floored. Why didn't they tell me she was so pretty? What beautiful eyes! Beautiful hair. Beautiful everything. You know what I mean? The Whole Enchilada!

Oh my God! How do I make an impression with her? She drank a little, smoked pot, was completely independent at twenty-two, smart as hell, extremely sarcastic and would not let an idle comment pass. Damn, a challenge! And, by the way, she is the ONE! I knew it immediately.

The way she tells it, I stayed the night and never went home. Not exactly. We were off and on for two years. And when I say off, I mean the intention was to end it. When we were on, it was pure love. It started out full bore love at first night (yeah, no typo). I wrote her poems. I didn't have any money, just love.

Our first date was a classic. We went to a Nathan's hot dog joint across from the Mid-Island Mall in Hicksville. Classy, right? Well, Andrea pulled the classy move. Nathan has their own logo-imprinted napkins, mostly green with some brown and yellow. Hot dog colors. We had delicious dogs smothered in mustard and their very green relish. She loves their thick, crinkle-cut fries.

After finishing, I looked at her and wished I'd had a camera. Half her face was green. It wasn't from the relish or getting sick. Rather, she had wiped her mouth with the logo side of the napkin. Apparently, our batch of napkins was freshly printed or overloaded with ink. She had that alien look. Charming first date, huh? I love this girl.

But this was a woman who had very strong opinions about everything, and, seemingly, opinions about every word that came out of my mouth. At the time, every word seemed worth discussing – and losing that discussion. We lived together about two out of every four weeks over the two years.

Tumultuous is a word that comes to mind. We were opposites in many ways, but you know how opposites go. We clashed about a million things. When we were good, we were very good. When we were bad, we split up, sometimes for several weeks. Talk about a trial period – every couple should try it before that big commitment.

The commute to Stony Brook sucked but I arranged my classes so that I only had to go twice a week, no classes before noon and one at 8PM. That helped me get through another year and then back to Jones Beach for one more summer.

College started to become tedious. Oh, I truly loved the philosophy courses but all the other fill-in classes were a waste of time. I was dropping classes left and right. The commute to Stony Brook from Mineola, when Andrea and I were good, and my parents' home in Bellmore was getting very tiring. By the time I was due to graduate in December 1975, I was nine credits short of a degree.

By then, I had lost my love of academia, thinking it was, like the Catholic Church, a place to provide jobs to smart people who didn't find work very appealing. Fuck it. I was done. On to the real world.

Unless you have a gift for gab and no conscience, jobs other than sales are few and far between for almost-college graduates in 1976, unless construction appeals to you. I had no idea what I wanted to do.

Though my cynicism of the academic system was, to me, clearly deserved, I knew my path into a major course of studies that had no end game, unless I plowed forth into teaching the bullshit I was now revolting against, was my own fault. I had found great pleasure in absorbing the ideology of well-regarded thinkers. I identified with these people. But now reality loomed. I had to earn a living.

The Real World

My skills in expressing myself were mostly by way of the pen. No computers then and my high school typewriting class was ancient history. I could talk one-on-one with anyone about my personal philosophy and debate points of contention. But, put me in front of a group and I clammed up.

That old shyness, or perhaps, fear of rejection creeped back into my psyche. Hey you shrinks, talk amongst yourselves - that fear held me back for a long time. Public speaking should have been on my course list. At any rate, the list of appealing jobs was pretty small.

Thus, though I was told yet again I was over qualified, I pleaded for the job of shipping clerk at Wallach's, a clothing store in the very upscale Long

Island community of Manhasset. At the same time, January, 1976, Andrea moved out of the Mineola apartment and into the waterfront village of Manorhaven, right down the block from Manhasset.

Bye, Bye, Bonnie

In late April of '76, we were together when we got an early morning phone call. My brother was in a bad car accident a few hours earlier. He had been working the night before, parking cars at the Huntington Town House until about two.

On the way home, in our father's prized '65 Pontiac Bonneville with it's 389 engine that could leave rubber in a second (I would know that how?), he fell asleep at the wheel on the Wantagh-Oyster Bay Expressway, as it was known then, or more affectionately now, the SOB, renamed as the Seaford-Oyster Bay Expressway because, it turns out, that it really started in Seaford, and slammed into the rear of a tractor-trailer. The engine ended up in the front seat, crushing his hip, pelvis, spleen. You couldn't name a part of his body that didn't have a broken bone.

He was in surgery all day. I don't think we got to see him until the following day. He was in that hospital on Hempstead Turnpike just off the expressway - I think it was called Mid-Island Hospital then. It's called St Joseph now. Anyway, Michael looked like a mummy. He was wrapped in bandage from head to toe.

The hospital had some rules about only allowing two people at a time to see him. I recall us waiting outside the room while a friend of his was visiting. She was discussing a concert she had been to the night before and the headliner. She said, and you can't make this shit up, "We went to see 'Asleep At The Wheel' last night."

I was stunned. Didn't she know? Or did she think my brother would be amused? He was a fan also, so I suppose it was ok. I will never forget that. Made me add to life's rules – if you visit someone in the hospital, try to come up with something witty and topical related to the person's reason for being there. Don't remind them that they did something problematic. Like, "Sorry about the lung cancer. You know, I was hospitalized last week for asthma and those cock-suckers told me to stop smoking Camels. Do you have a butt?"

He spent a year on his back. At some point, Andrea and I brought him some pot brownies which he recalls were some of the most potent edibles he has, to this day, ever had. I don't remember that because I didn't eat them - or maybe I did.

I do recall bringing him a new toy, a waterproof pipe that did not allow smoke to escape. It was a solid plastic tube about eight inches long, an inch in diameter, with a wooden joint holder at one end that plugged into the tube, and at the other end was a wooden piece containing a rubber flap that allowed air in, when inhaled, and prevented smoke from exiting when not inhaling.

This was perfect for someone trapped in a hospital bed, or in a shower, which is how I employed mine. We loved new paraphernalia back then. The ideal birthday and Christmas presents for stoners.

During his long hospital stay, my brother was visited by a high school friend, Linda. She turned out to be an angel of sorts. She was there all the time and after he was sent home to recover. She was there every time he got drunk and fell down stairs - getting used to one leg shorter than the other wasn't easy. A couple of years later they married. Still are.

As I said, Andrea and I were off and on for two years, very far off by the summer of '76. I wanted to run away again. Artie and Joe had broken off their relationships also so we started planning our escape. But first, we had to celebrate the two hundredth anniversary of the country.

We had become huge fans of using a one-hit bong to get high. Economics! When you inhaled and burned up all the weed, the ashes got sucked into the water. If you used the right amount of pot for your lungs, the smoke would fill them and none would be coughed up or otherwise wasted. A perfect delivery system for that era. Vape pens hadn't been invented yet. If they were, we couldn't afford them.

Anyway, in the last couple of years we had taken bonging to a new level. Efficiency was the name of the game. The idea was to get high, and get high fast, or maybe just get really high and not piss around. So, you pulled out ten or fifteen matches from a matchbook - I think they held twenty, and laid them out next to the bong, or maybe in a bong well.

Some of the cooler ceramic bongs had a little well on the left and right side. One side would hold your pot, the other, if you had one, those matches. The pot should be ground up a bit, but not so much that it would fall into the bong water. Put enough pot in the well to last ten or fifteen bongs. Then you light a candle within easy reach, and make sure you have enough music queued up to play continuously through the session.

Three steps: load the bong with one hit's worth of pot; pick up a match and light it via the candle; hold match over pot in bong and inhale until all weed is burned and ashes are sucked into bong water. Repeat for all ten or fifteen matches. Important: do not be distracted before next hit.

Ten bongs would give you a decent high, very quickly, and efficiently. But we had time on our hands as responsibility-free students. At some point in those years, Joe had introduced us to the Rupert Mile. This was a drinking game named after Rupert Miller, founder of Miller Beer. T

The idea was, drink a shot of beer every minute for an hour. No big deal, right? Even if you only pour an ounce, that's sixty ounces, or five cans of beer in an hour. That will fuck you up. By putting you on the clock, you forget about everything else but the task at hand. An hour later and you are ripped.

How Many Bong Hits Can You Do In a Half Hour?

Well, I took the Rupert Mile concept and applied it to bongs, but figured a half hour was long enough. That's thirty bongs. That will fuck you up. Then Joe took it to another level - how many can you do in a half hour? You needed to have a very full bowl of pot and several books of matches. Joe set the record at seventy-four. I'm not sure if he's come down yet.

We were getting very high, even if the pot was shitty. I suppose some of that ability to deal with being so stoned had to do with surviving and thriving through all those hyper-drive acid trips.

By 1975, I had stopped tripping. Artie and I had created a reel-to-reel tape that auto-reversed after three hours. The idea was that you did not have to make a decision about what to play next. Like going to a six hour concert. Making decisions in the middle of an acid trip can seem monumental. Reduce them so you can let your mind go.

The music was recorded in four "phases" of about an hour and a half each. The first contained songs that had definite references to getting high or LSD like 'Magical Mystery Tour', 'Purple Haze', and The Moody Blues' 'Higher and Higher'. The second grouping was like the second stage of a rocket, designed to take you "out there" while starting to consider your inner space as well. Stage three brings you to the intense peak hour and beyond, keeping you focused on reaching that magic moment. The fourth phase offers some mellower tunes to help bring you down gently while the lyrics continue to provide food for thought.

The Last Trip

Anyway, we set aside a day where we had his house to ourselves and ran that tape. We discussed our thoughts about the experience, played some chess, smoked a bunch of doobies, and well after we should have been peaking wondered when we would. It was good acid.

We had just succeeded in creating an environment so comfortable that we didn't feel high. I had complete control over those million thoughts per second. I knew they would come. I knew how to keep each massive grouping of thoughts in context. Without that strangeness and detachment from reality, there was no high. This reality is where it's happening. Right now!

That is a strange concept to grasp – peaking on acid and feeling normal! Yet, when I closed my eyes and got on that multidimensional transport of a billion thoughts per second, I could be screaming through the universe – totally content either way. I got IT!

Of course, that begs the question, "What is IT?" Peter Gabriel delved into it on the last track of the Genesis double album, 'The Lamb Lies Down On Broadway'. "It has no home in words or goal…It is here, it is now…It is real…" You can find the entire album's lyrics on genius.com, or on the album sleeves.

I felt I had nothing more to learn from acid trips and that was my last. Boom! THE life changer, and now I'm done. LSD brought me out of the deepest, darkest world that one can descend to. Suicide was no longer in my vocabulary. IT put me back in charge of the life vehicle. (One more quote from Peter Gabriel's song 'it!', "…, it is purple haze".) Those fifty-plus, whatever the accurate number, seemed to culminate with the question, "Is that all there is, my friend, is that all there is?"

And the answer? Yeah, but you should have been there. "It don't come easy, you know it don't come easy!"

Now, let's get back to celebrating the two hundredth anniversary of our country. On July 4th, 1976, I started the day with about twenty bongs before I went downstairs for coffee. My goal was to do two hundred by day's end. And I did. By early evening I had done about a hundred fifty. The headache began but I braved wave after wave of shooting pain from the front to the back of my skull. We, Artie and family, went to a fireworks display in Sea Cliff and just before midnight, I sucked down number two hundred. I remember very little about that day. The headache was most memorable.

The Road Trip

Then we prepared for our exit from Long Island. In mid-August, Artie, Joe, and I packed up our earthly possessions and caravanned to San Diego. The weather and the whole concept of sunny, southern California won us over.

Off we went, first to visit the brothers' cousin in Tennessee. A day or two later, not too much beyond Hot Springs, Arkansas, the recently rebuilt Volkswagen engine in Joe's van gave up the ghost in the Smokey Mountains. We spent a week in a state park near Clarksville, Arkansas, a little town off interstate 40 that just happened to have a shop that specialized in Volkswagen repair, and, was in a dry county, twenty miles from beer. We managed.

Once on the road again, we bolted with very little sleep until we got to the Grand Canyon. That was our only sight-seeing side trip and one that would plant a seed which would one day alter lives. It should be a trip everyone makes. Just do it.

We then drove non-stop to San Diego, actually, to Escondido, between LA and San Diego, camped out for a week, dressed up in suits in tents to go on job interviews, and had our first Taco Bell meals.

I was all set to start a job at a Radio Shack in a shitty area of San Diego when I came to my senses and called Andrea. At ten that Friday night I packed up my stuff, wished Artie and Joe luck, popped my last hit of speed, and hit the road.

Every four hours I stopped to pee, gas up, and get two cups of coffee to go, sometimes lingering to eat something substantial. I slept about four hours just east of Denver and two more in Indianapolis. At seven thirty Monday evening, I pulled up to the apartment in Manorhaven.

For years I said it took sixty-nine and a half hours but now, when I include the three hour time change, it comes out to be sixty-six and a half. Not bad for two thousand eight hundred and seventy miles. Love will motivate you. Artie and Joe stuck around San Diego for a few more weeks and then they came back too.

That was the end of Andrea and I's last "off" period. All of a sudden we were on and there was no off switch. Real world here I come.

Chapter 19 - The Final Cut

Story Over

You know, I'm going to cut this off now. End of the first journey. I found her. My wandering, the

searching – over. We found the right notes to play.

Ok, the two of you still reading might ask, "What happened next?" Well, Andrea and I became a serious couple. We went out to nice dinners with her father and had him over for dinner a few times. I recall, specifically, one special night among those home dinners.

I was making lasagna with very thinly sliced pepperoni included in the layers – just one of those details that is very clear. Memory is funny like that. While I was still making it, Alan was browsing through our bookshelves. Most of them were my textbooks from college along with the complete sets of Hermann Hesse and Carlos Casteneda as well as a smattering of popular science fiction of the day.

Holding a copy of Martin Buber's 'I and Thou', Alan asked, "Have you read all these?"

"Yes," I answered, "some more than once. Some of those guys, you have to read a couple of times. You have to get out there with them. Some are very clear and one reading is enough. Some are like good movies."

I loved those books when first introduced to me. I didn't really sour on any one of them. It was all of them. They were all brilliant yet all approached this life thing from a new and "unique" perspective.

WRONG! They were all just proposing an argument for existence, morality, and reality. Basically, what is this, how do I do this, and what do I do with it? That became, to me, an enormous waste of time since none of them provided an answer I could believe in. And by that time, religion had become a disgusting abomination of the truth. It was always buried in "faith", in blind belief.

The Church, oops, here I go again, and any religion that asks you for a penny, should be banned, or at least regulated – show some proof that the shit you are preaching can be proven to be true. That would put an end to the bullshit that has been around since some wise ass five thousand years ago was able to sell the idea of god to another. Faith? Why? So we can accept another mass murder?

Can we finally be done with religion? It has no place in a truly civilized world except as just another business out to make a profit. Tax the mother fuckers!

That more or less sums up my deepest negative passion. On the positive side, that rejection of religion has shifted my path a bit towards a whatever-works mentality, though not forgetting Metahedonism – which you better start taking seriously or you'll never have a good trip again… oh, that would be a nasty brainworm (you know, earworm but a thought that creeps into your head when you're eight miles high and start worrying if you've hurt anybody recently).

As I was saying, my philosophy now tends to be utilitarianism – was I saying that? Any philosophers I agree with? Yeah, lots, as long as they don't veer off into bullshit. I suppose George Santayana is one I wondered about at first but now think of as brilliant. A true skeptic and pragmatist, "Those that cannot remember the past are condemned to repeat it." You've heard that line time and again – but here we are with yet another nihilist in a clowning performance as a world leader disgracing the concept of truth (talking about Trumpty-Dumpty again).

Well, here's where Jesus fucked up – he basically said forgive and forget. I say don't ever forget! And don't let your stupid friends who voted for the douchebag-in-charge to ever forget. They are not your friends. But, I digress. Now you know where that famous quote came from. Say his name again and don't confuse him with a rock star – George Santayana. Got it?

Rather ironic, no? A believer-wannabe, a starship trooper of the inner universe, the god of odd himself, now the ultimate skeptic grounded firmly in getting from point A to point B – and don't get me started on shitty drivers!

I think of myself as an efficiency expert though Andrea would disagree and say my OCD tendencies – can you say "Rainman"? – slow me down to a crawl pace. My whole thing now is – just fix it! Life! Your life, your kid's lives, any fucking thing that needs fixing. Never, ever – NEVER - look for blame – just fix it! And if it ain't broke, enjoy. Have fun. That is the whole fucking point. Period!

The adventurous spirit of that space and time traveler we knew and loved in the early seventies is still there. It just needs some coaxing to get that aching body moving. My brain still feels like it did back then. Pretty sure I'm twenty-four. That's 24 years old!. I just have a lot more experience stored up in those memory cells to keep me from jumping at opportunities or reacting to adversity immediately.

One thing I have learned over the years to be a valuable mental tool is patience. As a matter of fact, if I'm ever asked what the key is to staying married so long, I always have a one word answer – patience. Not that anybody asks. I mean, who can take an old coot who took acid as much as I did seriously? I just smile and wonder myself. And now I'm laughing inside, perhaps a slight audible chuckle. It's been quite a trip!

But, I digress. A few days after that dinner with Alan, Andrea got a call from her sister, Tricia. She said that Alan floated the idea that he'd be interested in bringing me into the family business if Andrea and I ever got married. We kicked that idea around for a few weeks.

At the time, late fall of 1976, Andrea was making a decent living working for her childhood doctor and soon to be adult molester. I had my shitty job at Wallach's. Tricia, two years younger than Andrea, was engaged to Stanley and their wedding was coming up in January. Her older sister, Carol, was already a mother with then-husband Peter. Carol had attended Cornell and never came home to Long Island. Tricia was living with Stanley in Old Bethpage on Long Island. Tricia and Andrea were best friends as sisters, still are.

Perhaps Tricia's marriage had some influence. Perhaps it was the prospect of joining the family business. Perhaps we felt we were finally ready after two years of figuring it out.

We, and it wasn't a surprise-here's-a-ring thing, decided that, sure, let's get married. We might as well be. We've lived together off and on for over two years. That's better than a lot of marriages. (As I am going through my final edit, we are celebrating forty-two years in Oia on the Greek island of Santorini.)

Marriage?

So Alan got stuck with two weddings in the space of six months.

Ours was a beautiful day on the 15th of May in 1977 when cars rolled up to the Sans Suici in Sea Cliff on the north shore of Long Island with pot smoke billowing out of the doors as guests were unexpectedly welcomed by all-valet parking.

Notorious cousin Richard laid out his magic carpet on the beautiful lawn and with turban and foot-long beard looked the part of a rising Iranian cleric. His brother Gary called him the Ayatollah. Everyone ignored him and got high in their separate groups.

The wedding was a civil service conducted on the lawn looking out over Roslyn Harbor.

Andrea always looked that good. It took a store full of a clothing store's employees to put a tie on me.

By all accounts, a good time was had by all. Pretty much everyone between the ages of sixteen and thirty got high, most lighting up out on the lawn but a few brazenly puffing away at the tables indoor. The maitre'd told us that we had such "characters" out there and we shrugged.

We didn't light up all day. We didn't need to. We were naturally high. Best day of my life.

Married life is a whole new life. I tell young people approaching marriage that all the time - life as you know it is over. It Ain't Me Babe - it's WE! You know what I mean (ok, more Turtles, "can you read in between the lines?")? Kids? You think "your" life was over when you got married? A child brings "we" to a new level. Another new life for what's left of "you".

Yep, married forty-two years (in 2019). I still think I'm that invincible guy in his twenties who knows nothing but doesn't care. I got my two and a half rules that still work. Life happened through it all.

Then to Now:

That's it for those stories of yesteryear. The Hunter Thompson-like life blended slowly into a life of your almost average Joe. You really want to know what happened next? Long story short, or maybe, many, many short stories, condensed, it went like this:

We bought a house in Bayville, Long Island in 1979 and lived there until 2001. I came to my senses, regarding that dumb idea that maybe I am not supposed to fly, and got my pilot's license right after we were married, but stopped flying after we bought the house. Couldn't afford both.

After Andrea's father filed for chapter eleven bankruptcy in 1980, the job sucked and I hated commuting four hours every day. Andrea suggested I try computers and so I did. In 1981, with her taking over my job in her father's failing business, I went full-time to computer programming school at Grumman Data Systems.

In the spring of '82, I started writing code for the New York Shipping Association, a kind of go-between organization that handled payroll and benefits for the Longshoremen's' union. It was at that job that I got a full introduction to thoroughbred horse racing through Mr. Monroe Baum. We spent nearly every lunch at an OTB.

I refined my programming skills by writing code for an IBM 360 that would take the concepts of Andy Beyer's now legendary "figs" and produce a "fig" for each horse in a race, provided enough prior race data was entered. It helped me become a better programmer more than it picked winners.

That allure of the racetrack took us to Saratoga Springs that summer, and every summer until we moved to Colorado.

In January, 1984, I had paid my dues as an entry level programmer and took a job at Con Edison, THE electric utility in New York City. On my application I told them I had a degree.

In fact, in the years I worked at Sleepwear, I had taken a couple of college courses but I knew my computer programming courses were worth about twenty-three credits. So, though I didn't have the paper, I knew I had the credits for a degree. Fucking Con Ed wanted to see the diploma.

So, I applied for it. Turns out, rules change over the years. All those Farmingdale aviation credits that they originally didn't accept at Nassau Community College and Stony Brook University, were now good. When all my education was added up, I was three credits short of a masters, though I would have needed a class or two to fulfill a major requirement. All this was one more validation to my thought that the academic world is as full of shit as the rest of us. We make it up as we go along.

Anyway, in March of '84, my mother died, very unexpectedly – heart failure with an asthma inhaler in hand. I was at work when I got the call. It made me feel like I needed to be closer to family – on Long Island. Not sure why. It takes forever to get anywhere in the tri-state area. It sort of re-inforced my hate of commuting two hours each way.

One of the biggest allures to the computer profession was the location of computer jobs – they were everywhere.

In June I took a job with Slater Electric in Glen Cove, ten miles down the road from Bayville. After finding that we couldn't produce children with

1980's science, we adopted Briana three days after her birth in August, 1984.

This was Halloween '84.

Charles and Diana had just had Harry.

So Bree went as Harry.

It was a year earlier that Andrea and I went to a family Halloween party as Jesus and Mary. I knocked on the front door carrying a six foot crucifix and my Aunt Clare started screaming "Blasphemy". Successful costume, I took that to mean. The whole family was big on Halloween.

Andrea had a successful career in real estate in the local area. She got very involved in the school system, ran for school board, and was eventually elected president of the tony, Locust Valley Board of Education.

We took loads of great vacations and that wanderlust peaked in 1998. We took a sixteen day vacation to visit seven national parks, a few national monuments, some state parks, while driving scenic highways whenever possible in a tour of the southwest that changed our lives.

That trip moved me so much, we literally moved west, to Monument, Colorado in 2001. My computer career had, coincidentally - I don't believe in fate (or coincidence - you make it happen), opened a door at a software company in Colorado Springs. That year, Andrea convinced me to try an RV trip to Yellowstone. A year later we bought an RV and shortly thereafter knew we would full-time someday.

Andrea began a new career in oil and gas, a self-taught GIS analyst. I ended up working exclusively from home. Andrea's job led us to a two year stint in a vacation-like home in a suburb of Houston, League City on Clear Lake, across from NASA. That move was preceded by my being diagnosed with moderately aggressive prostate cancer.

In Houston, in August of 2010, I had my prostate removed – luckily, it was Friday the 13th. Unfortunately, the follow-up discovered that the cancer had tried to make a break for it and I needed forty-four days of radiation treatment. That had a big influence on our decision to retire early and hit the road in 2014.

Then my back started corroding as did my hip. In the span of one hundred days in 2016, I had spinal fusion (L4-S1), right side hernia, and total right hip replacement. You never know when the shit will hit the fan. Wait, PS: Final edit – the first back surgery put undo pressure on the already-deteriorating L3-L4 bone/disc/support junk (it ain't just disc). It became intolerable. Well, had that final fusion. The erector set now stretches from the top of my butt crack, the S1 vertebrae, to the mid-lumbar section, L3. Anyway, it worked! First time in, maybe eight years, that my back and/or legs feel normal, continually. Like coming down from a bad acid trip. Normal is the best. Thank you, Dr. Bhatti.

That, my friends, is 1977 to today in a nutshell. Lots of stories along the way but those forty years seemingly went by as fast as the prior seven. Kind of a blur.

The first pass of this book was finished in May of 2017 while we were reveling in the afterglow of a second grandchild. Life goes on. We went to see Roger Waters in June that year. A few days later, I went to Red Rocks, the natural amphitheater near Denver, to see Brit Floyd again. Some things don't change.

And here I am editing this two years later in Santorini, Greece (and one more clean-up in fall, 2019 (Impeach, convict, and subject Agent Orange to the punishment intended for one convicted of treason, and, I don't know facts, but I KNOW – Trump was hired by the Military Industrial Complex. That will, undoubtedly, never be exposed. Yes, I confess – I believe that Ike was right, about the Military Industrial Complex, and it has gone completely global.)) Oh, I digress. Damn, I just got high for the first time in weeks. Got lost on the tail end of a double ended parens after encouragement to actually print this sucker. By the way, feedback is appreciated. I wouldn't have had the balls to publish this if it hadn't been for some unexpected comments from the peanut gallery.

Love it all folks. It goes by in a flash. This is IT. Just get it right. Write your stories down soon after they happen. You'll thank me in forty years. And remember, besides being patient with that asshole sitting next to you:

Don't hurt anyone.

Have a good time.

And, IF you can help someone along the way, DO IT!

(Cut to the final guitar solo of 'Comfortably Numb')

An Epiloguey Thingie

Some Last Licks

It's really over. I can't believe I actually did something my grandchildren will lo... Well, maybe I'll write the PG version next. I hope I'm still alive when my grandkids do get to read this.

How about you? Did you have fun? I guess if you got this far you don't hate me. Did you ever want to be in my shoes? OK, some of you, maybe, when Ronnie asked me in for a drink. That wasn't her real name. I honestly don't remember it. And maybe when Joy surprised me in her birthday suit, on our first date? And when Zoe came back from that porn movie ready to try out what she learned? But maybe not when her mother opened the door on a porn show. You know, it ain't all fun and games.

Some of the names have been changed, but you know who you are, and didn't we have fun, while it lasted? The names for Zoe and Joy are like crossword puzzle hints. Ronnie? No, I lost her real name in my cobwebs, and yeah, I know, how could I forget her name? ~shrug~ Yes, everything happened as described. You don't forget those firsts, and some sloppy seconds. Oh, come on! You never did? Wait, it was just me?

Most first names were real, as were the main characters from the Army, Stan, Dave and, my improbable savior's full name, Michael T. Gross of Philadelphia, Pennsylvania.

Thank you, Michael for, besides saving my life, introducing me to Pink Floyd. I haven't counted lately but I believe I have around thirty Pink Floyd themed t-shirts, much to Andrea's dismay (and disapproval. "You're a grandfather for God's sake. Grow up!").

I've seen them live about ten times, Roger Waters four or five times, David Gilmour once, and been to numerous tribute band performances. My phone has eight or nine live versions of 'Comfortably Numb', live and studio versions of 'The Dark Side of The Moon' and 'The Wall', and, besides all the studio albums, various versions of many other album cuts including the dress rehearsal of the opening number, 'Obscured By Clouds', for one of the great shows of all time, the March 17th, 1973 Radio City concert. There's also a complete 1971 concert that includes a cut from 'Animals' which wouldn't be released on vinyl until 1977. Michael, my musical world was never the same after I met you. I will always love you for that.

To you, thank you for taking this journey with me. Hope you had a good ride. Please write a review.

One more thanks to Coleen Ehrensmann. She runs the 'Writing Your Life Story' class at Canyon Vistas RV Resort in Gold Canyon, AZ. Upon entering the class, in January 2019, she told us that she would guarantee publishing our books. I jumped all in. Truth be told, I wrote 95% of this in 2017 but had no idea what to do with it. She jump started the jalopy in January, 2019 and helped drive it to the finish.

To LG, the phone maker - How about sending me some money for plugging your phone? I wrote 99% of this in QuickMemo+. I might sue you for the steroid shots I'm going to need in my left hand from holding the phone continuously for several years. I started with the LG G2 and then transferred all those memos over to the current LG

V20, in my hand now. Once completed, I copied each chapter into a Word doc. The Word app is available on Android.

In Word, Coleen showed me how to format the doc for book printing. To get the docs onto my laptop, I moved the files to a removable SD card, a great feature on the LG V20, and plugged that card into the PC. After copying to the laptop, I also backed up the files onto a thumb drive. But, I'm still doing the bulk of the work on my LG V20.

So LG, are you there? What a great ad for your phones! You need endorsements? Commercials? Come knocking! I'm here.

Of course, the biggest thanks goes to my wife of forty-two years, Andrea. I was going downhill once more when she came into my life. You wonder where you would have ended up had certain events not fallen into place. Meeting her was the best thing that ever happened to me.

Back up a sentence - You wonder where you would have ended up had certain events not fallen into place. I think about that a lot, but I do not regret any of it. Would I do it again? In a heartbeat. And I do, when I re-read pieces. I hope you were there with me and hope even more that it became, "I am there". Then we really would be sharing some unity.

Lastly, I do know something. At the pinnacle of understanding, I am, there in a flash, a timeless moment of infinite awareness. I got it.

See you down the road, campers.

And now, upload to Amazon!

And Now This:

Concert History

- July 12, 1969 The Brooklyn Bridge – State University of NY Ag & Tech College at Farmingdale

- January 31, 1970 Santana – State University of NY Ag & Tech College at Farmingdale

- June (approx), 1971 The Guess Who – Shreveport, LA (ok, it was just the final encore number, 'No Time'

- April 9, 1972 John McLaughlin and the Mahavishnu Orchestra - Philharmonic Hall

- May 1, 1972. Pink Floyd - Carnegie Hall - A Piece For Assorted Lunatics

- May 20, 1972 John McLaughlin and the Mahavishnu Orchestra - Capitol Theater, Passaic, NJ

- August 12, 1972 Festival at Roosevelt Raceway, Westbury, NY - Jefferson Airplane, Chuck Berry, James Brown, Commander Cody, The James Gang, Elephant's Memory, McKendree Spring, and Stephen Stills with Manasas)

- October 23, 1972 Matinee - Moody Blues – Madison Square Garden

- November 15, 1972 - Pink Floyd movie Live at Pompeii - Stony Brook University

- March 2, 1973 Genesis - Carnegie Hall (Foxtrot).

- March 17, 1973 Pink Floyd - Radio City (DSOTM). The greatest concert of all time.

- May 18, 1973 - Frank Zappa and The Mothers of Invention AND John McLaughlin and The Mahavishnu Orchestra - Nassau Coliseum Floor First Row in front of left speaker column - tinnitus

- June 18, 1973 Pink Floyd - Roosevelt Stadium, NJ

- November 22, 1973 Genesis - Felt Forum (Selling England By The Pound)

- December 21, 1973 ELP - Madison Square Garden (Brain Salad Surgery)

- February 14, 1974 Yes - Nassau Coliseum (Tales From Topographic Oceans) – How did this story not get into the body of the book? The Tripping Spaghetti Dinner served by Artie's Mom to 10 Zombies: this was a great concert. Artie, Joe, Martha, maybe even George went, with friends. We gathered at their home in the late afternoon, got very high and then everybody dropped acid at about five PM. Their mother, Gertie, prepared a spaghetti and meatball dinner for about a dozen. At six, dinner was served, just as the starship troopers were getting off. At one hour in, your appetite on acid flies away. You start getting slight stomach pangs, depending on the amount of foreign ingredients the chemist used. I would often get a sensation of having a number two bout, but it would pass. Anyway, here are a bunch of stoners with zero appetite, lining up for a bowl of crawling worms and round, brown balls, dripping with a bloody goo. At least, that's what my swirling head saw. Being somewhat of an expert at handling life at eight miles high, and knowing a load of carbohydrates would be a good thing for the next eight hours of being fucked up beyond belief, I stepped up to the plate, literally, took a big bowlful, hoping to set an example, though having no clue what others were going through in their attempt to act normal, and chomped down on those worms. I can't say that I tasted anything. I was just trying hard to swallow. Finally, we all finished and bolted for the show. We had floor seats, eight or ten rows back, and proceeded to smoke a few numbers to reset the high. As was customary then, the sound system played current music, appropriate for the crowd. The last piece they played was the first side of Mike Oldfield's album, 'Tubular Bells'. Did you know that he was twenty years old when the record was released a year earlier? Well, as the album side neared the end, the volume increased to a level that made conversation difficult, "And, Tubular Bells", the few lyrics announced. Gongs away go the Tubular Bells. As the track slowly fades out, the lights dim and a new recording, much louder, seeps out of the full blown sound system. The violins of, I believe it was, but I won't swear by it, The London Symphony Orchestra's version of Stravinsky's 'The Firebird', gently fill the basketball/ice hockey arena. The volume increases as the orchestra dramatically blasts out an introduction to, with the last note taken up by Rick Wakeman's synthesizer, 'Siberian Khatru'. Wham! The concert intro of intros. The spaghetti concert. Fantastic.

- March 6, 1974 - Hunter College - Carlos Santana and John McLaughlin

- June 14, 1974 - Beach Boys - Nassau Coliseum. During Good Vibrations, I saw musical notes emerge from the pedal steel guitar and fly to the ceiling. Great show. My original date ditched me so I took a friend's younger sister. She was a bit younger and I felt weird with my friend's sister. She was attractive but I couldn't get past that friend's sister thing. I think she got that. I wonder now. Not really a date. We both tripped and, I think we, at least I did, had a great time.

- September 28, 1974 - Nektar - Academy of Music (Remember The Future) Power Outage - also recorded by Artie's brother, George, as it was broadcast by WNEW. The amount of power needed for the audio and the light show overwhelmed the facility. It took about ten minutes to resume the show. It was cool having that recording for decades.

- November 2, 1974 - Hawkwind - Academy of Music

- December 7, 1974 - Genesis - Academy of Music (The Lamb Lies Down On Broadway)

- 1974 – I think, Rick Wakemen, keyboardist for Yes, released his second solo album earlier in the year, 'Journey To The Centre Of The Earth'. My memory says it was cold so let's go with Nov-Dec, and I can't find a concert date on-line – if you were there or can find the date, let me know – but I know it was at The Hayden Planetarium at the New York Museum of Natural History. It was great, for all 50 minutes or so. After a standing ovation of the few hundred that the planetarium can seat, he said, "That's all we know, so how about if we play side one again?" The audience all looked around at each other with a WTF-look on their faces, applauded more, wondering WTF they were going to do with six more hours of acid to go, and then zombied out on the star show that accompanied the music. Some seriously fucked up people were deposited out on Central Park West that night. Who was counting? It's fucking New York.

- June 15, 1975 - Pink Floyd - Roosevelt Stadium (Wish You Were Here)

- June 16-17th - Pink Floyd - Nassau Coliseum - Got free tickets from WNEW (named 5 songs they played one day) for the 16th. Bought floor seats the second night.

- July 25, 1975 - Yes - Roosevelt Stadium (Relayer)

- May 8, 1976 - Blue Oyster Cult and Slade - Capitol Theater, Passaic, NJ - Free Tickets from Gisela, a friend Andrea and I had lived with at some point., who worked at RCA Records. Artie and I walked out with Slade screaming something about "We're all crazy". They sucked.

- Spring, 1978 (or 79, 80) – RCA studios at Rockefeller Center, George Thorogood and The Destroyers – Courtesy of friend, Gisela, at an "employees and friends" casual lunch on the 5th floor, about the size of a small gymnasium. He rocked the shit out of the Question Mark and The Mysterian's song, '96 Tears'. Blew me away. Thank you, Gisela.

- August 19 & 21, 1988 - Pink Floyd - Nassau Coliseum

- July 17, 1994 - Pink Floyd - Giants Stadium

- April 1997 – Crosby, Stills & Nash – San Diego Convention Center (Oracle Conference)

- October 1997 – The Beach Boys - San Diego Convention Center (Oracle Conference)

- October 1997 – The Charlie Daniels Band - San Diego Convention Center (Oracle Conference)

- April 1998 – The Steve Miller Band – Hawaii Hilton (Oracle Conference)

- April 2000 – Huey Lewis and The News – Philadelphia (Oracle Conference)

- Spring 2001: Outdoor south Denver. Brian Wilson (Beach Boys) robotic performance as the opening act for Paul Simon who I learned to hate. He soaked up audience applause for four encores. Egotistical little jerk!

- Fall 2001: Pepsi Arena Denver. Neil Young. Rocked the hell out of it. Seemingly ended every song with a giant guitar and drums crescendo. Give him an A, even if they all sounded the same. As he has said, "It's all one song". Very philosophical.

- Roger Waters - mid-2000's - Dark Side of the Moon, at the Pepsi Center, Denver and MGM in Las Vegas

- Roger Waters – June 2012 - The Wall, at the Toyota Center in Houston, then a few months later at the Pepsi Center in Denver

Pink Floyd tribute bands:

- Pink Floyd Experience at the US Air Force Academy

- Australian Pink Floyd in Colorado Springs Arts Center and Mohegan Sun Casino near New London, CT

- Brit Floyd, three times at Red Rocks in Morrison, CO, outside of Denver

- And a local Houston band in a bar with an absolutely spot on 'Great Gig in The Sky'.

- I saw a couple of other tribute bands but I can't recall their names and one "laser light show" where they merged Dark Side with The Wizard of Oz. Cool.

- There was one amazing show in Las Vegas by The Musical Box, a Genesis, Peter Gabriel era, tribute band around 2002. My sister, Susan, a fan of post-Peter Gabriel Genesis, led by Phil Collins, saw the ad for the show in their lobby, The Hotel, and suggested we – Andrea and I, and her husband, Jack – all go. I had seen an ad also and was really curious as the show promised a full reprisal of 'The Lamb Lies Down on Broadway'. However, I knew this was not the Genesis she knew and warned half-heartedly against. She won, we went, they hated it, and I loved it. What made the show most memorable was a tribute band groupie (yeah, a tribute band groupie) sitting next to poor brother-in-law Jack. This guy kept making hilarious comments, such as this one, as an encore song was announced, "I just died and went to heaven." Great fucking show!

- In March, 2016, we saw David Gilmour at The LA Forum. Best "Astronomy Domine' I ever heard. Relentless, attacking guitar.

- Roger Waters at the Pepsi Center in June, 2017. Fucking ridiculous ticket prices. One ticket cost more than my first car, that piece of shit 1960 Ford Fairlane. My appetite for their music is insatiable. The good news about all these shows is that most of the crowd is as old as we are and they sit.

- I'll keep going as long as I can. In 2016, a month after having spinal fusion and two months before hip replacement, I still staggered up and down the sixty-four rows of the Red Rocks Amphitheater to see Brit Floyd, alone. No one else would go with me. I'm pathetic.

Love your music. It loves you back.